FADE IN:

For My Father,
STANLEY J. BERMAN,
August 15, 1909 to July 30, 1983

FADE IN:

THE SCREENWRITING PROCESS
2ND EDITION

ROBERT A. BERMAN

Published by Michael Wiese Productions, 11288 Ventura Blvd., Suite 821, Studio City, CA 91604, (818) 379-8799 Fax (818) 986-3408.
E-mail: wiese@earthlink.net
http://websites.earthlink.net/-mwp

Cover design by Wade Lageose, Art Hotel
Author's photograph by Ron Caruso
David Brown's photograph by David Derex
Ethan Wiley's photograph by Timothy O. Teague
Copyediting by Robin Quinn

David Brown's article, "The Creators," reprinted with permission from Variety, Inc. © 1996.
S. Ish-Kishor's story, "Appointment with Love," reprinted with permission of Johanna Hurwitz, literary executrix of the estate of Sulamith Ish-Kishor.

Printed by Braun-Brumfield, Inc., Ann Arbor, Michigan
Manufactured in the United States of America
The publisher plants two trees for every tree used in the manufacturing of this book. Printed on recycled stock.

Library of Congress Cataloging in Publication Data

Berman, Robert A.
       Fade In: the screenwriting process / Robert A. Berman. 2nd ed.
         p.   cm.
       Includes bibliographical references and index.
       ISBN: 0-941188-58-2
       1. Motion picture authorship. 2. Motion picture plays -- Technique.
I. Title.
PN1996.B465   1997
808.2'3--dc21   96-29509
                                             CIP

Books from
MICHAEL WIESE PRODUCTIONS

Directing Actors
Persistence of Vision
The Digital Videomaker's Guide
Shaking the Money Tree
Film Directing: Shot by Shot
Film Directing: Cinematic Motion
Fade In: The Screenwriting Process
The Writer's Journey
Producer to Producer
Film & Video Financing
Film & Video Marketing
Film & Video Budgets
The Independent Film & Videomaker's Guide

FADE IN:
THE SCREENWRITING PROCESS
BY ROBERT A. BERMAN

TABLE OF CONTENTS*

*In addition to the Index, the Table of Contents has been prepared with as much detail as possible to better assist you in finding things.

Acknowledgments

My relationship with Michael Wiese, my publisher, goes back to 1987, and having surpassed the duration of so many people's marriages, this says a great deal. His support, guidance, and friendship is greatly appreciated. Working with him has always been a positive experience.

Thanks to...

Lauren Schnitzer for her encouragement and proofreading assistance.

Robin Quinn for her editorial skills and helpful input.

Donald and Ann Haney for rescuing me from my software problems.

Bob Belli, my first manager, who has remained one of my most important influences.

Gil Backerman for his support.

Carl Ferrazza who has so graciously helped me over the past two years.

David Brown for taking time out of his busy schedule to meet with me and contribute to this book.

Ethan Wiley for his contribution and friendship.

Most importantly, a very special thanks to Susan, my wife of twenty-eight years. Her continuous love, support, sacrifice, and understanding has allowed me to pursue my dream. Someday soon, we will share in my success.

INTRODUCTION

The second edition of *Fade In* draws from eight years of experience with writing and in dealing with agents and production companies. The screenwriting method in this edition has been highly refined and presented with far greater clarity. The scope of the book has also been expanded to function as a *career guide* to aid you in all aspects of a screenwriting career. And to that end, two interviews have been added. The first is with David Brown, whose partnership with Richard Zanuck produced some of Hollywood's most successful movies. The second is with screenwriter Ethan Wiley, a twelve-year veteran whose experience and insight into both writing and the business side of the profession will be extremely helpful to you. Another major plus: the second edition of *Fade In* addresses the harsh realities of screenwriting, not to discourage you, but to make you well-informed about what to expect. Of greatest importance, I will share with you my proven *system* to help you penetrate agencies and production companies and get them to read your work—a big part of the battle.

In looking back at the past decade*, I have to wonder if Paul Simon had me in mind when he wrote, "Still Crazy After All These Years." It's important for you to know my background and experiences with screenwriting, since my story reflects what other writers have gone through, are going through, and will go through in this highly competitive field... if they are willing to persevere.

In September of 1986, at the age of forty-two, I walked away from a successful sales management career to pursue screenwriting. I was not only walking away from a hefty paycheck, but leaving at a time when major career opportunities were in my future. Making a change at this point would be analogous to someone going through all the years and hardships of college, med school and internship, only to quit before reaping the prime rewards of the profession. Since my decision was a spur-of-the-moment thing, I didn't have the benefit of building up a bank account to cushion the loss of income that still has not resolved itself. That's right—it's been ten years and I'm still pursuing the success which has so far eluded me.

*My screenwriting career officially started in October of 1986, but there was a period of two years when I did things other than screenwriting.

1

Having written for national magazines as a hobby during my business career, I approached screenwriting with a basic talent for writing and a high level of confidence. But there were problems. My work for national magazines was primarily interviewing people and writing how-to articles which require different writing skills. Also, in growing up and going through grade school, high school, and a brief stint at college, I was never a big reader—a prerequisite for being a fiction writer. So, in taking on screenwriting, I was at a major disadvantage and didn't know it. Another problem—I knew nothing about screen-writing and even less about how Hollywood worked.

On the personal side, I am married for twenty-eight years to a very supportive wife. Having no children, we were initially in a position to survive on her earnings so I could pursue screenwriting. This, of course, was provided we made major adjustments in our lifestyle and I took care of household chores and did the food shopping. Anyone wanna swap coupons? I'll trade you two Johnny Mops and a Mr. Clean for a Haagen-Dazs!

After digesting several screenwriting books, I struggled through writing my first screenplay, *The 12/20 Club*—an original idea that I had been thinking about for years. In writing that script using the most popular screenwriting book as a guide, it became apparent there was a better way of teaching this unique form of writing. In my business career, my responsibilities included rewriting company sales manuals and creating training programs. So having a knack for that type of writing prompted me to make notes on screenwriting techniques as I discovered them.

Browsing through a bookstore, I happened upon *The Independent Film & Videomakers Guide* by Michael Wiese. Having enjoyed his informative book, I decided to contact Michael. During a conversation over lunch, I mentioned my ideas about screenwriting. After reading my first script and being aware of my other writing experiences, Michael asked me to outline my thoughts on a screenwriting book. When two weeks passed and he had not responded to my proposal, I assumed he was not interested. The next day, to my surprise, a letter and contract arrived in the mail.

After completing *Fade In: The Screenwriting Process*, I went back to writing screenplays, two per year. Did my writing improve? Yes, but slowly. Submissions of early screenplays to those few agents and production companies who agreed to read them were met with flat-out rejection. This means they made no offer to see anything else in the future. In a few cases, I received coverage—the reader's critique of my script. Some were written objectively while others were outright malicious.

After three years, my work gradually improved but in such small increments it seemed hardly noticeable to anyone, least of all to me. As frustrations were setting in, a job offer came my way in January of 1990. While I was not looking for work or willing to give up on screenwriting, it was an opportunity to help replenish our much-depleted bank account. From February of 1990 to March of 1991, I worked eighty hours a week. My responsibilities not only included running a twenty-three state region with personnel reporting to me, but assisting the President of the company in upgrading the national sales organization. This meant flying to California every month in addition to jumping on airplanes every other week to work the East Coast markets. During this hectic thirteen-month period, my writing was focused on only one thing—developing sales and marketing programs. In a way, it was a blessing because it gave me a much needed break from screenwriting. When the company president ended up returning to the European headquarters, he replaced himself with two *empty suits*. The first thing they did was fire me. It was *adios* to my business career and back to the computer.

Rejuvenated by the thirteen-month hiatus, I worked even harder at writing screenplays. Again the work was improving but not good enough to attract an agent or interest a production company. By 1993, my scripts were being better received by a few agents but, again, no one would sign me. I was disappointed but not discouraged.

Drifting into 1995, I wrote *Last to Die*, a character-driven action script with a highly original premise that was enthusiastically received by my hard-to-please readers. Bolstered by their praise, I worked my way into one of the three big agencies, confidence high. Four weeks later, the script was returned along with a brief letter. They liked the characters but not the plot. *Hasta la vista*, baby. At that point, I went into the tank for six months. I can't remember how I spent the time except for one thing: I didn't write a word. Constant rejection, which is a *BIG* part of being a screenwriter, is tough and, quite frankly, something I wasn't used to receiving. With my sales career, which was not easy by any stretch, I was successful the vast majority of the time.

In January of 1996, with my confidence restored, I made a giant leap forward by writing two screenplays—from concepts to third drafts—in sixty days. Prior to writing these scripts, it took me, on average, six months to complete a third draft screenplay that was not nearly as good as these new ones, or so I thought. I handed out dozens of these scripts to people who were never previously enthusiastic about my work or who never got back to me after reading.

Within weeks, without calling anyone, the compliments began pouring in. I then decided it was time to go to Los Angeles. Not wanting to touch household money, I sold some of my musical instruments and ran a fishing tackle garage sale to raise the trip money. Over a period of three weeks, I made a full court press on fifty L.A.-based agencies and got twenty-one to accept scripts. Not bad. Shortly thereafter, I went to Los Angeles for a week that can be best described as an emotional roller coaster ride. Details to come later.

While financial pressures have not made things easy for my wife and me, we both realize that devoting all my time and energy to writing is the best way to maximize my opportunities with screenwriting. Some friends found it hard to believe that I left my business career just as I was moving into my peak years, and some even wonder why I haven't gone back. I look at it this way. Having invested almost ten years into screenwriting, do I walk away from this career just as my writing hits its stride? I say, "No way!" I know I have the talent and now the writing skills, the ability to network, the energy and enthusiasm of someone half my age, the personality to win people over, and the confidence to persevere. It's a question of coming up with the right script and finding more creative ways to earn that all-important first break. And you know what? I will. You can bet on it.

Before you attempt to write your first screenplay, it is my recommendation that you read this book and become totally comfortable with all the procedures. Then, read as many screenplays of successful films as you can. Read them until you understand each one intimately. This is all part of the learning process and an absolute necessity. Any attempt to cut corners here will cost you dearly when it comes time to tackle your first screenplay.

It's very important to have confidence in your own abilities. You must ultimately trust and rely upon your own judgment, taste, and intuition. Advice from others can be extremely helpful in the research stages and after the first draft screenplay is completed, but not while you are actually writing. If you receive bad advice or negative comments on what you have already written, it can be inhibiting and have an adverse effect on your attitude and, subsequently, your writing. You must always approach your work from a position of confidence. While you are writing your first screenplay, you may desire input or feedback as to how to approach a given problem. If you put your faith in the screenwriting method outlined here, you will answer those questions as you complete the necessary exercises.

In dealing with people inside and outside of the film industry, it is important to know and understand—and to constantly remind yourself—that *very few people can accurately assess any form of creative writing and provide the writer with helpful, constructive criticism.* What you most frequently get is someone else's take as to how *YOUR STORY* should be *CHANGED*—not made better, just made different. Of course, there will be those rare occasions when someone will have incredible insight into your story and provide you with helpful comments. And you will immediately know it. Embrace the advice and cherish the moment because it happens all too infrequently.

In the first edition of *Fade In*, my original screenplay, *The Crimson Moon*, was reprinted in its entirety to help illustrate various aspects of screenwriting. Since it was only my second script and my screenwriting skills were very limited at the time, it was poorly executed. In preparing the second edition of *Fade In*, I decided to use one of my most recent scripts, *Dead Man's Dance*. While I wanted to improve it before including it in the book, I felt it would be more beneficial to use the actual third draft copy which was submitted to agents and to present their specific comments on it. And since you are unfamiliar with the story, you will be able to read it from an unbiased point of view and later compare your reactions to the script with those of agents, as well as my own analysis.

Of greatest importance—*don't begin to write your screenplay until you are thoroughly prepared; and once you start, don't stop to polish, correct, or rewrite until the first draft is completed.*

Screenwriting is a true art form and craft mastered by a handful of talented people. Will you be one of them?

Author's Note: Throughout the text, certain points have been frequently repeated and restated in slightly different language in order to stress their importance.

THE SCREENPLAY

Films are the most influential medium in society today. Without a word of dialogue, images rendered on a screen can evoke many different emotional responses.

While film is a collaborative art form dependent upon the skills and talents of many artists and technicians, the strength of every film project lies with the screenplay.

A screenplay is a structural plan for a motion picture encompassing seven primary elements:

1. Story
2. Plot (structure)
3. Scenes
4. Characters
5. Dialogue
6. Emotional action
7. Physical action

When it comes to writing a novel, the author has total freedom and control over every aspect. A screenwriter must adhere to the unique screenplay form, the terse style of writing, and demonstrate great skill in structuring and executing a story within a specific number of pages.

As a general rule, *each page of screenplay is equal to one minute of film time*. This applies to both action scenes and those that are dialogue-driven. The minimum length for a feature film is 90 minutes which translates into 90 pages of screenplay. Some feature films can exceed two hours while others, especially comedies, tend to run between 90 and 100 minutes. Be prepared to write at least 90 pages but let your story determine the final length.

Regardless of how interesting a story's premise might be, *it is ultimately the writer's treatment of all the elements—collectively—that determines the final quality of the screenplay and how well it is received.*

After reading screenplays written by famous screenwriters, you will quickly identify the individual styles and liberties each has taken in completing his or her work.

James L. Brooks's screenwriting style is almost that of a novelist. *In Terms of Endearment*, he describes the emotional feelings of the characters in the scene descriptions. It greatly enhances the read and provides the actors with far more insight into the characters.

Horton Foote's screenwriting style in *Tender Mercies* demonstrates tremendous skill with minimal use of scene descriptions and the most effective treatment of dialogue. In some scenes, his sporadic use of dialogue initially seems inadequate—until you study it carefully. Then you realize how brilliantly it works.

As an unknown writer, you would be well-advised to stick to the basic screenwriting form and write as economically as possible. Your goal is to write a *tight script* that will be both appealing to the eye and easy to read.

THE BENEFITS OF READING SCREENPLAYS

Reading screenplays is a required step in the learning process. *In form, every screenplay looks the same, but in the treatment of characters and subject matter, each is distinctly different.*

In the Appendix, there is a list of stores specializing in selling screenplays as well as film books. Read as many scripts as you can since they will provide helpful insight into screenwriting and speed up the learning process. Whether you are writing a drama, comedy, action, sci-fi, or whatever, acquire screenplays in that genre. Reading them will help you determine how scene descriptions are handled as well as how much detail is used.

Reading scripts of successful films gives the reader a sense of form, the author's style, and how the various elements are treated. It also provides an opportunity to compare the script to the final results—the film. The screenplays you acquire may be a second draft, revised third draft, or even a shooting script as the legend indicates on the title page.

In reading screenplays of successful films which are in various stages of development, you may be exposed to deleted scenes or scenes which might have been filmed but later edited out. In many instances, the deleted or edited-out scenes were excellent judgments, regardless of who made the decision. Some scenes might have been deleted or edited out because they didn't move the story forward; or taking a particular scene out might actually enhance the story.

In the second draft of *Lethal Weapon*, there were a lot of funny, smart-ass wisecracks that were eventually deleted or edited out. Maybe Richard Donner, the director, wanted to keep a tight edge on the story so he cut back on some of the humor.

In some scripts, you will notice—in comparison to the film—that whole segments of dialogue have been deleted from scenes. Quite possibly, the director was able to make the scene work through the visual expressions of the actors—thus eliminating entire segments of dialogue. Some actors, like Clint Eastwood and Charles Bronson, are noted for communicating their thoughts to the audience with just a glance or the narrowing of their eyes.

If you can lay your hands on a third draft copy of Robert Towne's Academy-Award-winning screenplay, *Chinatown*, you will discover a number of interesting things. First, there are at least six scenes or major segments from scenes that were deleted from the film. These scenes, while interesting, were clearly not needed because they didn't advance the story. Also, within many segments of dialogue, the sequence of sentences was rearranged in order to present the information more logically.

By reading and analyzing scripts, you can begin to assimilate the writing form and the intricate techniques involved.

After seeing a terrible movie, many people incorrectly assume that they can write something better. The same logic is applied to great films which often create an unrealistic impression of being rather simplistic and, therefore, easy to write. That is not the case.

Anyone who plays golf can relate to this analogy. If you have no experience with the sport, you can quickly gain a false sense of confidence by observing the ease with which a professional swings a club. Not until you actually try playing golf do you realize the great skill, technique, and timing which are involved. The correct golf swing is totally foreign to natural body rhythm, making it very difficult to master without instruction, a lot of practice, and a positive mental attitude. Screenwriting, like golf, may look easy, but it is not. It is a complex form of writing requiring a delicate balance of many intricate details. If any one detail is not properly treated, it can derail the entire screenplay. Instead of having what could have been a great script, you end up with something which is ultimately a big disappointment.

It's important to understand the difficult aspects of screenwriting and, at the same time, know that you have the knowledge and means to succeed.

FILM REVIEWS AS A LEARNING TOOL

A good film review addresses both the positive and negative aspects of a film and provides moviegoers with reasonable expectations. How many times have you read, "The story drags in the last thirty minutes but thanks to so-and-so's magnificent performance, it is worth seeing." You certainly know what to expect.

Film reviews are a great learning tool for screenwriters because they can often trigger a conscious awareness to a problem in your own script—something you were unaware of until reading a review. "We never really understand the character's motivation." In thinking about your own script, you may suddenly realize that you have a similar problem. Film reviews can provide accurate insight into what makes a film appealing, or detracts from it, and may even prompt ideas. Read them.

HOW TO READ A SCREENPLAY

Reading a screenplay for the first time can be awkward. But once you understand the basic form and get by the terse style of writing, a good story will propel you to the end.

Each SCENE HEADING indicates either INT. (Interior) or EXT. (Exterior) LOCATION as well as time—DAY or NIGHT. Directly below the SCENE HEADING is the SCENE DESCRIPTION where characters and/or the action of the scene is described in paragraph form.

The CHARACTER speaking is capitalized and placed in the center of the page. STAGE DIRECTIONS are written one space below the character in parentheses. The DIALOGUE forms a block in the center of the page under the character's name or stage directions, when used.

Unlike novels and short stories written in the past tense, screenplays are written in the present.

Here is a brief illustration of screenplay form.

EXT. HOUSE - NIGHT

ARNIE EVANS, walking his dog, stops in front of a house and nervously looks around. BILL KIRK explodes from behind the bushes with a FLASHLIGHT and shines it in Evans's startled face. The DOG BARKS.

>   KIRK
>   What's the idea of letting your
>   dog do his business in front of my
>   house?

>   EVANS
>   (defensively)
>   He's got to go somewhere.

>   KIRK
>   (pointing)
>   Fine. Then take him over to
>   Behan's house, because I'm not too
>   fond of him either!

Evans walks off with his dog in tow under Kirk's watchful eye. (End of illustration.)

About Reading Screenplays

Before you read my original screenplay, *Dead Man's Dance*, there are a few points I'd like to bring to your attention about reading film scripts.

Reading a script you have not already seen as a film will prompt the most subjective reaction possible because you are relying only upon your own imagination. Whereas when you view a film, you are seeing the director's take or interpretation of the material.

No matter how many people read the same script or watch the same movie, you can bet there will be a divergence of opinions because personal taste dictates how each of us responds. At the same time, there are five basic reactions we all share when it comes to film.

There are:

1.   those we really like and can view over and over again.
2.   those we enjoy at the moment but don't care to see again.
3.   those we don't like at first but later learn to appreciate.
4.   those we are sorry to have seen and never care to see again.
5.   those that, in spite of major flaws, appeal to us because of memorable scenes. And whenever we view these films later, we wait in anticipation of those special scenes.

For the most part, films we enjoy at the moment but don't care to see again are primarily action pictures or those driven by special effects—usually at the expense of good characters and a strong plot. These films are typically referred to by critics as *popcorn movies* because of their entertainment value. Of course, using a metaphor, *popcorn movie* can also mean something light and of little substance—which obviously fulfills the needs of many viewers given the heavy-duty box office receipts of films in that category.

Of all the movies you have seen, think of the ones you have liked and why. Some sustain your interest from beginning to end with very few *dead spots*—areas where the story drags or for other reasons is just not appealing to you. These are the films you enjoy viewing over and over again. For me, *In the Heat of the Night* is just such a film and the one which probably initiated a subconscious interest in screenwriting back in 1967 when it was released—and it hasn't dated itself one bit.

This four-star film, one of director Norman Jewison's best, won five Academy Awards: Best Picture, Best Actor (Rod Steiger), Best Screenplay from Another Source (Stirling Silliphant), Best Editing (Hal Ashby), and Best Sound (Samuel Goldwyn Studio Sound Department). (Mike Nichols won Best Director that year for *The Graduate*.)

In the Heat of the Night, an atmospheric thriller set in the south, very effectively deals with two issues: racial bigotry and a mystery involving the murder of a prominent developer. Up to this point, most films had portrayed blacks in demeaning roles. In this story, however, Sidney Poitier plays a highly intelligent homicide detective from Pennsylvania. In passing through the sleepy southern town of Sparta, Mississippi, he becomes a suspect in the murder and locks horns with a less-than-able redneck police chief, magnificently played by Rod Steiger.

On parallel lines, the murder mystery and the issue of racial intolerance are developed with incredible style and believability. Over the course of the story, the black detective and the police chief gradually come to not only respect each other, but establish a friendship. If you haven't seen *In the Heat of the Night*, check it out and study it carefully. It not only effectively balances all seven primary elements of a screenplay, but evokes a strong emotional response. For my money, films don't get any better than *In the Heat of the Night*.

There is one distinct difference between seeing a movie and reading a script that you have not seen as a film (or has yet to be made into a film). And this works to the writer's advantage. *A person who doesn't enjoy a movie will not likely praise the screenwriter; but in reading a script, someone may recognize that the writing is good even though the story does not appeal to him or her*. A producer may not like your story but is impressed enough with your writing to offer you an assignment.

After he read one of my scripts, my nephew, David Randall, called and said, "I liked your script, Uncle Bob, but I don't know what to compare it to." "Why compare it to anything?" was my response. I pointed out to David that if he wanted to have a criteria for reading a screenplay, it would be this. After reading one, ask yourself three questions: "Did the story grab me right away?" "Did it sustain my interest all the way through?" "In the end, do I feel satisfied?"

COMMENTS ON THE READING ASSIGNMENT

Reading *Dead Man's Dance* has two purposes. First, it will help you gain familiarity with the screenwriting form. And second, you must be familiar with the story since all the elements will be frequently referenced throughout the book to illustrate different points.

Over the years, I have realized the value of streamlining my screenplays to make them better reads. During the rewriting phase, one of my goals—in addition to making improvements—is to reduce the length of scene descriptions and cut back dialogue. There are just a few abbreviated terms in my script, so if you have any doubts, refer to "Screenwriting Terminology" in Chapter 6. In writing my scripts, I visualize the characters, hear the dialogue in counterpoint, and imagine the action. For me, it's a very real experience, like going to the movies.

In regard to creating characters, I sometimes write with an actor in mind, but not always. With *Dead Man's Dance*, I had no actress in mind when I created the Kerry Parker role. Nevertheless I still form a very strong visual image of each character as I write my scripts.

Dead Man's Dance appears in the back of the book. To preserve the look and feel of the screenplay, the *Fade In* page headings were omitted. Please read the screenplay now in its entirety since it is an important part of the learning process and it will be frequently referenced from this point on. After you finish, return to the next chapter and continue from there.

DEAD MAN'S DANCE: SCRIPT ANALYSIS

The focus of this chapter will be to analyze *Dead Man's Dance* (DMD). All of my comments, as well as those of friends and agents, are based upon the third draft script presented here.

FEEDBACK FROM FRIENDS

The feedback from friends on *DMD* was not very elaborate since most read strictly for entertainment. The general comments were: "good read," "interesting plot," "would like to know more about Kerry and see her personal situation somehow resolved in the end." A few friends liked the mystery aspect of the story since they were unable to figure out what was going on. They also stressed that the last sixteen pages, once the policeman delivers Kerry to the Mafia house, were really fast-paced and very exciting—which enhanced the ending when everything was revealed.

FEEDBACK FROM AGENTS

By having to respond to one agent's two-page critique of *DMD* while writing this chapter, I was forced to really think about his comments. And because nine months have passed since completing the third draft script, I am now seeing things very objectively. My question is this: how much better will the script be after rewriting it based upon what is presented in this chapter—plus other changes I might make during the rewrite? If you didn't like the third draft script, would your opinion or that of an agent change after reading the fourth draft?

I will first present the general comments made by agents and then outline the two-page critique of *Dead Man's Dance* that one agent was kind enough to share with me. For obvious reasons, agents will not be acknowledged by name.

Most agents I had contact with, even with coaxing, would not elaborate on their criticism of the script, and the reason became obvious— someone else probably read it. The collective response in the form of major criticism was: the script was not commercial enough because it didn't have an *EDGE* like the movie *Seven*. By the way, *edge* is currently the most-used buzzword in Hollywood.

In a conversation with one agent, I asked him to explain what edge meant to him. 'He said, "You know, edge." After thinking about *DMD* for a moment and comparing it to *Seven*, I had a sudden realization which I confirmed with the agent. 'I said to him, "You mean it doesn't have enough sex, violence and profanity?" 'The agent said, "Right." Edge encompasses far more than those three elements, but I will, for now, address them first.

Does sex sell? The answer is *YES*, big time. And how about violence? Same. Of course, profanity is not an element to drive a film. It is a component of dialogue. In developing *DMD*, I made no conscious effort to avoid sex, violence and profanity. My focus was on creating a well-paced thriller utilizing those elements that would best drive the plot.

Would a hot love scene between Kerry and Mike enhance the story? No doubt, a flash cut from a hot love scene might make a tantalizing sequence in a movie trailer, but as far as a love scene making the story stronger, that all depends upon the character treatment. This issue will be explored in great depth later on in this chapter.

On the issue of graphic violence, I felt it wasn't necessary to show it. A movie that very effectively dealt with violence without showing it was the 1979 thriller, *When a Stranger Calls*. While this film has problems and was panned by many critics, it does have two sequences that will jolt you right out of your seat. Now to my point. *When a Stranger Calls* is a story about a baby-sitter, Carol Kane. While she is in a house, watching television in the living room and talking on the phone, two young children are brutally murdered upstairs. The brutality of these murders is communicated to the audience by the reactions of the police who investigate the murder scene. There was no need to show it. I came to the same conclusion about not using excessive violence in *DMD*. It has nothing to do with standing on higher moral ground. It's just that showing excessive violence would add nothing to the story.

When it came to writing dialogue for *DMD*, profanity simply didn't fit in given the characters and the story's setting. As you know, the story starts in California but quickly moves to a small town in western Massachusetts. The fictional town of Westbridge was created with the actual town of Great Barrington, Massachusetts, in mind. In this setting, the use of profanity would be totally inappropriate. Do I have a problem with profanity? Only when it is used excessively and gratuitously. Profanity has permeated films to the point that it has almost become a prerequisite. Look at the 1986 hit, *Stand by Me*, a story about the friendship of four twelve-year-old boys during the 1950s. This highly-praised film received one major complaint from critics—an excessive use of four-letter words that were not characteristic of the 1950s.

Sex, violence and profanity are elements which add gritty textures to a film—or if you will, an edge. Not using them in *DMD* might have created the impression it was written for television.

Maybe that was your reaction, too—or maybe you didn't even think about it until I just mentioned it. Or maybe, it just doesn't matter at all. Consider this: Given the subject matter, scope of the story, and modest budget requirements, *Kramer vs. Kramer* was perfect fare for television. The only reason it didn't go to television is because it had Dustin Hoffman and Meryl Streep, two major stars and gifted actors.

While *DMD* could go to television or cable, I feel confident that after making the improvements soon to be addressed here, it would be a satisfying experience for theatergoers and well worth the price of admission.

The following comments were presented to me in a rejection letter from an agent's assistant who read both *Dead Man's Dance* and *Screechers*, my sci-fi screenplay.

"Overall, I thought your writing was very good. *Dead Man's Dance* is an especially well-written piece. I do feel however, considering current trends, that the plot does not have enough conflict to make it commercial. But I want to stress how impressed I was and am with your characters and your ability to move the plot along."

The assistant's comments that the *plot* does not have enough *conflict* is one aspect of *EDGE*. The other has to do with the treatment of the main character, Kerry Parker. Both issues will be addressed after this segment of the chapter.

AGENT'S CRITIQUE

I will now present an agent's two-page letter of rejection outlining his specific criticism. His letter will be presented word-for-word. For the sake of clarity, it appears in sections, followed by my comments.

"I had a chance to look at your screenplay. While the premise intrigued me, unfortunately, I had enough problems with the execution to return it to you. The first problem I had was that I felt Kerry's character was not developed enough to really make us like her. The brief incident at the catering company where she shows compassion for her low-paid associate was nice, but ultimately it didn't seem to connect in any real way with the behavior she exhibited from then on. She was far too stubborn about taking anyone else's help or advice. It was as if a caterer had become Columbo. She needs to show more vulnerability and we need to see her fallibility."

There are two major elements where improvements would greatly enhance *DMD* —and one is Kerry's character. Therefore I feel that most of what the agent said here is valid and insightful. Since the agent addresses the character issue with even more specifics by scene, I will hold my comments until those scenes are presented.

"In the course of the story it comes out that Elaine pulled similar stunts four times before. Why then, after 24 hours, was Kerry on the way to find out what happened to her sister? Experience would have made Kerry more low-keyed about this. Had something recently happened to Elaine to make this time different?"

Good questions—good point. When Elaine tells Kerry she is going to the police in Westbridge, Massachusetts, about Hobart, Kerry tells Elaine to call her after she does. When she doesn't hear from Elaine, Kerry then decides to go to Massachusetts and look for her. In a conversation with Sgt. Daily on page 22, she explains that Elaine has emotional problems. In turn, the sergeant asks, "She's disappeared before?" Kerry says, "Yes, but never more than a few days without contacting me." Here is the disparity the agent was getting at. If

Elaine previously disappeared for a few days, why then is Kerry going to look for her after only one day? This problem could be easily corrected by one additional line of dialogue in that same scene with Sgt. Daily. Kerry could point out that Elaine's emotional problems were progressing and that she sounded far more erratic than before— thus prompting a greater concern for her sister at this time.

"Pg. 35. Kerry's conversation with Mike about Kathy seems too confidential and personal for this time in Kerry's life."

The conversation the agent is referring to happens just after a weepy-eyed Kathy reminisces with Kerry about Elaine and what her friendship meant to her. Given Kerry's emotional state at the time, still spinning from Elaine's rape and murder, the agent is right. The scene where Kerry brings up Kathy's problems with Mike would be more appropriate later in the story.

"Pg. 37. After Daily's death, why doesn't Kerry voice her suspicions to Chief Lavery, even if he is retiring?"

I don't agree with the agent on this point. When Kerry suggests to Sgt. Daily that he go to the chief, the sergeant says, "Chief Lavery's six weeks away from retiring. Forget him. For the past year, he's let the Lieutenant run the department."

Given the fact that Sgt. Daily *knows* the chief and says, "Forget him," would be enough for me to heed his advice. The chief could be incompetent and, therefore, not trusted to do the right thing. Sgt. Daily might assume that the chief would approach Lt. Haskins directly, if told about the lieutenant being seen with the murder victim and his later denying it. Thus Sgt. Daily would be revealed as the source of the complaint. On top of that, the sergeant tells Kerry he will approach a detective with the State Police for advice. For those reasons, Kerry would not go to the chief.

The following observation was made by the agent before addressing the next specific scene.

"There is an overall need to develop the relationship between Elaine and Kerry, as the script assumes too much as to the reader's emotional involvement with the pair and the tragedy that follows. Perhaps a longer scene on the phone might give us some insight into that relationship or maybe a conversation Kerry has with Mike."

No doubt about it, another good point made by the agent. As to a longer phone conversation between Kerry and Elaine, it would slow down and diffuse one of the most important scenes in the entire script. This scene and the one which follows set up the story, so they have to be extremely focused and right to the point. Also, given Elaine's emotional state, distraught and desperate, the telephone conversation scene does not lend itself to any kind of personal discussion where their real affection for each other is expressed. The agent's second suggestion is far more viable. At a later point, in a quiet scene between Kerry and Mike, or better yet Kathy, she can talk about her sister and the closeness they once had.

"Pg. 81. Mike's suggestion that Kerry stay with Kathy after Kerry has laid the bombshell on Haskins is putting his wife and children in danger along with Kerry. Would any father really do this—especially after he just chewed her out about being a risk taker?"

The agent has a point and the problem could be easily remedied by deleting that portion of the scene.

"Pg. 82/3. For someone who thinks she is as smart as a private eye, Kerry falls too quickly for the 'Mike's had an accident' gag."

I definitely disagree here. At this point, neither Kerry nor the audience has any way of knowing other policemen are involved. There is nothing previously in the story that might even indicate that. When Officer Dansk shows up at Kathy's house, you might guess him to be a bad guy, but I don't think the way the scene is handled gives it away. Here is this clean-cut, twenty-five-year-old policeman showing up at the house. Seeing Kerry, he asks, "Mrs. Burrows?" It all seems natural. In answering Kerry's question about how Mike was hurt, Dansk says, "I don't know. I was dispatched to take her to the hospital. I was told she doesn't drive." A logical assumption here would be that Mike, not fatally injured, was able to give that information to the medics.

"Pg. 96. Hobart is too quick to spill what he knows about the Mafia relocation program to Kerry. Also, there is a need to give Hobart additional scenes before the third act so that his villainy can be truly and clearly defined and thus the audience will feel that he gets what he deserves."

I disagree with the idea that Hobart discusses the relocation program too quickly. First, it is the end of the story and things have to be wrapped up quickly with the least amount of elaboration. It is obvious that Hobart talks freely with Kerry about the Mafia relocation program because he intends to kill her as soon as he thinks he has eluded his pursuers. I also have a problem with the agent's second point—giving Hobart additional scenes before the third act to show what a nasty guy he is. There are really two issues here: showing more of Hobart before the end and making him more despicable.

In regard to the first issue, Dennis Ludlow—Hobart's assumed identity—is only shown once (page 39) prior to the ending when his real identity is revealed. He was *played down* as to not give away who he really is. As logic dictates, the Hobart character has to show up or there would be no story. It would be easy to guess that Ludlow, because he has only one brief scene and doesn't show up until the end, is Hobart. If you read the script looking at the details, that would appear to be obvious. However, if you read the script simply for entertainment, you probably forget about Ludlow altogether until page 90 when it is mentioned that he was seen earlier (page 39) with Lt. Haskins.

Is there a way to give Hobart, as the Dennis Ludlow character, a more prominent role without giving away who he really is? The answer is yes. As long as Ludlow (Hobart) is not in the same scene as Kerry, because she knows him, he can be in many scenes. However, at that point, it might become too obvious as to who he really is. There is a way of getting around that problem.

Ludlow/Hobart is fifty—about the same age as Kerry's deceased father. If he is shown interacting with men his age, he would not stand out. Under these circumstances, I could even have Lt. Haskins approach Ludlow and have a full-blown discussion with him about something to do with the town. With that kind of treatment, Ludlow would come across as one of the more prominent citizens—someone the shrewd Lieutenant would cultivate a relationship with.

However, in giving this issue careful consideration, I have come to one very important conclusion and that is not to show Hobart until the very end. Why? First, it is logical to assume that he is maintaining a low profile since Kerry is in town. Second, it adds that extra jolt when he shows up at the end and reveals himself and all the details about the Mafia criminal relocation program. Third, I don't have to mislead the audience by presenting him as the Dennis Ludlow character.

Does it matter that my treatment of Hobart violates one of the important rules of dramatic writing—having only one clear-cut villain? Only as long as it works. As pointed out in the first chapter, it is the treatment of all the elements, collectively, that determines how well a story works. It should be every writer's objective to find the most unique and interesting way of developing his or her stories to create originality.

Since *Dead Man's Dance* has two villains—Kenneth Hobart and Lt. William Haskins—this point will be reviewed now. It works, but will work much better after making all the changes (the collective issues) proposed in this chapter.

TRANSITIONING THE VILLAINS

The story starts off with Hobart prompting the action because Elaine supposedly sees him in this remote New England town. Of course, once she is murdered and the finger of guilt is pointed at Lt. Haskins (page 29), the action follows him and takes an abrupt turn when it is revealed (page 76) that his DNA doesn't match that of Elaine's murderer. Then, at the end, it is Hobart whom Kerry faces and kills. Again, this is perfectly logical because Hobart is hiding out in this small New England community, maintaining a very low profile. And with Kerry in the area, it is easy to assume that Lt. Haskins advises Hobart about her presence and suggests that he stay out of town until she leaves or is removed.

Regarding his film *Absence of Malice*, which starred Paul Newman and Sally Field, screenwriter Kurt Luedtke remarked in an interview that he created a major error/problem in his treatment of the story's villain.

Until he mentioned it, I never gave it a thought. Field, playing a reporter, is duped by a scheming federal investigator into writing an article saying that Newman is being investigated by the organized crime and racketeering strike force. When Newman discovers that this federal investigator is the one responsible for all the grief in his life, he doesn't go after him. Instead he pursues the U.S. District Attorney. The scheming federal investigator is dismissed at the end through indirect action. By all reasoning, Newman should have pursued him and not the D.A. Nevertheless the story works which clearly supports the point that it comes down to *how* all the elements within a story are treated.

Now to the agent's second issue. He feels it is important to reveal Hobart's identity earlier in order to make him more despicable so that when he is killed the audience is pulling the trigger along with Kerry. If I followed the agent's suggestion, I would be identifying Hobart too early and ruining the surprise at the story's conclusion. Since it is now my intention not to show Hobart until the very end, here are two other points regarding the agent's comment about introducing him earlier so he will be more despised by the audience. My position is that it doesn't matter.

In the 1975 thriller, *Three Days of the Condor*, starring Robert Redford and Faye Dunaway, the villain is a character named Atwood (Lionel Atwell)—a director in the CIA in charge of the Middle East. About forty-five minutes into the film, he is revealed to be the bad guy. In this scene with Max von Sydow, who plays a contract killer hired by Atwood, the Atwood character comes across as a mild-mannered man. There is absolutely no animosity created towards Atwood from the viewer's perspective. The next time Atwood shows up is at the end when he is murdered by the contract killer in front of Joe Turner, the Redford character. And even in that scene, there is absolutely no sense of satisfaction from the viewer's point of view when Atwood is killed. The fact that the Atwood character, as the villain, was treated as a non-menacing type had no bearing on how well the story worked. Again, this comes right back to the issue of making all the elements work collectively.

Now point two on making Hobart more despicable. First, the audience knows that Hobart has literally ruined Kerry's life. After all, her father was convicted of embezzlement and murder and died in prison; her mother is institutionalized; and her sister is raped and murdered—all because of him. All this is reinforced when she confronts him at the end. After Hobart (page 96) boasts about how he beat justice, Kerry vents her hatred towards him. She says, "You... you killed my father!"

As that scene continues (page 97) and Hobart tells her why he blames her father for what happened, Kerry says, "So you framed him for embezzling and for your murder!" A good actress can project Kerry's pain, suffering, and anger, while a good actor can make us loath the Hobart character. In the last scene with her, Hobart is gloating and proud of how he managed to make her father pay for his crimes. Collectively all these issues establish him as a rotten S.O.B. So when he is killed by Kerry, it will be a vicarious thrill for the audience.

I am very grateful to the agent for sharing his comments with me on *Dead Man's Dance*. He not only brought to my attention things that require improving—things I might not have noticed right away—but forced me to see other issues at the same time.

REWRITE STRATEGY

For *DMD* to realize its maximum potential as a thriller, both the characters and the plot require improvements. Some improvements will be very subtle changes, others will be quite significant. In this portion of the chapter, I will go back and forth between character and plot issues as logic dictates.

In Linda Seger's book, *Making a Good Script Great*, she presented a case study on the rewrite of the 1985 Academy-Award-winning script, *Witness*. One point she made was that Rachel, the Kelly McGillis character, was very feisty and confrontational in early drafts of the script. When these scenes were shot with John Book, the Harrison Ford character, Rachel came across as being too irritating. New scenes were then written and shot to make Rachel more sympathetic. With just a little tweaking, a character's personality and *likability* can be greatly enhanced to the point that the entire script is improved. This is one of my objectives with the Kerry Parker character.

Studio readers focus a lot of attention on the main *character's arc*—the gradual change a character goes through in pursuit of his or her goal.

No doubt about it, a character's change can greatly enhance a story if it is appropriate and natural. For example, a disillusioned man on the brink of suicide finds hope from a blind girl. Based upon that premise, the man would be expected to go through a change or there would be no story.

On the other hand, look at *Hud*, the 1963 four-star film starring Paul Newman as a Texas heel. His character does not change one iota and, for that reason, his nephew and housekeeper leave him because he is unfit to live with.

In the 1960s, you could present unsympathetic characters and downbeat endings because it was acceptable then—it tied into the mood (economy) of the country. Today the studios are looking for sympathetic characters and upbeat endings because that is what the audience wants. Having said that, I will now say that for every rule, there is always an exception.

In *DMD*, Kerry does not go through a change in the third draft script because I lost my focus on her by putting too much emphasis on the plot. Also I didn't step back from the script long enough to see those problems. (I wrote it in thirty days and shipped it right out the door. It was a big mistake... one I will never make again.) Another factor contributing to the script problems was not getting the right feedback. With this project, I responded to the compliments of friends who read it for entertainment. The script should have been given to someone with a keen eye who would have taken it apart. Many points made from here to the end of this chapter were strongly influenced by the recent input from Ethan Wiley, my screenwriting friend whose interview appears in Chapter 9. While I didn't agree with everything he said, the vast majority of his observations, comments, and suggestions were extremely accurate. His insight into my story and characters clearly opened my eyes. As you will learn, the most difficult part of rewriting is knowing what to rewrite.

Before getting into Kerry's character, I want to address the issue of *EDGE* again because it has application to many different aspects of a story, including character and plot.

A segment of *Dead Man's Dance* is clearly lacking in suspense, which is not good because it is supposed to be a thriller. How will this problem be addressed? By creating more suspense-type scenes in that segment without going over the top. In Chapter 5, the plot points for *DMD* are outlined from the story's setup to its resolution. When you look at them carefully, you will see that the action and suspense in the story gradually builds. There are three major plot points at the end of the first act and at the beginning of the second: Elaine's body is found; it turns out that Lt. Haskins was the last to see her alive; and then Sgt. Daily is killed. After that, from pages 37 to 56, the amount of tension in the story is minimal. With that in mind, I will create three suspense scenes in that segment of the script that will have two functions: to increase the tension and to lead the audience to the possibility that a conspiracy (the Mafia criminal relocation program) is in the making without giving anything away.

The first suspense scene would be showing Sgt. Daily being killed. In this scene, he will be dispatched, late at night, to investigate a complaint about a prowler. He goes to a dark house and rings the doorbell. No answer. He walks around the house and tries the back door. It's locked. From behind, the sound of a twig snapping. As Sgt. Daily swings around, a handgun, held by a dark figure, flashes in the night. This scene would add considerable suspense since the sergeant's death, in the third draft, was treated through exposition.

A second scene would be set in downtown Westbridge. At 2:30 a.m., Kerry—who is unable to sleep—wanders down Main Street and glances into stores. A scar-faced man crosses the street, heading her way. The scar-faced man will be Sonny Lello, the Mafia hit man. His menacing posture prompts Kerry to hurry. As she picks up her pace, so does her pursuer. When she turns the corner to make a run for it, she bumps into a seedy-looking, homeless man, which gives her a fright. As Kerry tells the homeless man that she was being followed, Lello disappears. That scene can give the audience a nice *jolt* and foreshadow other things to come.

A third scene would be handled in this way. It's late at night and Kerry is sound asleep in her room at the bed and breakfast inn. Something disturbs her. She wakes as someone is trying to enter her room. As the suspense builds, wham! The sound of a door slamming shut down the hall shatters the tension. At the sound of retreating footsteps, Kerry gets out of bed and goes to the window.

Looking outside, she sees a man moving swiftly for a car. It's Sonny Lello, the Mafia hit man who shows up at the end. This works in two ways. First, it diverts direct suspicion from Lt. Haskins. And second, it adds to the conspiracy factor. It will also make Haskins's role in whatever is going on more confusing to the audience when Kerry learns that his DNA doesn't match that of her sister's murderer.

OTHER PLOT-RELATED ISSUES

When and how information is related to the audience determines its impact. On page 5, Kerry tells Dan that Elaine is in Massachusetts and claims to have seen Kenneth Hobart. Knowing who Hobart is, Dan reacts and says, "Jesus..." On the very next page, it is explained that Hobart is the man that Kerry's father supposedly murdered. That certainly grabs the audience's attention, but as Ethan Wiley suggested, "Why don't you hold back that information until later and let the audience remain curious and guess who he is. It gets them more involved in your story." Immediately I knew he was right. Therefore that fact will be revealed more towards the end of the first act to string things out.

Another point about Hobart as a plot issue. When Kerry goes to the police station (pages 7/8) about Elaine, she does not mention him by name. That scene will be changed to Kerry mentioning Hobart and having Sergeant Quill respond that he doesn't know anyone by that name in town. This gets the Hobart issue out front, and since this sergeant is not part of the conspiracy, it works even better.

Towards the end of the first act, Kerry will explain who Hobart is in her conversation with Sgt. Daily when he tells her about Lt. Haskins. The audience would then be given a double dose of information, making those other plot points even stronger.

By adding those suspense scenes, changing when and how information is given to the audience, and not showing Hobart until the end, the plot would be greatly enhanced.

THE CHARACTER ISSUE

One of the most important steps in improving *DMD* would be the treatment of Kerry Parker's character. From the very beginning, she will be placed in a crisis situation in two ways—with her own life and in dealing with her sister's murder. From the outset of the story, Kerry will be in a strained relationship with Dan Wallace—only this time, he will be her fiancé, as well as her partner. This will create all kinds of conflict and tension from the get-go.

Remember the scene on page 2 when Kerry tells John Mathews, her older employee, that she didn't forget to deduct from his pay all the time he took off when Mark (his son) was in the hospital? That scene will be written like this. Dan will barge into Kerry's office complaining about her not docking John's pay. She will defend her decision by saying that John is a loyal, hard-working employee, who deserves special consideration. Their meeting will end showing an incredible strain between them. And when the time comes for Kerry to leave for Massachusetts, Dan will argue with her over going. He will say that her leaving at this time would place an unfair burden upon him and everyone else given all the catering jobs on the books. Kerry's troubled relationship with Dan also strengthens her motive for leaving. Is she going because of her sister, or because she wants to get away from her life which is unraveling?

An important turning point in the story happens not after Elaine is discovered murdered, but after Kerry learns that Lt. Haskins could be the murderer. This is the moment when the investigation begins and her goal is established—to see that the murderer is brought to justice. But why must she do this herself?

Her motive, which will be subtly introduced in a conversation with Mike Burrows later in the story, is this: she is looking for a way to vent all her anger and frustrations from seeing her once-happy family destroyed. She couldn't do anything about her father or mother's situations, but she now has the opportunity to avenge her sister's rape and murder.

On page 27, the second scene description reads: Kerry is walking down the sidewalk, half-dazed. In the fifth scene description, on that same page, it reads: Unlike before, Daily is not the calm professional—and Kerry is no longer out of focus, but highly alert. When Kerry senses that Sgt. Daily has something to tell her about Elaine's murder, she is no longer consumed with grief at that moment, but highly focused. This is a very natural response to real-life situations. When the family of a victim learns who the perpetrator is, grief is suddenly transferred into intense anger and a desire for revenge.

How much the audience likes Kerry and accepts her actions will be determined by *how* and *how well* her character is defined. Her character will go through a radical change in the fourth draft. My goal will be to accurately balance and portray her likability, vulnerability, and faults. This, of course, will alter how she responds to the different situations she will encounter. Her brazen act of entering Lt. Haskins home (page 56), in trying to acquire a hair sample for DNA testing, will be made more spontaneous and impulsive.

Thus in her scene (page 66) with Mike Burrows in which he censures her for her reckless behavior, she would not respond defiantly, but with humility agree that what she had done was wrong. This approach to Kerry's character would be maintained throughout the entire script.

REVEALING MORE ABOUT KERRY

Here are a few ways to reveal more about Kerry, especially her relationship with Elaine and Dan. This would be accomplished by integrating a few well-crafted, well-placed scenes into the second act.

The first scene would be Kerry—in a very subtle way, maybe being caught off guard—talking about the tragic events that have torn her once-close family apart. It could occur during a quiet moment when she is alone with Kathy Burrows, and because Kathy is slightly under the influence, Kerry drops her guard and speaks from the heart. Since Kathy and Elaine were the best of friends, Kathy would know the family history and could be the one to bring up that topic, which would then allow Kerry to reluctantly respond, etc.

At another time, Kerry could talk about her strained relationship with Dan, stressing that the problem is primarily due to all the hours they spend together, etc. Kerry could also express her desire for a change in her life other than working fourteen-hour days. Maybe she could make the point that, at twenty-eight, the urge for motherhood is stronger than ever, but given her family's painful history it makes it difficult for her to seek happiness at this time. With whom, when, and how she shares these intimate thoughts would be critical to making them believable.

KERRY'S RELATIONSHIPS WITH DAN, KATHY, AND MIKE

Let's look at Kerry's character from the standpoint of her relationships with Dan Wallace, Kathy Burrows, and Mike Burrows.

Midway through the story, Kerry would get into a heated argument with Dan during a phone conversation. She would tell him that she wants out of not only their business arrangement, but out of their engagement. This would be a very logical move given her strained relationship with him and the pressure she is dealing with regarding her sister's rape and murder. Obviously all those friendly phone chats between Kerry and Dan that are presently in the screenplay would be dropped.

With other goals in mind, such as having Kerry go through some kind of transformation by the end of the story, my treatment of her would require a profound change in her relationship with both Kathy Burrows and Kathy's ex-husband, Mike.

With Kathy, the connection will be twofold. First, since Kathy and Elaine were best friends—and Elaine is now dead—Kerry finds herself needing to have a relationship with Kathy. Her second motivation will be to try, in some way, to help Kathy deal with her problems. This is a form of redemption since Kerry feels a sense of guilt over not helping her own sister more.

It will require a delicate balance to create these small personal/subplot scenes—to enhance Kerry's likability and vulnerability—without derailing the action of the main plot... Kerry's pursuit of Lt. Haskins.

Kerry's relationship with Mike Burrows will also change. In my first draft of *DMD*, I had them make love, but it didn't feel right given all the circumstances surrounding the relationships of the three characters—Kerry, Kathy, and Mike. In the fourth draft of *DMD*, Kerry and Mike *will* make love. One major change will be required or it will totally destroy Kerry's likability with the audience, and that is— Mike and Kathy's relationship must change.

In the third draft, Mike is still in love with Kathy. That is the reason Kerry doesn't go through with making love to him, in spite of the attraction and feelings they have for each other. In the fourth draft, it will be made clear that both Kathy and Mike want no part of getting back together. They are in a relationship where they tolerate each other for the sake of their children. In this case, it would be appropriate for Kerry and Mike to make love. My instincts tell me that they won't get together at the end for the following reasons. Given their opposite backgrounds and the circumstances at the end of the story, it is more logical for Kerry and Mike to remain friends and go their separate ways. Kerry was born into wealth, is college-educated, self-sufficient, and would find life in a small town, at this stage in her life, boring. Mike is an honest working-class man who is deeply devoted to his sons and wouldn't leave the area because of his need to be close to them. Kerry would have a second reason for not staying: living in the Westbridge area would be a constant reminder of Elaine's untimely death.

Kerry's life would be resolved in a number of ways at the end of *DMD*. The first thing she would do is clear her father's name. This point would be made as she is leaving town. Second, she would leave having established a relationship with Kathy—similar to the way Elaine did. Third, with her family history behind her, her relationship with Dan Wallace over, and being out of the catering business, she would be able to start her life over. All these points could be handled quickly and subtly at the conclusion of the story, and made believable through conversations she has with Kathy and Mike during the second act.

When I get through rewriting *Dead Man's Dance*, it will read like a *new story* because, essentially, that is what it will be. It will have a completely different tone—an edge, if you will; and it will function using a different set of dynamics, making the most out of both the characters and the plot.

Two Small Issues

One obvious issue that should be clarified in the story, but was never brought to my attention by anyone, was how did Lt. Haskins find out Sgt. Daily was going to the State Police? The answer is: Daily was friendly with Sgt. Walcott, the other dirty cop, and confided in him.

Here's a mistake so obvious it's embarrassing. It happens on the last page of the script and it involves the last piece of critical exposition.

As Kathy Burrows picks up the newspaper from the front porch, she glances at the headlines, then the article. Both are shown in CLOSE UP which means the audience has to read it. I give myself an *F* for that one. The scene will be changed this way. Kathy will go into the kitchen after Mike leaves with Kerry for the airport. While she cleans up the counter, the radio will be on broadcasting all the details outlined in the newspaper article. This is a far more effective way of presenting the information to the audience.

THE PLUS SIDE OF REJECTION

Is there a plus side to rejection? Yes and it's twofold. First. Agents and producers who rejected *DMD* said they liked the writing and expressed an interest to read future scripts. Having an open door is an asset because you don't have to go through all the *breaking-in* steps which are time-consuming and can be frustrating. The second benefit is this—sometimes you can get meaningful feedback as to why your script was rejected.

FINAL COMMENTS

Insightful comments given to a writer by an agent or producer are invaluable. And it is a shame that this *sharing* doesn't happen more frequently—especially with those writers who clearly exhibit talent. After all, with the right feedback, in some instances, a script could become something special after making only minor changes. No doubt, everyone would benefit. Writers would benefit from those observations that would allow them to improve their scripts; while agents and producers would benefit from having direct access to the scripts of those talented writers they have helped.

Taking it one step further, what could be even more beneficial would be the writer sitting down with the agent or producer who has actually read his or her script. Through that type of exchange, the writer could acquire even more input. Sure, it does happen, but not often enough.

Anytime your script is rejected, try to find out why—get the specifics if you can. Going back one step further, it is absolutely essential for a writer to get input on his or her script before sending it out to anyone in the industry.

POST SCRIPT

Four weeks after submitting this edition of *Fade In* to my publisher, I completed my rewrite of *Dead Man's Dance* and am now awaiting responses from agents. Prior to sending agents the revised draft, I gave a copy to friends who had read the draft presented here. They couldn't believe how much better it is and commented that a good portion of the script felt like a first-time read. Their reaction was based upon the significant improvements made to the Kerry Parker character which is supported by many revised scenes exploring and revealing, in far greater depth, her likability, vulnerability, and faults. She is now more sympathetic and interesting. They also noted how well the dialogue has been refined and how the streamlined plot, with a few subtle changes, works even better.

After doing the rewrite on *Dead Man's Dance*, it became apparent to me that my writing skills have reached a major turning point. One contributing factor was the time spent away from screenwriting—the six months it took me to write the second edition of this book. The second factor was shifting my emphasis from plot to character and maintaining that focus in the rewrite. Now that I am more than halfway through revising my first screenplay, *The 12/20 Club*, and see how well it is developing, I am convinced more than ever that success will be forthcoming.

THE STORY

THE BASIC RULES OF DRAMATIC WRITING

Once you understand the basic rules that apply to dramatic writing, it's easy to approach screenwriting and establish your course of direction with confidence.

In any story, there can only be one protagonist or main character: a person who has an urgent need to achieve something that is important to him or her. While there may be two characters who seemingly appear as *equals* in a story, one must have a more dominant role and greater need than the other. The reason for having only one main character is to provide clarity and focus in developing your story. Also, the viewer, as an individual, most readily identifies with another individual.

In *Lethal Weapon*, Martin Riggs (Mel Gibson) and Roger Murtaugh (Danny Glover) appear as equals and share almost the same amount of screen time. However the main character is clearly Riggs. Why? Because in trying to deal with his wife's death, he is suicidal. His need is to find a reason to live.

For the same reason, there can only be *one* antagonist or villain who will create obstacles in the path of the main character. By progressively increasing *conflict* between the main character and the adversary, you will create a story that will sustain the audience's attention and interest.

Conflict is the basis of all drama. Without conflict, there's no story.

If you choose to write a story about a man or woman battling a harsh wilderness environment or any other form of inanimate opposition, it will not work by itself.

Only when adversaries act and react through rising human conflict can an audience's attention and interest be sustained.

35

If your main character advances a step towards achieving his or her goal, there must be a setback or counter-thrust delivered by the adversary. This is the primary essence of dramatic writing—one person striving to achieve a goal while another attempts to defeat him or her. The action of both the main character and the adversary must be motivated by their individual needs. And you must find a way to establish their motives with the audience.

A distinction needs to be made between the forms of human conflict, as determined by the treatment of the characters in different film stories. Are there stories where inanimate opposition is the primary source of conflict? Yes. But the question is "How well do they really work?"

Places in the Heart is a moving story dramatizing the struggle of a woman trying to save her farm after the death of her husband. The harsh climate of the Depression era is *the* primary force creating conflict; which is inanimate opposition. What is interesting and unusual about the situation is this: the bank holding the mortgage on the woman's (Sally Field's) farm was actually supportive of her, thus reducing the most obvious potential for rising human conflict. Considering all the bank foreclosures during that period of history, the bank manager should have been merciless in demanding prompt payment. There are a few separate incidents where human conflict come into play, but they are very minor and not continuous from a standpoint of *one* character being the primary antagonist.

On Golden Pond deals with human conflict, but at a different level than other stories in the traditional sense. Henry Fonda's character is struggling with himself in dealing with old age. Jane Fonda's daughter character struggles with the need for her father's approval. There is strong friction between these two characters until the end of the story when they really talk to each other for the first time and come to an understanding. While the conflict in *On Golden Pond* is very dramatic within the context of the story, it is less dramatic in comparison to stories where the adversaries are a protagonist versus an antagonist.

Another example of conflict is the *antagonist within* premise which is best illustrated by two Rocky films: *Somebody Up There Likes Me*, based upon the real-life story of Rocky Graziano; and Sylvester Stallone's *Rocky*. Both of these film stories follow the same basic premise in that the characters are born losers coming from an environment of poverty and crime. Their backgrounds are *inanimate opposition*—the force working against them. Their goal is to overcome those aspects of their lives which label them losers. In that respect, the stories are identical. What essentially made Stallone's story different and fresh is one primary element, the story's *hook*. Stallone's Rocky, an unknown fighter, is given the opportunity to fight the world champion. Overcoming the loser within himself, his self-doubt, his life of poverty and crime, is *the* primary force of conflict in both Rocky stories.

In a later chapter, the various forms of conflict within *Dead Man's Dance* will be examined. There is rising human conflict, conflict which is indigenous to the story, as well as the main character's internal conflict (antagonist within) in dealing with personal demons.

Within every story, there are major and minor conflicts, obstacles, confrontations, and struggles. These forms of conflict will vary in degrees but, collectively, they provide the adhesive force sustaining the audience's attention and interest.

While film stories are similar in some respects, they are very unique in regard to the treatment of the characters, subject matter, and all the other important elements. Read and analyze screenplays of successful films until you clearly understand how and why each one works so well.

A LIKEABLE MAIN CHARACTER

The success of your story will also hinge upon creating a likeable main character—someone the audience can identify with, relate to, and root for. Early in your story, it is important to establish who your main character is, as well as his or her likability. Without using dialogue, you could show your main character giving assistance to a young child or possibly an elderly person. The scene can be as brief as four or five seconds but it will be long enough to plant a positive character image with the audience. Most importantly, scenes like this must fit naturally into the framework of your story without appearing to be obvious or contrived.

In *DMD*, Kerry Parker's likability is initially established by the kindness she shows an older employee by not docking his pay. As co-owner of the company, her act of generosity fits naturally into the story. Of course, as the agent pointed out in his critique of *DMD*, that scene didn't work for him because of my failure to enhance and develop Kerry's character later on in the story.

If your character shows any signs of being mean, nasty, or malicious, audience empathy will be lost and your story will fail right from the outset.

Jack Nicholson has a knack for making the audience like him even when he is playing an unsympathetic character. I once wrote a short film script creating a smart-ass character... à la Nicholson. In sharing it with friends and explaining how I modeled my character after him, it didn't make any difference. They didn't like the script because my main character was not sympathetic—which has nothing to do with whether or not it would *work* as a film and enjoy success.

If you deliberately make your main character unsympathetic, know that you are facing an uphill battle in trying to sell your screenplay.

The emotional action and dialogue spoken by your characters must be believable. In any situation, your characters must act and react as they would in real life.

While *creative license* allows for the taking of many liberties, every story must remain within the boundaries or realities it establishes from the beginning. This applies to every story from drama to sci-fi.

BELIEVABILITY VERSUS IMPLAUSIBILITY

An important objective in writing fiction, regardless of genre, is making things as believable as possible and to avoid *contrivances*—which is easy to do. Example: Your main character saves the President's life by shooting a sniper 800 yards away. Early in your story, you must establish your hero's expertise with a rifle or when that critical scene happens, it will appear totally contrived.

There are some *gray* areas where things may or may not be plausible—depending upon each person's point of view. In *DMD*, Kerry learns that the car leaving the scene of Sgt. Daily's murder has a fan belt that squeals. Later when she is leaving the supermarket with Kathy

Burrows and her children, she notices that Gail Haskins drives a station wagon with a squealing fan belt.

Only one reader questioned that point but accepted my explanation. Since the story is set in a very small town, it is highly likely that she could run into someone driving a car with a fan belt that squeals. However, had Kerry run into Haskins driving his wife's station wagon or his own vehicle with a squealing fan belt, that would have been too convenient.

When your story is finally resolved, nothing must be left unexplained, hanging, or resolved by coincidence. Everything must be tied together in one neat package.

THE STEP-BY-STEP SCREENWRITING PROCESS

When you consider the total amount of time involved in completing the actual first draft screenplay from the initial story concept, you may spend eighty percent of your time conceptualizing the story, researching the subject matter, and completing the various written exercises. Writing the actual first draft screenplay may only account for twenty percent of your total project time up to that point. (Rewriting is a separate issue.)

Those who apply themselves and follow the procedures outlined in this book will be capable of writing a good, solid screenplay.

Since writing is very personal and everyone has different levels of ability and skill, you will ultimately determine, through experience, what is valuable to you as far as the entire screenwriting method is concerned. Experienced writers may feel certain steps, such as the scene descriptions or narrative treatment, are not needed. That may be true for them, but not necessarily for you. Don't let anyone else influence you in that respect. Go through all the exercises until you are experienced enough to judge for yourself the value and necessity of each step.

Each step of screenwriting is overlapping and gradually enhances the development and clarity of your story.

With each successive step, things gradually become easier. If you follow all the exercises, you will be surprised at how effortless it seems to write that first draft script.

Taking a few shortcuts without having the experience first could set you up for disaster. Eliminating a step in the process doesn't save time if you end up stalling out or struggling halfway through your first screenplay.

EIGHT EXERCISES

There are eight exercises involved in creating a first draft screenplay from story concept—and they are:

1. Create a main character and then determine the character's need; that is, what does the main character want to achieve in your story?

2. Complete a character biography and outline the six aspects of good character. (More on this to come.)

3. Determine the ending of your story.

4. Outline the screenplay's structure from setup to resolution, from plot point to plot point.

5. Outline the scene descriptions.

6. Complete a narrative treatment of your story.

7. Complete the necessary research.*

8. Write your first draft screenplay.

You will find these exercises scattered throughout the book, noted with the same exercise numbers listed above.

---

*Some writers start the process by researching subject matter and create a story from what they discover. Therefore, research might be the *first step* in the process instead of the seventh.

EXERCISE TIME FACTOR

Don't set time goals for completing any exercise because it is difficult to predict how much time will be involved to finish any step.

While it is important to follow the exercise sequence, you may be able to tackle portions of the next listed exercise if you are having difficulties with the one you're doing. Sometimes jumping to the next step might force or prompt your creative powers to resolve the uncompleted exercise. Don't become unhinged if a particular step is taking longer than anticipated—you will find the solution.

HOW TO CREATE A SCREENPLAY STORY

Story ideas for screenplays come spontaneously for most writers. That is, a basic thought comes to mind and it is either developed or discarded. Screenplay ideas can come in two forms: SUBJECT MATTER—what the story is about, and/or CHARACTER. Regardless of where you start, *the entire process evolves from character*.

Let's say you decide to start with subject matter first; something that really appeals to you like football, auto racing, science, medicine, or whatever. What if you wanted to write about a group of businessmen, possibly ex-jocks, who want to put together a company football team and challenge other companies within their industry. That's fine. But remember, the process evolves from *one* character.

Once you determine who your main character will be, you then establish his or her *need*—that is, what that person wants to achieve. *Your character's need will create action as well as conflict, the basis of all drama*.

Once you know what your main character wants to achieve, it will be easy to create obstacles that will impede your hero or heroine from reaching his or her goal.

For your football story, your main character could be Brad Reynolds, a company executive and ex-jock who never accepted the fact that his football days are well behind him. Reynolds's need could be to put together a company football team to challenge and beat his college rival who works for a major competitor. Now that you know what

Reynolds's goal is, you are in a position to create obstacles—and the choices are numerous. In order to achieve his goal, it is true that Reynolds's own actions will naturally create conflict without resorting to any other human working against him, sort of the antagonist within premise, as well as conflict which is indigenous to the story itself.

In certain stories, such as *Rocky*, the antagonist within premise works very effectively. Another example might be a story where a character fights to overcome a major physical handicap in order to achieve his or her goal.

Since Brad Reynolds is an average guy, it is necessary to create a human adversary in order *to strengthen the story's conflict*. Reynolds could have: a tough time trying to recruit other players; difficulties at home with his family over his outside activities; or possibly problems with his boss who doesn't share his enthusiasm for sports. Those are conflicts influenced by Reynolds's own actions and are inherent in the story. Having a flesh-and-blood adversary is an absolute necessity that will bolster the story's conflict. What if one of his peers openly works against Reynolds achieving his goal—or possibly, behind his back? His nemesis may even benefit if he can discredit Reynolds whose actions quite possibly create a conflict of interest at work. It's easy to see how rising conflict between two people can be extremely stimulating and have the strength to sustain an audience's attention and interest from the story's beginning to its end.

Your story could be a drama, a comedy, or possibly both. What if Brad Reynolds had some kind of medical problem where playing football might jeopardize his life, yet he recklessly pursues his goal anyway? How and when information like that is revealed to the audience would have significant impact on the story. You make those decisions out of choice.

In developing a story, the process starts with CHARACTER, NEED, and SUBJECT MATTER. As concisely as possible, outline your story.

If you titled your football story, *Six-Yard Penalty*, your description would be treated like this.

Six-Yard Penalty is the story of Brad Reynolds, an ex-jock executive, who puts together a company football team to challenge his college rival.

That sentence tells you who the main CHARACTER is (Brad Reynolds, an ex-jock executive); what the SUBJECT MATTER is (football); and the CHARACTER'S NEED (to put together a company football team to challenge his college rival). That description provides the direction for developing the story—and everything is built from that premise.

Dead Man's Dance is a story about Kerry Parker searching for her sister who disappears after supposedly seeing the man their father murdered.

That one sentence tells you that Kerry Parker is the main character; her need is to find her sister; and the subject matter—*what it is about*— is her sister supposedly seeing the man their father murdered.

ANOTHER WAY TO CREATE A SCREENPLAY STORY

If you're not sure of what to write about, there is a simple exercise you can complete. And remember, every story begins with and evolves from character. Select a career field that you have expertise in or one that appeals to you—such as teaching, medicine, science, law, aviation, whatever—and determine a dramatic need for that given profession.

That would stimulate the creative process leading to the next step. It's really that simple. Through bulldog determination, you can make any story work once you understand the basics of dramatic writing.

If you decided to write a story about a journalist, what would be the main character's need? Something really dramatic. What if the journalist wanted to interview a world-famous terrorist? Think of the possibilities, the challenge of making contact, and the danger involved. The opportunity to create action and conflict around this situation makes it potentially a great story—that is, if you can develop it.

Make a list of career fields and select one that appeals to you. Through research, reading, and/or interviewing experts in that field, you might find a number of interesting elements that provide the basis for a story.

CHARACTER

CHARACTER, THE BASIC FACTS

How people act and react reveals a lot about their character. And, of course, if you don't know someone, it would be impossible to predict his or her behavior under any given circumstances. This same principle holds true for the main character in your story.

You must know your main character intimately so you can accurately and naturally determine how he or she will act and react to any given situation in your story.

If you don't know your main character, you will ultimately *force* him or her to act and react. And as a result, his or her actions will come across as being contrived and not believable.

How would a stranger react to being approached by a panhandler on the street? You may know how you would respond, but what about a perfect stranger? The hero or heroine in your story is a stranger until you define the character and establish his or her identity. It's not enough to know how your character will *react* to the panhandler; you must know how he or she will *act*. ***The primary function of the main character in any story is to act—to take action***. Therefore you must know your main character intimately.

Creating a three-dimensional character (information to follow) is a major step in the screenwriting process which may seem initially unimportant. Don't make that assumption—consider it a tool and a major asset that will contribute greatly to the development of your character and your story.

ONE MAIN CHARACTER

If your story is about four brothers, there still can be only one main character from which your story evolves. Pick the brother with the greatest need—possibly one who is dying from a terminal illness and wants to be reunited with his brothers one last time. Or the story could be about one brother convincing the other three to search for their sister who is missing and presumed dead. The possibilities are endless. If your story was about four brothers, you would have to complete a biography on each. Your objective would be to define the different elements in each personality that would establish the right blend of those forces that would bring them close together and, at the same time, create friction and conflict.

The first brother could be aggressive and domineering, while the second brother is somewhat reserved and resentful. The third brother could be very hyper and prone to arguing at the drop of a hat. The fourth brother could be financially well off but stingy and not willing to share his good fortune with the other three.

EXERCISE I: CREATE THE MAIN CHARACTER/NEED

Create a main character and then determine the character's need (what that person wants to achieve during the course of your story). As concisely as possible, outline the basic premise of your story—character, need, and subject matter.

THE THREE-DIMENSIONAL CHARACTER

Human behavior—everything we do, why we do it, how we think, and how we feel—is strongly influenced by our three dimensions, which are:

PHYSIOLOGICAL, SOCIOLOGICAL, and PSYCHOLOGICAL.

PHYSICAL makeup influences our viewpoint on life. A short person sees things a lot differently than one who is tall; as does someone who is fat in comparison to someone who is physically fit. Whether we are good-looking, average-looking, or homely—these are just some of the elements comprising our physical makeup which affect our viewpoints and attitudes towards life.

SOCIOLOGICAL background affects how we respond to life's situations. Think of the contrast between growing up in poverty as opposed to wealth. Imagine life on the city streets in comparison to life at the country club. In some instances, a person growing up without material assets may be emotionally healthier and ultimately more successful because of that innate desire to make a better life. The basic premise of sociological background is all-important in determining how we act and react to various situations.

The PSYCHOLOGICAL dimension is a combination of the first two which influences our attitudes, degree of ambition, the level of frustration we experience and express, our complexes, and so on.

Understanding the three dimensions of character provides insight into human behavior and establishes the foundation of building a well-defined main character.

Since you make every decision concerning your main character's background, you ultimately influence how your main character will act and react.

THE CHARACTER BIOGRAPHY BY DIMENSION

PHYSIOLOGY PROFILE

> Sex
> Age
> Height and weight
> Color of hair, eyes, skin
> General appearance (good-looking, average, homely, sloppy, neat, disheveled)
> General health
> Any abnormalities (defects)

SOCIOLOGY PROFILE

> Class background: lower, middle, upper
> Home life: relationship with parents; influence of parents; parents still living; divorced; any brothers and sisters and, if so, relationship with them
> Relationships with friends: who, how long
> Education: how much, what schools, kind of grades, likes, dislikes, aptitudes

> Occupation: type of work, attitude towards work, basic abilities, leadership qualities
> Personal status: married, if so, how long; children, if so, how many, their ages, etc. If divorced, what is relationship with children and former spouse
> Race, nationality
> Religious beliefs, if any: what are they; and are they expressed
> Political views, if any: what are they; and are they expressed
> Hobbies/interests: sports, physical fitness, sailing, gardening, music, race track, gambling

PSYCHOLOGY PROFILE

> Sex life
> Ethics, values, moral standards
> Drive, ambition
> Frustrations, disappointments
> Temperament: pessimistic, optimistic, aggressive, easygoing
> Attitude towards life: resigned, militant, defeatist, enthusiastic, vigorous
> Complexes: obsessions, inhibitions, superstitions, phobias, quirks
> Extrovert, introvert, ambivert
> Qualities: imagination, judgment, taste, poise, social graces
> I.Q.

KERRY PARKER BIOGRAPHY

Here is a brief version of Kerry Parker's biography.

Physiology Profile

Name: Kerry Alison Parker
Age: 28
Height and Weight: 5'6" - 130 lbs.
Hair: Brown
Eyes: Hazel
Appearance: Attractive, physically fit
Health: Good, but sometimes battles fatigue from overwork.

Sociology Profile

<u>Class</u>: Comes from a wealthy family.

<u>Home life</u>: Was close to both parents and only sister until a tragedy changed everything. Ten years ago, her father, Richard, an investment banker, was convicted of embezzling millions from clients and murdering his partner, Kenneth Hobart. Two years ago, he died of a heart attack in prison at the age of fifty-three. Eighteen months ago, her mother, Ruth, fifty-two, was institutionalized for psychological problems. Her sister, Elaine, thirty, is divorced and working for a research company. In growing up, Elaine always looked after Kerry. Now, with Elaine suffering from emotional problems, it is Kerry who looks after her. In spite of fourteen-hour days, Kerry calls Elaine every day and sees her at least twice a week. Only recently, Kerry's hectic schedule precludes her from calling Elaine every day.

<u>Relationships</u>: Kerry has two close friends, Linda Thomas and Gail Laveros. Even though both friends are married and live in Chicago and Texas, respectively, she talks to them at least once a month and gets together with them around the Christmas holidays.

<u>Education</u>: B.A., UCLA. Kerry was always a good student but had to work hard for her grades. She excelled at science and math but struggled with foreign languages.

<u>Occupation</u>: Owns successful catering business with partner, Dan Wallace. Their clientele comprises both corporate accounts and celebrities. They have twenty-three employees and plans to expand. Kerry is a confident leader and sensitive to her employees. She handles the details of running the business with great skill and leaves the sales functions to Dan.

<u>Personal status</u>: At one point, Kerry and Dan were engaged but their relationship was strained by all the hours they spent together. They both realized that they had a better chance of making a partnership work than a marriage. Their breakup was amicable and to this day they are very supportive of each other. Given the demands of their business at this time, neither one has the time to date.

<u>Religious beliefs</u>: Non-practicing Catholic.

Political views: She is fiscally conservative and socially liberal and has voted for candidates of both parties. Because she can be stubborn when it comes to expressing her views, she avoids discussions on religion and politics.

Hobbies/interests: She was a very good tennis player. Now, with limited time, she goes to a local health club where she does aerobic workouts three times a week. She enjoys reading nonfiction such as historical biographies, but rarely has the time to read anything these days.

Psychology Profile

Sex life: Prior to Dan, Kerry had three previous lovers, and in all three cases, they were men she cared about.

Ethics: More than anything, she believes in remaining true to her word. Once she makes a commitment to someone, even herself, she will comply without fail.

Frustrations: She constantly feels the pain her family has suffered but refuses to talk about it with anyone.

Temperament: Sort of controlled hyper. Following her instincts, she pursues everything with a sense of purpose and without hesitation.

Attitude towards life: Resigned optimism: "Life is difficult—make the most of it every day." She prefers the company of close friends to going to big parties. As she says, "I really don't care for big parties. Too many people put on phony airs trying to impress. It's a big game... one I choose not to play."

Complexes: She is afraid of failure and of losing those close to her.

Qualities: She demonstrates good judgment in most matters and makes other people feel very comfortable around her.

I.Q.: Even though she is blessed with both intelligence and common sense, she can be easily swayed by her emotions.

Kerry's *mini* biography can give you a sense of what to do with your characters.

By elaborating on each character trait, it is easy to develop a character who has a very specific point of view—someone who will act and react to those situations you place them in. A well-sketched character will tell you how he or she will act in any given situation. You won't have to stop and think about it or force action that, at some point, will appear inconsistent and not believable.

EXERCISE 2A: THE CHARACTER BIOGRAPHY

Following the profile, prepare a character biography, with as much detail as possible, on your main character and two other key characters up to the time your story begins. Write until you exhaust all ideas for each character. One bio may end up two pages long, while another exceeds ten.

Many of the small biographical details will strongly influence your main character's behavior and provide a strong line of development for both character and story. As you develop your screenplay project, the value of the character biography will become very evident.

Once your main character has formed a real identity in your mind, you may only extract bits and pieces of the biographical details to enhance the character's treatment in your story. The character biography is very similar to research information in that you may only use a small portion of what you gather. But the information you use will be more meaningful than you initially realize.

THE MOST IMPORTANT ASPECTS OF GOOD CHARACTER

There are six individual aspects which influence the development of your character. For each, the point will be illustrated by presenting my treatment of Kerry Parker.

1. DRAMATIC NEED

The dramatic need of your main character provides the purpose, the focus, and the direction of your story. What does your main character want to achieve or accomplish during the course of your story?

Kerry Parker wants to find out who raped and murdered her sister. That is her dramatic need.

2. POINT OF VIEW

A strong character always expresses a *point of view* in how he or she sees the world.

Given her family history—her father was convicted of embezzlement and murder and died in prison; her mother is institutionalized; and her older sister has emotional problems—Kerry's point of view is: "Life is very difficult—make the most of it."

Her point of view is expressed by the way she lives. She owns her own business, is self-reliant, and controls every aspect of her life.

3. ATTITUDE

Every character has a basic attitude about life—be it positive or negative, superior or inferior—whatever trait is the most obvious.

Kerry's attitude is positive. Whatever she sets her mind to, she believes she can accomplish.

4. CHANGE

During the course of a story, a good character must grow and go through a progressive change in accordance with his or her needs. Depending upon the character, the change could be very minor or quite significant.

As addressed in the analysis of *Dead Man's Dance*, this is a prime objective in my planned rewrite of the script.

5. WEAKNESS/NEGATIVE TRAITS

As human beings, we all have weaknesses and negative traits that strongly influence our behavior.

A *flaw* makes our main character vulnerable. It also creates internal conflict—where the character's own action tends to work against him or her. If a person is indecisive, that negative trait might cause the loss of a great opportunity. Or, more dramatically, indecisive behavior may hinder a person from saving someone's life.

Kerrys stubbornness is a weakness and character flaw. Obsessed with trying to prove that Lt. Haskins murdered her sister, her reckless action puts her life at risk.

6. MANNERISMS/HABITS

We are creatures of habit. Certain mannerisms and habits reveal a lot about us. What's your impression of a man who smokes and then complains about his hacking cough?

When habits are consistent with a character's personality, they can be very effective and often enhance a scene.

Take a woman who is constantly twisting rubber bands in her fingers. She could be sitting at her desk, cradling a phone on her neck, while pulling and tugging on rubber bands. At one point, a rubber band could slip from her fingers, fly across the way, and knock over a Styrofoam cup, spilling coffee all over a desk top covered with reports—just as the occupant returns.

In developing Kerry, no one mannerism or habit jumped out so I left this character trait alone. Ultimately it was the right thing to do. Look at yourself and your friends. Some have obvious mannerisms, others don't.

EXERCISE 2B: THE SIX ASPECTS OF GOOD CHARACTER

For your main character, define the six aspects of good character using no more than a sentence or two for each.

Once you complete the biography and outline the important aspects of good character, your character's actions will be spontaneous and natural.

Early in your story, it is important for the audience to *know* the main character and form an empathetic bond with him or her. Creating good characters will make the job of telling your story much easier.

Emotional Expression

If the proper circumstances are created, a character will have the opportunity to display a wide range of emotions. However those emotional expressions should accurately depict the character's attitude, emotional state, and situations, which must appear natural, not forced. In a drama-based story, the primary emotional expression of the main character usually follows one strong plane. However, if the character is confined to playing at the same emotional level, such as always being serious, the performance, no matter how talented the actor, will come across as being flat or dull.

What about combining other emotional expressions, such as love, humor, conflict, anger, outrage, pity, etc.? During the course of a day, how many ways do you express yourself emotionally and what are the circumstances? Some emotional expressions can be very subtle, while others are more striking. In developing your story, you can utilize the contrast between various emotional expressions to create or release tension. A bitter argument can evolve into a tender love scene or vice versa. Kerry Parker displays a wide range of emotional expressions such as humor, anger, sorrow, outrage, hurt, fear, etc. Each one is a natural response to situations she encounters.

With a three-dimensional character, you never have to force reactions— the character will respond naturally to any given circumstance.

Revealing Character

Character can be revealed visually and through dialogue.

Visual impressions are very effective because they register immediately with the audience. In using visual techniques to reveal character, your approach can be subtle or very dramatic.

People visually display their personality through body language—the way they carry themselves. An individual can be outgoing, confident, shy, serious, witty, sloppy, aggressive, unsophisticated, whatever. Would you bend over to pick up a dime on the street? If so, would your action be spontaneous or would you look to see if anyone is observing you first? Or would you look at the dime and just walk away? No matter which way you react, it reveals something about your character.

Through visual techniques, you can reveal everything about a character from personality quirks to attitude. Whenever possible, as it applies to everything in your story, *don't say what you can show*.

In driving past the local track, I noticed there were 50 people walking and jogging in the normal counterclockwise direction, while one woman walked against the flow drawing odd looks. What does that say about her? While gassing up my car, I watched a man jaywalk across the street. He brazenly stopped in the middle of the road and blocked traffic to light up a smoke. When one vehicle honked at him, he flipped the driver the *bird* and then slowly strutted out of the way. It wouldn't take much of an imagination to figure out the attitudes of these two people. Make every effort to utilize visual techniques to reveal character.

One of the most effective uses of revealing character through visuals is in the 1969 Steve McQueen film, *The Cincinnati Kid*. Ann-Margret's character, Melba, is playing with a jigsaw puzzle in her hotel room while her husband, Shooter, Karl Malden's character, observes. As Melba struggles to finish, she cuts a piece of puzzle and forces it into place. Shooter says, "Do you have to cheat at everything?" In that one little moment, Melba's character is clearly established.

Character is best revealed under pressure. Does your character excite easily, or remain calm and composed under pressure? Think of ways of visually expressing your main character's action in a crisis situation. Revealing character through dialogue can be handled the same as the visual techniques—subtly or dramatically.

In film stories, as in real life, impressions are quickly formed about people by what they say and how they say it. One statement can immediately reveal a person's character and attitude. One individual might say, "While I enjoy jazz, I really prefer classical music." Another person says, "Heavy metal is great—everything else sucks!" From their dialogue, it wouldn't be difficult to make up a character biography outlining each person's background and physical description. This is another method of creating character by working backwards from a key element of character. If you know a person's attitude, it wouldn't be difficult to determine other things about him or her.

THE FOUR FUNCTIONS OF DIALOGUE

As we all know, in real life, people talk in run-on sentences expressing fragmented thoughts. Dialogue is not elegant prose. It is functional and has four primary purposes in your story.

1.   To reveal character.
2.   To reveal the character's emotional state.
3.   To communicate information to the audience.
4.   To move the story forward.

For inexperienced writers, dialogue is the most difficult part of writing. Initially your dialogue will probably be trite, awkward, clumsy, stilted, etc. But it can be improved through rewriting. Writing good dialogue is also a skill you develop and enhance with experience. When it comes time to writing that all-important first script, let the dialogue flow without prejudging it. During the rewriting stage, you will cut, refine, and polish it. One important point about writing dialogue— it is best to actually read it out loud. Speaking lines you expect actors to say really allows you to hear it. Of all the elements in a screenplay, you will probably spend more time rewriting and polishing dialogue.

PROFANITY

Profanity is an integral part of our language and culture. When it is used appropriately—to duplicate real-life situations—it adds a realistic dimension to your story.

In the early 1970s, when the *Dirty Harry* action-movie series started, there was hardly any profanity in films. Gradually, over the years, profanity was worked into movies to add more gritty texture and realism; thus making it a required element in certain genre pieces. Today, submitting an action script to Hollywood agents or production companies without any profanity will almost certainly influence a negative reaction from most. In one respect, it is a sad commentary, but oh so true.

SLANG PHRASES

Since dialogue is written to reflect how people really speak, here are some of the most popular slang phrases.

"Gimme that." for "Give me that."
"Whattaya say?" for "What do you say?"
"How ya doin'?" for "How are you doing?"
"I dunno." for "I don't know."
"Lemme see that." for "Let me see that."

How people speak—what they say and how they say it—reveals something about them.

In *DMD*, the British-born private investigator, H. C. Hibbs, speaks very proper English to the point that he rarely uses any contractions. On the subject of Hibbs, he is the only character in the entire script who received an elaborate character description as noted on page 37. Why? Because I wanted him to be very specific and stand out.

CHARACTER DESCRIPTIONS

Having read at least one hundred screenplays over the years, it is apparent to me that character descriptions are treated with far greater discretion than any other element. In some scripts, considerable detail is used to describe not only the physical aspects, but the character's emotional state as well. In other scripts, there are literally no descriptions, not even an indication of age, just the character's name. If your character's age is not important, then leave it out. The minute you determine a specific age for a character, you limit the number of actors who qualify by that factor. In some stories, it might not make any difference if the character is twenty-five or pushing forty. Having a broad age range provides far greater casting opportunities. Unless a detailed description is absolutely essential to establishing a very unique character, keep the description minimal and avoid using age whenever possible.

A well-sketched character, through dialogue and action, will reveal everything the audience needs to know.

In *Dead Man's Dance*, Kerry and Elaine's ages, twenty-eight and thirty, respectively, are critical to the story for two reasons. First, there are many actresses who are in that twenty-eight-year-old range. Second, those ages tie in logically to the story's background—meaning all the things that transpired prior to the story starting. At twenty-eight, Kerry closely reflects a lot of women today who are independent, own their own businesses or have successful careers, and have yet to marry.

SCREENPLAY STRUCTURE

STRUCTURING YOUR STORY

After you have completed all the character exercises, you are ready to begin the process of structuring your story.

Where do you begin? *You begin with the ending.* By knowing the ending of your story, you have a straight line of development to follow from the beginning to the resolution. You would no sooner get into a car and start driving without having a specific destination in mind. This same logic applies to your story. At all times, *you must know where you are going*.

If you attempt to *make up* your story as you go along, you will either run out of steam or force things to happen. As a result, your story will be contrived. You might be able to make up a story as you go along, but I doubt that it will be any good when it is finished.

Knowing the ending of your story allows you to work from two directions at the same time—forwards and backwards. *Working from the beginning, you create all the necessary scenes that will take you to your story's resolution that you have already predetermined.* That is simply called forward motion. *Knowing the ending of your story points out the necessity to go back and create scenes that are needed to justify the resolution.*

As previously illustrated... if your hero saves the day by accessing a computer system, it is essential that you establish his expertise with computers early in your story. If you don't, your character's action will come across as being totally contrived. If your hero is a computer expert, without a word of dialogue, you could show him sitting at a terminal, working on some complex problem. Or, using *exposition*, you could establish his expertise by having two people talk about how great he is with computers. (The meaning and use of exposition is explained in Chapter 6 under Screenwriting Techniques.)

All the interim action between the beginning of the story and the resolution is related and tied together by both forward and backward motion.

The pain Kerry feels after she learns that Elaine has been raped and murdered only works if there is a bond established between them because ***the audience reacts emotionally, not intellectually, to a film story.***

While they only share a brief phone conversation, Kerry's concern for her sister is apparent. Kerry's last words to her are: "Elaine. I love you." Obviously their bond would have been established much stronger had I shown them interacting together in pleasant circumstances. However, that would have required additional scenes that would have impeded the plot and diminished the impact of seeing Elaine outside her distraught persona. Since the audience only sees Elaine once, I want them questioning her behavior—is she rational or not?

Defining the needs of your main character ultimately provides you with the ending of your story. It then becomes an exercise of fleshing out all of the details that lead to the story's resolution.

Kerry's need is to find out who raped and murdered her sister. Given the complexity of the ending to *DMD* and all the details leading to the story's resolution, I will not illustrate the point at this time. However, many of the details and how they were worked out will be addressed in Chapter 10, in a section called "The Creative Steps Behind *Dead Man's Dance.*"

EXERCISE 3: DETERMINE THE ENDING TO YOUR STORY

Determine the ending to your story with as much detail as possible. Once you figure it out, you fill in the space between the beginning and ending by working from two directions—forwards and backwards.

STORY LENGTH

The minimum length of a feature film is 90 minutes, which converts into approximately 90 pages. Use that as a guideline. Your story will ultimately determine the actual length, but keep one thing in mind: ***It is a lot easier to cut back excess scenes rather than add new ones later.***

STORY TIME PERIOD

Each screenplay story covers a specific amount of time in the main character's life. It could be 90 minutes, the length of the film, or two days, three weeks, or possibly a lifetime from childhood to old age. In planning your project, it helps to define the exact time period your story covers even though you may not make it known to the audience. Knowing your story's time period will significantly aid you in determining how you treat the development of your main character and the progressive change he or she goes through.

If you stopped to count the number of days in *Dead Man's Dance*, you would learn that the story takes place over an actual two-week period.

TIME AS A FACTOR

As long as your story *moves forward* following a straight line of development from beginning to end, there are no requirements with regard to any time factors other than what common sense dictates. This applies to the length of scenes, the transition of day from night, days from days, etc. In other words, you have total freedom in jumping from one scene to another. In your story, one character tells another that they will meet in two days. Without accounting for the interim time, the next scene could be those characters meeting. By defining the amount of time your story will cover, it makes the entire screenwriting process much easier. You know how much space there will be, in story time, between the beginning and the resolution.

TIME DEADLINE – THE TICKING CLOCK

If a *deadline* is established where a predetermined action will take place at a specific time, it can effectively create additional tension and suspense. A deadline intensifies a sense of urgency. If the heroine doesn't discover the antidote for a poison in twenty-four hours, 300,000 people will die. A time deadline is just one facet of dramatic writing. It should only be used if it fits naturally into your story without creating the impression of being forced.

BACK STORY

The action that takes place just before a story begins is called a *back story*. It's not part of the story, it's just a reference point or aid for the writer. By knowing what your main character is doing prior to the opening scene, it allows you to enter your story more confidently.

Here is the back story for *Dead Man's Dance*. Kerry had gone to her health club in the early morning and had a vigorous aerobic workout. From there, she visited with her institutionalized mother, then went to work. Since this information is not part of the script, it has absolutely no value to anyone other than me. Knowing those things gave me a clear understanding of Kerry's emotional state as the story began.

One of the most important elements in writing a good script is screenplay structure because it ensures a smooth and even development of your story from beginning to end.

If a picture is worth a thousand words, then the following overview of screenplay structure in its entirety is the best illustration of that point.

SCREENPLAY STRUCTURE

Page(s)	Description Of Action
1-25	ACT I (Setting up the story)
1-10	Introduce the main character, establish the premise of the story, what it is about, and the circumstances surrounding the action
11-17	Focus on the main character
18-20	Introduce the first major plot point
25	End of Act I
26-70	ACT II (Confrontations/Obstacles)
35	Introduce another plot point

45	Introduce midway plot point
55	Introduce another plot point
65	Introduce the second major plot point
70	End of Act II
71-90	ACT III (The Resolution)
75	Introduce another plot point
85-90	Resolution of story
90	End of Act III

SCREENPLAY STRUCTURE-AN OVERVIEW

As previously established, each page of screenplay is equal to one minute of film time. Therefore positioning plot points within a screenplay, at *specific intervals*, ensures the smooth development and even pacing of your story.

What is a plot point? It is a significant incident or revelation that propels the story forward, a segment of dramatic action.

As it applies to plot points, every story is different. Some will have many, others will have few. If a story has few plot points, will it lack solid pacing? That depends upon the story and the strength of the other elements—the characters, the dialogue, how funny or dramatic it might be, etc.

Traditionally, mysteries have many plot points. As the story develops, the detective uncovers one clue that leads to another, then another, etc. Ensemble pieces, like *The Big Chill*, have very few plot points since the focus of the story is on the characters and their relationships.

Dead Man's Dance will be used to illustrate screenplay structure from the story's setup to resolution.

THE SETUP

You can do it in less, but *you have ten pages or ten minutes to set up your story*. And that is to:

1.   Introduce the main character.
2.   Establish what the story is about.
3.   Establish the dramatic circumstances surrounding the action.

THE SETUP - *DEAD MAN'S DANCE*

In the first six pages, you learn the following: Kerry Parker owns a catering business and has a sister, Elaine. While Elaine is planning to visit a friend in Massachusetts—after attending a business meeting—she calls Kerry and tells her she has seen Kenneth Hobart. You learn that their father was convicted of embezzlement and of murdering his partner (Hobart), and subsequently died in prison. You also learn that Kerry is going to Massachusetts when her sister fails to get back to her after saying she is going to the police there.

From this setup, we understand three things:

1.   Kerry Parker is the main character.
2.   The story is about her sister claiming to see Kenneth Hobart—the man their father supposedly murdered.
3.   The fact that Kerry is going to Massachusetts to find her sister when she doesn't hear from her establishes the dramatic circumstances surrounding the action.

After the setup, the focus is then on moving the story forward while revealing more about the character.

PLOT POINTS - *DEAD MAN'S DANCE*

On pages 7/8, Kerry goes to the police station in Westbridge, Massachusetts, and confirms that Elaine never contacted them.

On pages 12/13, she finds Elaine's childhood friend, Kathy Burrows, and learns that Elaine never contacted her either.

On page 16, Kerry tells Dan in a phone conversation that Elaine has claimed to have seen Kenneth Hobart on four previous occasions since their father died in prison. This twist sets up the possibility that Elaine is imbalanced and subject to hallucinations.

On page 17, Kerry learns that Elaine's rental car was found abandoned in the woods.

On page 23, Elaine's body is found behind a cemetery. This is the first major plot point that sets up the action for the second act.

On page 29, Sgt. Daily informs Kerry that he saw Lt. Haskins talking to Elaine the very day she disappeared and that the Lieutenant later denied it was him. Because of its significance, this is also a major plot point.

On pages 36/37, we discover that Sgt. Daily has been killed in a routine traffic stop. This, of course, given its importance, is another major plot point.

On page 43, Kerry visits Lt. Haskins's home and discovers that his wife, Gail, is abused.

On page 45, Kerry learns that the car leaving the scene of Sgt. Daily's murder had a fan belt that squealed.

On page 46, Kerry is almost run over by a speeding van when she carelessly crosses Main Street in the middle of the block.

On page 51, while helping Kathy Burrows with food shopping, Kerry discovers that Gail Haskins drives a station wagon with a squealing fan belt. This is the midway plot point.

On pages 56 to 58, Kerry sneaks into Lt. Haskins's house and obtains a hair sample for DNA testing.

On page 59, Kerry tells Mike Burrows she learned from the private investigator that Lt. Haskins was accused of raping one woman and beating two others when he was on the New York City Police Department.

On page 62, Kerry confirms the fact that Lt. Haskins occasionally drives his wife's station wagon.

On page 63, Kerry is nearly killed when a truck forces her car off the road.

On page 66, Mike informs Kerry that a sergeant said the truck which ran her off the road was probably stolen by teenagers out for a joyride.

On page 70, when Mike and Kerry are leaving a restaurant, they are almost killed by a tractor trailer truck.

On pages 73/74, Kerry confronts Lt. Haskins and tells him that he is not going to get away with killing her sister and Sgt. Daily.

On page 76, Kerry learns that Lt. Haskins's DNA doesn't match the DNA from her sister's murder. This is both a twist and another major plot point that spins the story into another direction, setting up the action for the third act.

On page 79, Kerry—trying to rattle Lt. Haskins—bluffs him by claiming she has a tape of Sgt. Daily detailing the facts about the Lieutenant meeting Elaine and that he was the last person to see her alive.

On pages 82 to 84, Kerry is picked up at Kathy Burrow's home by a policeman and taken to the house where the Mafia hit men are waiting for her.

On pages 95 to 97, Dennis Ludlow is revealed to be Kenneth Hobart. He tells Kerry how he framed her father and moved to this remote town under the protection of the Mafia.

On page 99, Kerry kills Hobart when he struggles with Mike Burrows.

On page 100, Mike sees Kerry off at Logan Airport.

SUMMARY OF PLOT POINTS -*DEAD MAN'S DANCE*

After the story's setup on pages 1 through 6, there are twenty-one plot points from page 7 to page 84—essentially one every four pages. The story's resolution begins on page 84 and continues to page 100. Between pages 23 to 37, there are three major plot points that really strengthen the end of the first act and the beginning of the second.

While most of the plot points in *DMD* are minor, they are significant enough, collectively, to propel the story forward and hold the reader's interest right to the end.

COMMENTS ON PLOT POINTS

In the illustration of screenplay structure, the plot points fall, after the first major one, at intervals of every 10 pages or, in film time, every 10 minutes.

Can you have more or less plot points? Are they flexible? Can they be moved? Of course! It's your story. The objective in writing a screenplay is holding a reader's interest from page one to the story's resolution and making it a satisfying experience. How you treat and balance the seven elements—which are described in Chapter 1—is up to you. And as you will learn, every script you write will favor different elements. The plot, action sequences, or humor might be the strongest element sustaining the audience's attention—even if you have well-sketched characters.

Plot points, if they are meaningful, help sustain the audience's interest in your story. The sooner you set up your story and introduce the first major plot point, the better. If you wait too long to introduce your *hook*, your story might start to drag. And if it does, your audience will be squirming in their seats and bouncing their popcorn containers off the head of the person sitting in front of them.

Screenplay structure is only a guideline to illustrate the ideal arrangement of the plot points. As you will learn from reading scripts, the number of plot points and where they fall are determined by the type of story that it is.

Take a movie you have never seen—one that is critically acclaimed and widely available on video—pick up a script, and do a complete analysis of it before viewing the film. Make notes as to what stands out in the script. What makes you curious? What makes you laugh or cry? Note the plot points by page number and how significant each one is. Focus on the characters, their development, and the dialogue.

In a plot-driven story, the plot alone won't sustain the audience's interest. The focus of every story has to be on the characters and a well-executed balance between all the elements in a screenplay.

Does Screenplay Structure Apply To Comedy?

Screenplay structure applies to every film genre. A story must progressively move forward at regular intervals (plot points) or it will bog down and stall.

Even if the humor is good, a comedy will ultimately fail without the proper screenplay structure to move the story forward as well as an antagonist creating obstacles (conflict) in the path of the main character.

Exercise 4: Outlining Screenplay Structure

Once you've determined the ending to your story, develop the screenplay structure by outlining all the plot points from beginning to end.

It isn't necessary to use a lot of details but just enough information to understand the purpose of each plot point. By reading just the plot points, you should have a clear and concise synopsis of your story that can be easily understood from setup to resolution. Again, the number of plot points and significance of each will vary from story to story. Some will be very dramatic while others will be less important. However, they all share equal importance in helping move your story forward.

It could take days or a week to complete the screenplay structure to your story. The more you think about it, the easier it gets. All of a sudden, ideas start to formulate and things fall into place, piece by piece, until your story is structured. But before you start, you must first know your ending.

Scene Descriptions

A scene is best defined as a specific segment of dramatic action. Every scene in your story has to have a purpose: *to reveal character, information about the plot*, and, most importantly, *to move the story forward*. Most scenes rarely accomplish more than one function.

Outlining scene descriptions is a step designed to *fill in* more details about your character and story.

Scene length will vary from possibly one brief visual to three pages and *there is no required number of scenes in any screenplay*. Your story will determine how many are needed as you write your script. However, in the planning stages, it is important to outline a number of scenes as a guideline to develop your story. Figure on two pages for every scene, as a rough average. Therefore, for each thirty-page segment, outline fifteen scenes. How many you use later is immaterial. Scenes will be deleted, added, rewritten, moved to other areas, or combined.

The exercise for outlining scene descriptions is broken down into four segments which look like this:

Act I runs from page 1 to page 25, from story setup to the first major plot point.

The first half of Act II runs from page 26 to page 45, to the midway plot point.

The second half of Act II runs from page 46 to page 70, to the second major plot point.

Act III runs from page 71 to page 90, to the story's end.

You don't need a lot of details to outline scene descriptions, just brief comments as to what you want to accomplish in a given scene. By outlining the basic premise for a scene, you stimulate the creative process which prompts the next step—focusing on how to develop them.

Listed below are the scene descriptions for the first act of *Dead Man's Dance*.

Scene Descriptions - *Dead Man's Dance*

Act 1 - *Dead Man's Dance*

1. Catering business (establish California location).

2. Introduce Kerry Parker interfacing with employees.

3. Kerry receives a phone call from Elaine who is in Massachusetts.

4.   Exposition on Hobart and Kerry's father.

5.   Kerry flies to Boston.

6.   Kerry goes to police station in Westbridge, Massachusetts.

7.   Kerry tries to find Kathy Marks.

8.   Kerry finds Kathy. Meets her ex-husband and kids.

9.   Kerry calls Dan. Not coming back. Tells him about Elaine seeing Hobart before.

10.   Elaine's rental car is found abandoned.

11.   Kerry runs into Kathy's ex-husband.

12.   Elaine's body is discovered.

13.   Kerry grieves for her murdered sister.

14.   Sgt. Daily tells Kerry about seeing Lt. Haskins talking with Elaine.

15.   Sgt. Daily is killed in a routine traffic stop.

In the end, some scene descriptions will be developed as outlined while others will be altered or discarded or their sequence will change. In some cases, you might combine two scenes into one or recognize the need to create another scene. Again the length of any scene will be determined by the purpose of the scene.

As to the length of any scene, here is one piece of sound advice. If a scene is heavily dialogue-oriented, try not to exceed three pages unless the dialogue is riveting or very funny. If you have a long scene filled with tedious dialogue, the reader may slip into a coma and never regain consciousness to finish your script.

As your project develops, you acquire a greater sense of clarity so it becomes easier to identify those changes that will enhance the development of your story. Most of the time, you are only making minor adjustments.

EXERCISE 5: OUTLINING SCENE DESCRIPTIONS

Using the completed screenplay structure as a guideline, outline the scene descriptions. Remember, each scene has to have a specific function—to reveal information about your character, the plot, and to move the story forward to its resolution.

Scene descriptions are best outlined on 3" X 5" index cards so you can reorganize their sequence at any time. Also, with index cards, you can scribble notes on both sides as ideas come to mind for a given scene.

THE NARRATIVE TREATMENT

Having completed all the previous exercises, you are now ready to address one of the most important steps before tackling the first draft screenplay—*the narrative treatment*. It is essentially a short-story version of your screenplay story. The purpose of this procedure is to expand, elaborate, and clarify your story from beginning to end.

In writing your narrative, just let it flow naturally. As far as length is concerned, you need at least four pages to properly lay out your story, but it could end up being a lot longer. Some writers feel that exceeding twenty pages is totally unnecessary. Not true. If it naturally develops into even thirty or forty pages—following the guidelines outlined here—it will be extremely helpful to the writer. Each project requires a different volume of narrative depending upon how complicated the plot might be.

With each step in the screenwriting process, you attain more knowledge about your characters and story which, in turn, stimulates the creative juices, making the next step that much easier. By the time you finish the narrative treatment, you will be able to write that first draft screenplay with incredible confidence and far greater speed because of your intimate knowledge of the story.

If you follow each step in the screenwriting process, it may only take you two weeks to complete a first draft screenplay. However, if you happen to skip a few steps and wing it, you may be struggling to finish your first draft and ultimately end up with a big disappointment.

How much depth should the narrative treatment contain? Should you use dialogue? Or what about character or scene descriptions? The whole point of the narrative treatment is to outline your story from beginning to end with as much clarity as possible, but without a lot of details. With the exception of key scenes, I don't write any dialogue because it greatly extends the length of the narrative. Also, there is a tendency to spend too much time on dialogue as opposed to just getting the story out.

On the next page, there is a one-page sample of a narrative treatment from *Dead Man's Dance*. Given the importance of the first ten pages in setting up the story, I use a little more detail than what is necessary. After that, I confine my treatment to only the essential elements of the story as outlined in the exercise procedures.

NARRATIVE TREATMENT SAMPLE

DEAD MAN'S DANCE

Kerry Parker, 28, stands outside the entrance to her business, Sunset Catering, giving instructions to two young men loading a panel truck.

Inside, she checks the kitchen staff as they prepare food trays. An employee enters and tells Kerry that Elaine, her older sister, is on the phone and sounds rather distraught.

Kerry goes to her office and closes the door. In a highly excited voice, Elaine tells Kerry that she saw Kenneth Hobart. A stunned Kerry replies, "That's impossible. He's dead!" Elaine remains unmoved. Kerry learns that Elaine is in Westbridge, Massachusetts, on business, and that she plans to visit Kathy Marks—an old childhood friend. The conversation ends with Elaine telling Kerry that she is going to the police in Westbridge. Unable to talk her out of it, Kerry asks Elaine to call her after she does.

When Kerry leaves work looking distressed, an employee questions Kerry's partner, Dan Wallace. It comes out that Kerry and Elaine's father, an investment banker, was convicted of embezzling millions from his clients and of murdering his partner, Kenneth Hobart. It is also revealed that their father died in prison two years ago.

When Kerry doesn't hear from Elaine the next day and can't find a phone number to reach Kathy Marks, she tells Dan that she is going to Massachusetts to find her sister.

Kerry arrives in Westbridge, Massachusetts, a small town in the Berkshires in the western part of the state, and goes directly to the police station. The desk sergeant tells her that Elaine never filed a report.

The following day, visiting stores on Main Street, Kerry runs into someone who knows Kathy and learns that her married name is Burrows. She goes to Kathy's home and is warmly greeted because Elaine is Kathy's best friend. Since Elaine had not contacted Kathy, Kerry's concern becomes more evident.

The next day, Elaine's rental car is found abandoned in the woods. When the police fail to conduct a search because they don't suspect foul play, Kerry becomes insistent and forces them to do so.

The narrative treatment for *Dead Man's Dance* is straightforward, with just enough detail to establish a clear line of development for the plot.

EXERCISE 6: THE NARRATIVE TREATMENT

Your objective in writing the narrative treatment is to concentrate on the development of your main character and move your story forward from plot point to plot point, from setup to resolution. Take no detours. That is, don't attempt to fill in any unnecessary details. Use of dialogue in your treatment is optional. However, if you do use dialogue, keep it brief. From a standpoint of being practical, it is best to save dialogue for your script. Without using extensive details, describe the visual aspects of key scenes.

Novels and short stories are written in the past tense such as "John ran down the street and stopped next to the phone booth." Since screenplays are written in the present tense, your narrative treatment should be, too. Thus, the description above is presented as "John runs down the street and stops next to the phone booth."

While you are writing the narrative treatment in prose style, don't get fancy; your writing is purely functional. It should not be an attempt to gain literary recognition; you are just telling your story.

Unlike all the previous steps, *the narrative treatment provides the broadest expansion of your story because it combines and links all the separate elements together: character, plot points, and scene descriptions*.

It's quite possible that your story might make a fabulous novel. If that is the case—and you have the writing skills—you could change your course of direction.

RESEARCH

Research is required whenever you are unfamiliar with the subject matter you are using in your story. In certain stories, *technical* or *procedural research*

74

is an absolute necessity if credibility is to be established. Try writing a story about medicine, law, or science without knowledge of the subject matter and the benefit of research. It's impossible. Technical or procedural inaccuracies ultimately ruin a good story.

Some writers spend months researching and conceptualizing a project before putting a word on paper. Unfortunately, many inexperienced writers incorrectly assume that if they are not actually writing, they are being unproductive. Nothing could be further from the truth. Research is a tool of good writing, so don't make the mistake of considering it a burden or inconvenience.

Research opens the door of opportunity because it often uncovers information that you could have only discovered through the process itself. You may be looking for one specific fact but ultimately find other information that is more meaningful. Also, extensive research allows you far greater choices of facts to help support and strengthen your story.

The type of research you do will vary from project to project. You could be looking for technical or procedural facts or bits of esoteric information. You might be able to find everything you need at the public library or via the Internet. Sometimes a newspaper or magazine article might be a great source. Interviewing *experts* in a given field is probably the most valuable type of research you can do. Since one-on-one interviews are spontaneous, they are often extremely effective. An answer to one question usually prompts another, and so on. In the end, you can often acquire more meaningful information with far greater depth and understanding.

While research is listed as the seventh step in the screenwriting process, it might be your starting point. *It is quite possible to develop a story out of researching unfamiliar subject matter.* Elements within the subject matter may have a certain appeal which sparks the creative juices. Next thing you know, you are developing a story line and sketching out a main character.

With *Dead Man's Dance*, I researched DNA evidence to confirm my understanding as to how samples are collected and processed. In interviewing a DNA expert over the phone, I collected a lot of additional information. There were a lot of interesting facts and technical jargon that would have sounded impressive and could easily have been worked into those scenes between Kerry and Dr. Compton, the medical examiner. But for the sake of keeping those scenes tight, I decided not to use the information.

The fictional town of Westbridge, Massachusetts—where *Dead Man's Dance* takes place—in my mind is the town of Great Barrington, Massachusetts. It is a small community in the Berkshires and an ideal setting for my story.

The cult classic, *Pretty Poison*, starring Anthony Perkins and Tuesday Weld, was filmed in Great Barrington in 1968. I drove there one day and visited the police department to get a sense of how it operates in a small community. The officer on duty, Rocky Scarbro, was quite helpful in explaining everything from their radio procedures to the subtle nuances of the town.

THE VALUE OF RESEARCH

To illustrate the value of research, I will briefly address my original action script, *Last to Die*, because this project came about as the direct result of research: my ongoing practice of scanning newspapers every day for interesting articles.

The New York Times ran a piece on the Pushkin Museum in Moscow. The Pushkin displays priceless art treasures—paintings and drawings by El Greco, Goya, Renoir, Degas, etc.—that had been plundered by Nazi Germany, and subsequently were taken by the Soviet Army as spoils of war. Several days later, there was an article (not connected to the Pushkin) on the *Organizatsiya*—the Russian Mafia—and how they impact crime in the United States through narcotics-trafficking, extortion, auto theft, and document fraud. From there, I followed the "what if" exercise. What if the Russian Mafia broke into the Pushkin Museum and stole all the priceless art treasures and sold them to a high-profile art dealer in Beverly Hills? Then, in turn, what if the art dealer ran *underground* auctions for wealthy but unscrupulous people—people who would be willing to pay millions in cash to own priceless, one-of-a-kind art treasures? From those extrapolations, a story was created. Also, by following art reviews in the *Times*, I was able to extract some very useful information that was incorporated into a key scene. Before outlining that scene, here is some background on the plot, characters, and the scene itself.

Last to Die is about a murder investigation that leads two P.I.s to a high-profile art dealer and a cache of art treasures plundered by Nazi Germany. The story focuses on the two P.I.s who are former husband and wife ... á la Tracy and Hepburn. Since she has remarried and he is resentful of her new husband, there is constant friction in their relationship. He, Joe Verbeck, comes from a blue collar background, while she, Beverly Hawley, is college-educated.

The scene takes place at a Beverly Hills art gallery where Verbeck and Bev are questioning the owner, Malcolm Stewart, regarding the murder of one of his employees. The P.I.s are working for the father of the victim.

The purpose of the scene is to have the villain, Malcolm Stewart, interact with the P.I.s in an informal setting, and to provide a moment of levity by having Stewart focus all his attention upon Bev while ignoring Verbeck.

INT. MALCOLM STEWART GALLERY-STORAGE ROOM-DAY

A long table stretches the length of the room covered with vases, ceramics, and odd-shaped pottery.

With intense concentration, Stewart examines each piece, then writes his comments on a list he carries.

> STEWART
> Lynn was not only knowledgeable,
> but had an incredible, discerning
> eye. A rare talent. I have yet
> to find a suitable replacement.

> BEV
> Can you add anything to what Mr. Chase
> has told us?

> STEWART
> I'm afraid not.

He notices Bev curiously eyeing a ceramic pot.

> STEWART (cont'd)
> Are you familiar with this piece?

> BEV
> It looks like it could be from the
> Yangshao era. Maybe 1500 B.C.

As impressed as Stewart is -- Verbeck is taken aback.

> STEWART
> How can you tell?

> BEV
> It's decorated with geometric
> motifs similar to those on African
> and archaic Greek pottery.

Verbeck looks at Bev in total amazement.

> STEWART
> What can you tell me about the
> Shang and Chou Dynasties?

> BEV
> It was the great age of Chinese
> bronzes -- and the ceramics of
> that period are often the same
> shape as the bronze vessels.
> However, they seem to have more
> linear decorative motifs.

Stewart smiles appreciatively. Verbeck is staggered.

> STEWART
> May I ask your background?

> BEV
> I was an art major in college.

> STEWART
> (smiling)
> Maybe I should talk to you about
> Lynn's position.

> VERBECK
> (abruptly)
> We've got to get going.

> STEWART
> (shaking Bev's hand)
> It's been a real pleasure.

Verbeck frowns -- end of scene.

That scene was made possible by research.

EXERCISE 7: RESEARCH

If you are writing about unfamiliar subject matter, you must take the time to research it properly. Start at the public library. If you can't find the information there, the librarian can probably direct you to other sources.

Interviewing an expert in a given field is enormously helpful. Through detective work, you can probably find someone in your immediate area who is both qualified in the subject matter you need to research and willing to help you. Do your research!

Form, Techniques & Terminology

Screenplay Form

Having completed the first seven exercises, you should be very eager to write your screenplay. But before you do, you need to understand and be familiar with screenplay form as well as screenwriting techniques and terminology.

With any word processing program or even a typewriter, you can quickly determine the correct spacings to establish the proper screenplay formatting as described in this chapter. (Note: Our illustration may not reflect recommended standard measurements due to book binding constraints and page size.) Of course, if you invest in a screenwriting software program, all the formatting is taken care of. See the Appendix for information on screenplay software.

Since there is no uniformity in measuring space on a page between the various brands of typewriters and computers, screenplay margins and spacings will be outlined using ruler measurements for the standard paper size of 8-1/2" x 11". From there, it will be very easy to determine the proper settings on your own equipment.

> Each screenplay page should begin 3/4" (three-fourths of an inch) from the top of the paper. With a page length of 58 single lines, there will again be 3/4" at the bottom of the page. Some pages may be shorter, depending on where a scene ends, but the maximum length from the top is 58 single lines starting from the screenplay *page number*.

> On the next page, the layout of a screenplay page is illustrated. Keep in mind that A, the line where the screenplay page number appears, represents the top of the screenplay page, which is 3/4" from the top of the paper.

A. (First line, 3/4" from top of paper)   1.

B. FADE IN:

C. EXT. SUBURBAN NEIGHBORHOOD - DAY

D. Children run down the street playing tag.

C. EXT. HOUSE - DAY

D. A black sedan parks in front of a white house with a giant oak tree in the front yard. In the b.g., the SOUND of a GARBAGE TRUCK making pickups.

D. GEORGE HOWARD, 35, average-looking, gets out of the black sedan. He cautiously looks around, then glances towards the house and smiles.

D. ANN PARKER, early 30s, attractive, with long, shapely legs, exits the house. She slowly approaches George and kisses him passionately.

D. As they break their embrace.

E.
F.   GEORGE
G.   (suggestively)
                          You look terrific.

E.   ANN
G.   I know.

D. George flashes a smile.

E.   GEORGE
G   What's Bill doing today?

E.   ANN
G   Working in Jersey.

E.   GEORGE
G   Well then -- what are we waiting for?

D. George and Ann drive off together in his car.

                            END OF SCENE

                                82

A. The PAGE NUMBER appears in the top right-hand corner approximately 3/4" from the top of the paper. The page length of 58 single spaces begins on this line. Use a 1-3/4" margin on the left side of the page with a 1-1/4" margin on the right.

B   FADE IN: is the traditional term used to indicate the opening of your story.

C. The SCENE HEADING is two single spaces below FADE IN. The SCENE HEADING indicates either INT. (Interior) or EXT. (Exterior) LOCATION followed by a dash and TIME; either DAY or NIGHT.

D. The SCENE DESCRIPTION appears two single spaces below the SCENE HEADING. This area is used to describe the action taking place within the scene, single-spaced, in lowercase letters. Anything pertaining to SOUND is CAPITALIZED as illustrated.

   Character descriptions are also presented in the scene description section. The very first time a character appears in the screenplay, the character's name (GEORGE HOWARD) is CAPITALIZED. From that point on, whenever the name appears again in the scene description, use lowercase spelling: George Howard or just George.

   The SCENE DESCRIPTIONS should be as brief as possible. If a lot of detail is required, write two or three short paragraphs as opposed to one long one—making it a lot easier to read. The SCENE DESCRIPTION margin is the same as the SCENE HEADING.

E. The CHARACTER speaking appears in CAPITAL LETTERS in the center of the page, starting 4-1/4" from the left-handside of the page; two single spaces below the ending of the SCENE DESCRIPTION.

F. STAGE DIRECTIONS appear one single space below the CHARACTER'S NAME in "parentheses," starting 3-1/4"from the left-hand side of the page. It can *wrap* to two or even three lines with the right margin 3-1/4" from the right side of the page.

G.   DIALOGUE appears one single space below the CHARACTER'S NAME (or the STAGE DIRECTIONS, when used). Dialogue forms a block in the center of the page with a 2-7/8" margin from both sides of the page.

General rule: whenever possible, numbers should be spelled out in dialogue instead of shown numerically.

H.   Line 58 is the last line on the page.

>   If you have a long passage of dialogue that runs over to the next page, it is handled like this.

BILL
(into phone)
I can't help it -- that's how I
feel. If you want, we can sit
down and discuss it, but believe
(MORE)

(MORE) comes on line 58 or above—whichever line is most practical to split your dialogue.

The character's dialogue then continues on the next page as illustrated below—with the character's name on line 3—which is two spaces below the page number. To the right of the character's name you put (cont'd) in parentheses.

BILL (cont'd)
me, you won't change my mind.

In *Dead Man's Dance*, I utilize this dialogue carryover on the bottom of page 80.

>   (CONTINUED) - CONTINUED:

In a shooting script, if a scene carries over to the next page, (CONTINUED) appears in capital letters with parentheses around it; two single spaces below the last portion of the uncompleted scene at the bottom of the page, flush with the right margin.

When the scene continues on the next page, CONTINUED: appears in capital letters followed by a colon, two single spaces below the page number on the top left side of the page.

Unless you are preparing a shooting script, don't use CONTINUED. As in the *Dead Man's Dance* screenplay, the text is continuous and CONTINUED is not used.

Also, with a shooting script, every scene is numbered in the margins on both sides of the page. This is done to help the production manager develop the film's budget and prepare the production schedule.

> In contemporary screenplays, CAMERA ANGLES are rarely used for two reasons. First, they are not necessary because the subject of the camera is what is described in the scene description. And second, use of camera angles is confusing and impedes the read.

The only time a camera angle should be used is when you need to emphasize something important in CLOSE UP—such as a newspaper column, a pen, or photograph. It would be presented like this within the scene description section:

INSERT OF PHOTOGRAPH (or CLOSE ON PHOTO)

revealing two young boys standing together.

BACK TO SCENE

as George puts the photograph down.

After describing the subject of an INSERT SHOT, use BACK TO SCENE to indicate where the scene actually continues. This is done for clarity.

On page 43 in *Dead Man's Dance*, I used the CLOSE ON technique to highlight a newspaper article.

I would like to make a point about why camera angles are not needed by illustrating the above-mentioned scene which runs over to page 44.

The scene takes place inside Kerry's parked car. The first line in the scene description reads: Kerry is looking at the front page of a newspaper. It is obvious that she, looking at the paper, is the subject of the camera. In the CLOSE ONs, the subject of the camera is first the newspaper headline, then the article. The next shot would be—as BACK TO SCENE indicates—of Kerry reacting startled to Mike Burrow's voice; he is OFF SCREEN. A few moments later, as written in the scene description on page 44, Kerry happens to glance at the house. Here, the camera is using her POV (point of view) looking at Gail Haskins who is looking their way.

As it applies to camera angles, it is the director's decision to determine how scenes will be shot. Just describe what you want in the scene description and leave it at that.

SCREENWRITING TECHNIQUES

Screenwriting techniques are those mandatory/optional facets of screenwriting that support a screenplay. Each will be explained and, in some cases, fully illustrated. Certain elements, such as the scene, are primary and essential to the screenplay and are therefore mandatory. Others—such as flashback, montage, or reversal—are optional and should only be used when they fit naturally into your story. Don't feel obligated to use any optional technique unless there is a definite need required by your story.

> THE SCENE

> After screenplay structure, the scene is the most important element in your script. *Word of mouth* can make or break a film and even has more impact than the millions of dollars spent on advertising and promoting a movie. When people leave the theater, they talk about specific scenes. If you write a good story with strong characters and create a half-dozen memorable scenes, your film has the potential to be successful.

Each and every scene should be treated with great care, so here are the most important details and guidelines relating to the treatment of scenes.

> A scene is a specific segment of dramatic action which has a beginning, middle, and end—just like your story. Every scene must have a specific purpose, such as revealing character or information about the plot. But most importantly, every scene must move the story forward towards its resolution.

> SCENE HEADINGS note two things—location and time of day, i.e., EXT. HOUSE - DAY or INT. HOUSE - NIGHT. Whenever location or time changes, you have a new scene. If your scene begins with INT. KITCHEN - DAY and moves to INT. DINING ROOM - DAY, you have a new scene. If your scene begins with INT. BEDROOM - NIGHT and the next one is INT. BEDROOM - DAY, it's a new scene.

> How will you open each scene? Will it be visually dynamic, like a shot in the great outdoors? Or will it be one expressing mood and atmosphere, like the inside of a dark house or a cemetery at night?

In *Dead Man's Dance*, I wanted to accomplish two things in the opening scene: introduce the main character, Kerry Parker; and establish the Southern California location because the story quickly transitions to Massachusetts.

Of course, setting that first scene in the outdoors makes it easy to convey the location and it is also visually impressive.

Since every scene deals with visual elements, be creative. If you think of a detail that can enhance a scene, write it in, but don't be too elaborate.

> There are no rules governing how short or long a scene can be other than what common sense dictates. In *DMD*, look at the scene near the top of page 6, at Kerry's apartment, where she anxiously awaits Elaine's phone call. Through a quick visual scene like that, the audience is given very specific information.

Directly below the scene in Kerry's apartment on page 6 are two short scenes. While they are not significant in moving the story forward, they do have a specific purpose in providing TRANSITORY ACTION. What is *transitory action*? It is action designed to connect scenes as well as provide CONTRAST BETWEEN SCENES, another important technique. Both issues will be addressed shortly.

> It is strongly suggested that heavy dialogue scenes be kept under three pages. Dialogue scenes exceeding three pages can be overwhelming and somewhat tedious; that is, with the possible exception of a high-voltage courtroom scene, etc.

> When should you enter a scene? At the last possible moment just before the *ending* of some specific action. If the purpose of a scene is to reveal information about a character or the plot, don't waste half a page leading to that point. Build that scene so the information can be presented immediately.

In *DMD*, look at the scene in Kerry's office that runs from the bottom of page 4 to the top of page 6. Very concisely, it reveals critical background about Kerry's father and helps introduce the premise of the story.

> In building scenes and developing your story line, be careful of revealing too much information. Don't let the audience get ahead of your story and predict what will happen next. Learn to hold back information and gradually reveal things only as it becomes necessary. The audience should find out things at the same time as your main character, never before.

> Don't duplicate scenes. This is a very easy trap to fall into. Two characters get into a heated argument. In a new scene, one of them runs into a friend and relates, verbatim, what just happened.

How do you get around this problem? By entering the scene just after the character finishes telling the friend about the argument. And from there, their conversation continues without boring the audience with what they already know.

> A very important element related directly to scenes is the SEQUENCE. A sequence is a number of scenes tied together by one theme. In your script, you will use scenes as well as sequences to tell your story.

A sequence works like this. Two men begin a discussion on tennis. The sequence starts in one man's office, continues as they walk in the hallway, out to the parking lot, ride in a car, walk into a restaurant, have lunch together, and so on. Remember, every time you change location or time, it is a new scene. You can combine ten scenes in one sequence, whatever works.

There is no set number of scenes or sequences in your screenplay. While you outline one scene for every two pages of screenplay as a guideline, the number you actually use may vary considerably. You could end up with twelve or twenty scenes for Act I, the first 25 pages. In the first half of Act II, you might end up with only ten. If you are properly prepared as you write that first draft, your story will determine how many scenes you actually need.

You will often eliminate or combine scenes, thus reducing how many you use. Or you might see the need for adding a scene to bridge or link two others. Just trust the process.

> Film is a visual medium, so don't say what you can show.

Let's say you have a scene with one woman telling another how beautiful Montana is in excruciating detail. The point could be made more effectively by having the woman show her friend a few breathtaking photos while engaging in insipid gossip. This technique not only enhances the presentation of information, but provides a second function by introducing a bit of humor.

What if you were writing a romantic comedy and wanted to show a man and a woman meeting for the first time. If you are good at writing clever dialogue, that might be the way to go. Or you could build a scene that relies solely upon visual. Say the scene takes place at a party where dozens of people are mingling on the porch of a house. You could have the characters eyeing each other from across the way; then, the man, standing over a bunch of seated guests, becomes highly distracted in an effort to impress the woman. Trying to be cool and nonchalant, he accidentally dumps his drink into the lap of one of the seated guests.

You might have seen the following ten-second television commercial sponsored by The Partnership for a Drug-Free America. It's a party scene inside a house, where this good-looking teenage boy is moving through the crowd towards a pretty girl. She takes a hit on a joint and after she does, she happens to glance up and see him turn away in total disgust. The girl lowers her eyes in shame and disappointment. It's a very powerful message and one that doesn't need or rely upon a word of dialogue to make its point.

When you are developing scenes, think about those ways you can visually relate information about your characters and/or your plot.

> A story's pacing is strongly influenced by two factors: SCREENPLAY STRUCTURE (moving from plot point to plot point) and CONTRAST BETWEEN SCENES.

Most stories follow *two dynamics*: the *plot* (the story line) and a *subplot* (the characters' relationships).

In *Dead Man's Dance*, there are two dynamics: the plot driving the story and Kerry's relationships with Dan Wallace, Mike Burrows, and Kathy Burrows.

In my action screenplay, *Last to Die*, there are four primary dynamics because they share equal importance in strengthening the story—and they are: the plot, the characters, the action sequences, and the humor.

No matter how good a story may be, every film inherently has *dead space* or *slow time* from the perspective of each person viewing it. There are portions of every film, without exception, that just don't appeal to some individuals. You can reduce that problem, as much as possible, through CONTRAST BETWEEN SCENES—rotating the primary dynamics within a story to keep it interesting and flowing smoothly.

Don't panic or feel overwhelmed by all of this; soon enough it will become second nature to you.

> TRANSITORY ACTION provides the means of connecting scenes as well as CONTRAST BETWEEN SCENES. It simply means that you make every decision concerning how you tell your story. A scene ends, often abruptly, and another one begins.

Sometimes there is no *space* between scenes. You move from a house to the beach without showing how your character gets there. That's fine. But sometimes you may want to show that transitory action in order to *visually* open up your story and to provide some contrast between certain scenes.

If a scene moves from inside one house to another, you could provide a nice contrast between those scenes by showing the main character tooling down the highway in a convertible with the top down. That transitory scene may only run for *five seconds* but it can visually open up your story—especially if it separates two interior scenes which might tend to be claustrophobic.

If you had a scene that begins in a bedroom and then moves to the kitchen, there are a number of ways of handling it. One scene can cut directly to the next. Or you could use transitory action to connect the two scenes. Example: The bedroom and the kitchen scenes could be tied together by having your character walk down a hallway between the two rooms.

If you wanted to create a mini-sequence, two characters could start a conversation in the bedroom, continue it in the hallway, and resolve it in the kitchen. This is another way of treating transitory action while utilizing the sequence as well. Everything in screenwriting is related.

> EXPOSITION is the technique used to convey information about your character and story to the audience via dialogue or visual means. It's an integral part of screenwriting since it provides the necessary background information to set up your story and move it forward. When exposition is required, it should be handled naturally and, whenever possible, it is best to weave it into scenes involving conflict—which makes it more interesting.

If exposition involves a lot of boring details, it should not be the function of the main character. However, if it is exciting and dramatic, like the main character explaining how he or she will save everyone from impending danger, then it is desirable because it will enhance the character's image.

Exposition can be handled visually. Rather than have two people talk about how sloppy a person is, it would be far more effective to show it. Example: A father and mother visit their son's first apartment and find it a mess with dirty dishes, newspapers on the floor, soiled clothing draped over the furniture, etc. They exchange a look of disgust; the father shakes his head while the mother sighs in exasperation.

Even more dramatic, you have a story about a reporter chronicling the life of a famous man who has died. You could have a scene with the reporter wandering around the man's den where memorabilia from his life is on display. Using the reporter's point of view, the camera could scan family photos, a collection of pipes, a wall of books on psychiatric care—possibly written by the deceased, etc. All these things reveal character without relying upon a word of dialogue.

There are two key exposition scenes in *DMD*—one to set up the story; the other to wrap it up.

The first exposition scene, at Kerry's office, which runs from the bottom of page 4 to the top of page 6, is handled two ways. The first part is very dramatic because Kerry, in a state of distress, relates to Dan her disturbing phone conversation with Elaine. The second part, which reveals the critical background on Kerry's father, is presented in a conversation between Trish Mott and Dan Wallace.

The second exposition scene, at the bungalow where Hobart is hiding with Kerry, running from the middle of page 95 to the middle of page 97, was far more difficult to write. Since the story is winding down, the audience is anxious to know what there is to know with great expedience. I tried to make that scene as believable as possible by having Hobart act cautiously at first—looking out the window while he speaks to Kerry—

then confident when he believes he has eluded his pursuers. A great deal of tension is built into that scene since it is obvious that Hobart, having revealed himself to Kerry, will kill her at some point.

While the basic rule of film is: ***don't say what you can show***, there are times when you will want to use exposition to eliminate other scenes for the purpose of reducing screen time and saving money. Example: One character tells another, "I want you to see all the people on this list and find out what they know about the boy. And when you're done, report back to me." Now you could show the person interviewing some or all of the people on the list or just cut to the scene when the person is reporting back. It all depends upon what is critical to telling your story.

Using and not using exposition also affects the treatment of a scene. If your main character is walking into a dangerous situation and the audience is given those facts ahead of time, again, through exposition, *suspense* can be created because the audience *knows* something is going to happen. If the audience doesn't know of the impending danger ahead of time, their reaction will be one of *surprise* or *shock* when the main character walks into trouble.

Exposition is constantly used throughout a screenplay every time you relate facts or information to the audience about your character or story. When exposition is needed, find a way of treating it so it will appear to be natural, not obvious. The last thing you want to do is hang a sign on it.

> BACKGROUND ACTIVITY is another way of *texturing* a scene and creating DRAMATIC TENSION. If you created a scene with a man and woman arguing, you could show another man observing them in the background. If the audience knows that the second man is an intruder, not liked by the man arguing with the woman, it would create additional tension and enhance the scene.

If you were writing a comedy and created a scene where a man and woman were sharing an intimate moment and had a bunch of penguins waddling behind them in the background, it could be highly amusing. However, if you had a critical scene between two characters, you wouldn't want to use any background texturing to distract from the focus of the scene.

> DRAMATIC TENSION also can be created and released within a scene by changing the emotional state of the characters. A harmonious family scene can erupt into a heated argument or vice versa. This is another element of dramatic writing that also provides contrast within and between scenes.

> SUBTEXT is what happens below the surface of the scene. It is the emotional aspects—what the characters are actually feeling. Subtext represents the quality dimension of writing that should be an intricate part of every scene, whenever possible.

The most obvious illustration of subtext in *DMD* is the second scene on page 68 where Kerry is picking up another rental car. At this point, Kerry and Mike's relationship is changing. Beyond the physical attraction, there is an emotional connection between them prompting the desire for physical intimacy. When Mike asks Kerry, "Are you hungry?", she answers suggestively, "Starved." It's clear that they are not referring to dinner here. Of course, when the moment arises, Kerry realizes that making love isn't right and gently withdraws from their embrace.

> A REVERSAL is simply an outcome opposite to what is expected—and it is usually a surprise of some significance. It can work as a character twist, such as the main character's best friend turning out to be the bad guy. Or it could be a plot device involving the heroine's escape from the villain in a sequence filled with suspense. As the tension subsides and the audience believes she is now well out of danger, the villain steps out of the darkness and recaptures her. Reversals are a very effective technique, but don't get carried away with them. Too many in one story will wear thin on your audience and turn them off.

> FLASHBACK is another effective technique which requires special consideration and very creative application. As the term implies, flashback means going backwards. Therefore it can impede or hinder the forward motion of your story. If you

opened your story with a flashback, it should be at a critical point in the main character's life, possibly a life or death situation. As your story unfolds, the flashback would have to be strong enough to grab and sustain the audience's attention and interest until the final outcome is revealed. If you decided to use a quick flashback, it would be more effective if you relied upon the visual aspects only, no dialogue. Think about it. When memories are recalled, we usually visualize past experiences as opposed to actually remembering the things that were said. Unless it will enhance your story and you can be extremely creative, don't use the flashback.

While the flashback technique can be used anywhere in your story, it is usually most effective when introduced at the beginning to set up something very dramatic that will be resolved later. It can be a great teaser, but if you use it, there had better be a big payoff at the end. Also, if you wanted to open your story with a flashback, you wouldn't have to introduce it as such—it would be obvious once it is over. Here is an illustration of that point.

EXT. MOUNTAIN PATH - NIGHT

Under a shimmering moon, a MAN, consumed with terror, races along a narrow mountain path. In the b.g., and getting LOUDER, the SOUND of some CREATURE. The Man, looking back over his shoulder, trips and falls over the edge. As he drops several hundred feet into the darkness--

INT. BEDROOM - NIGHT

The Man jumps up in bed, soaked in sweat, heart pounding, gasping for breath.

It is obvious from the second scene that the one before it is a dream sequence—a derivative of the flashback. In the following illustration, the flashback is made obvious by the scene before it.

EXT. LAKE ROAD - DAY

A MAN, 70s, walks along the road. At one point, he reaches a clearing that provides an unobstructed view of the lake. He stops and gazes out at the surface, glistening in the late afternoon sun. Soon his expression takes on a reflective look.

EXT. LAKE - DAY

A BOY, about 10, wearing a bathing suit, sits on a float near a very PRETTY GIRL his age. The Boy, shy and self-conscious, looks away when she smiles at him. She, in a very sensitive gesture, reaches out and touches his arm.

EXT. LAKE ROAD - DAY

The old Man holds his arm where the Pretty Girl touched him and smiles wistfully. The SOUND of YOUNG BOYS approaching on bicycles from behind breaks his reverie. He smiles at them as they pass, then walks off ever so slowly.

> MONTAGE is the technique used to combine a series of cuts (visuals; no dialogue) to indicate a passage of time—a week, a month, a year, whatever. By being creative, you can establish the passage of time the montage covers in any number of ways. Here is one illustration using the scene before a montage sequence and the scene following the montage sequence.

INT. OFFICE - DAY

BILL GRAVES is packing up the contents of his desk into a large box while TOM ANDERSON observes.

> TOM
> I was really disappointed to hear
> that you were leaving.

> BILL
> I just couldn't stand working for
> Cochran anymore.

> TOM
> So when do you start your new job?

> BILL
> When I get back from vacation.

> TOM
> Good luck, Bill. I hope things
> work out for you.

Bill nods and flashes a tight smile -- his anxiety evident.

MONTAGE BEGINS:

Cut #1: Bill, his wife, and kids loading their
station wagon.

Cut #2: Bill's station wagon cruising down the
highway.

Cut #3: Bill gliding across a lake in a sailboat.

Cut #4: Bill swimming with his kids.

Cut #5: Bill burning up the family's dinner on the
barbecue grill.

Cut #6: Bill sleeping in a hammock under the shade
of two huge oak trees.

MONTAGE ENDS:

EXT. OFFICE BUILDING - DAY

Bill, dressed in suit, looking well-rested, happy,
heads for the front door. As he grabs the door, a
VOICE from behind calls out.

> MAN (O.S.)
> Bill! Wait up.

Bill swings around. His face drops.

> BILL
>
> JJJ..JJ... John Cochran. What are
> you doing here?

> COCHRAN
>
> I was recruited over. Looks like
> you'll be reporting to me again.

Bill's expression says it all. End of illustration.

The six cuts outlined in the montage could take less than two minutes of screen time. And yet, they very effectively transition the two scenes: Bill leaving his old job and starting his new one.

> PLANTING is introducing an object, character, or a situation early in a story which pays off later or affects the ending. This technique is essential to any story with a twist or unpredictable ending. And when the plant is introduced, it should not consciously register or appear to be obvious to the audience. They should not see the significance of the plant until it is used to resolve the story's ending.

A rule about planting. Throughout a story, especially mysteries, a writer plants subtle facts, hints, and suspicions about various characters showing their *potential* to be the villain. To be fair, don't deliberately mislead the audience using the *red herring* technique. If you point a finger at someone, there must be a credible reason to justify it.

> STAGE DIRECTIONS, as they appear in parentheses under the name of the character speaking, have three primary applications, and should be used judiciously.

> GEORGE
>
> (impatiently)
>
> Bill! What are you doing here?

Here, (impatiently) relates to the character's frame of mind.

> GEORGE
>
> (yelling loudly)
>
> Bill! What are you doing here?

Here, (yelling loudly) relates to how the character delivers the dialogue.

BILL
(walking away)
Goodbye, George.

(Walking away) describes the physical action of the character while delivering the dialogue.

GEORGE
(to Bill; embarrassed)
I'm sorry for losing my temper.

When there are more than two people in a scene and one character is addressing another, but not by name, you may want to clarify who is being addressed.

You do so by putting the name of the person being addressed in parentheses in the stage directions under the character speaking. At the same time, as illustrated above, additional stage directions can be given. In this case, (to Bill; embarrassed), George addresses Bill, while acting embarrassed.

If stage directions can't be expressed in two or three words, then describe them in the full margin used for scene descriptions, as the following illustrates.

GEORGE
(to Bill)
There's something important I want
to show you.

George walks over to the desk, opens a drawer, retrieves a piece of paper and hands it to Bill.

GEORGE (cont'd)
So, what do you think?

As illustrated, when the character's dialogue is split by stage directions, (cont'd) is placed in parentheses next to the character's name when the dialogue continues again.

Stage directions can be used to *cue* a character, and it works like this:

TOM
(on Linda's smile)
Why are you smiling?

This stage direction actually cues both Tom and Linda because Tom's line is prompted by Linda's smile.

Sometimes how a line should be delivered is rather ambiguous— in that case, clarify it by using stage directions. Look at the scene on page 4 when Kerry and Elaine are discussing Hobart. Here, stage directions are used four times because I wanted to make clear the emotional states of the characters at that point. Again, use stage directions only when it is absolutely necessary. In reading *DMD* and other scripts, you will soon acquire an understanding and feel for when and how these various screenwriting techniques are used.

There are applications that preclude the use of stage directions. In the second scene on page 84 in *DMD*, when Kerry is dragged from the back seat of the police car by the Mafia hit men, she yells, "Get your hands off me!" The use of the exclamation point (!) makes it clear she is angry. Therefore, it's not necessary to put (angrily) in stage directions under her name.

> VOICE-OVER NARRATION is a technique used in those great detective films of the 1940s. We would usually see the detective's car gliding down the highway while hearing him speak in voice-over narration, filling in details (exposition) about himself and/or his case.

Voice-over narration should always express something other than what is shown in the scene. Example:

EXT. DESERT GAS STATION - DAY

A dust-covered Ford pulls up to the gas pumps and stops. A weary-looking SAM SPADE gets out.

> SPADE (V.O.)
> I pulled into this gas station and
> got out of my car.

This voice-over duplicates the obvious. Here is a better way to handle this voice-over scene.

> SPADE (V.O.)
> I've been driving for three days
> on coffee and cigarettes. If I
> don't make L.A. tonight, I may
> never see Verna again.

Like flashbacks, the use of voice-over narration is very infrequent since the technique only lends itself to certain stories. One of the best illustrations of effective narration and flashback is in *Stand by Me*. Because the narration is used to express the thoughts and feelings of the main character, as well as to present information about the story, it adds a special touch.

> DIALOGUE TECHNIQUES are easy to understand and use. There are two primary ones used within dialogue. Three dots after a word (Hummm...) indicates a long pause; while two hyphen marks between words (maybe -- I could do it) indicates a slight interruption in the delivery of the dialogue.

If your character pauses before speaking, then use, in stage directions, any one of three primary phrases: (beat), (a beat; then), or (a pause; then).

Here is an example of the various dialogue techniques incorporated into one brief conversation.

> GEORGE
> (a beat; to Ann)
> Whattaya say we throw Bill down
> the elevator shaft at the World
> Trade Center?

> ANN
> Can't we find some place...
> higher?

As indicated in stage directions, (a beat; to Ann), George pauses before he speaks to Ann. Within Ann's dialogue, she pauses after the word *place*.

> TELEPHONE CALLS can be handled three different ways.

EXAMPLE NO. 1A

INT. RESTAURANT - DAY

George stands in the corner on a pay phone. In the b.g., waitresses hustle from table to table.

> GEORGE
> (into phone)
> ... Hi, Ann. What's up?...
> What?... It's impossible for
> anyone to survive a fall from one
> hundred and seven floors!

In the above scene, by having *waitresses hustle from table to table*, a little background (b.g.) activity was added. With this phone technique, the person on camera (in this case, George) pauses as if he were listening to Ann speak on the other end of the line.

If you wanted to dramatically set up the scene without revealing exactly what is being said, you'd have the character *on camera* react accordingly as he or she listens to the other party speak. It would look like this:

EXAMPLE 1B

> GEORGE
> (into phone; shocked)
> Oh, no!... Are you sure?...
> Okay, I'll be right there.

In that illustration, the audience doesn't hear the other character's dialogue, but they know, from George's reaction *on camera* that something significant has happened. This is a very effective way of introducing a crisis situation and building tension.

EXAMPLE NO. 2

INT. HOUSE - KITCHEN - NIGHT

George walks around the kitchen while he is on the phone. In the b.g., a BLENDER runs at high speed.

> GEORGE
> (into phone)
> So, when are the visiting hours?

> ANN (V.O.)
> From three to nine.

> GEORGE
> I guess we should pay him a visit.

> ANN (V.O.)
> Maybe we could throw him down the hospital elevator shaft.

> GEORGE
> Sounds like a plan to me.

With this phone technique, a little b.g. diversion is created with the blender running over the two characters speaking. During this scene, we are constantly looking at George as he speaks to Ann. Her voice is heard through voice-over (V.O.).

In this type of phone scene, you could have the character who is on camera doing something in addition to talking on the phone. If you wanted to create a humorous scene, you could have the character trying to make a sandwich while carrying on a conversation.

Imagine someone walking around the kitchen retrieving the various ingredients. At one point, the phone cord is too short so the character has to awkwardly reach for something that is just out of grasp. Crash! A jar of pickles explodes on the floor.

- EXAMPLE NO. 3

INT. HOSPITAL ROOM - NIGHT

Bill is lying in bed; in traction. One of his arms and both legs are suspended by cables. Wrapped up in bandages from head to toe, he looks like a mummy.

The PHONE besides his bed starts RINGING. A NURSE enters and picks it up.

                    NURSE
              (into phone)
        Hello?... Just a minute, please.
              (to Bill)
        It's for you.

The Nurse hands Bill the phone and exits.

                    BILL
              (into phone; lethargically)
        Hello?

INT. HOUSE - DEN - SAME TIME

George is seated in his lounge chair with the phone cradled on his neck. Ann, in a sheer nightgown, stands behind him rubbing his shoulders.

                    GEORGE
              (into phone)
        Bill? How ya doin', good buddy?

INTERCUT PHONE CONVERSATION

                    BILL
              (struggling to speak)
        Oh, hi, George, I guess I'm doing
        okay. I hope you're taking care
        of Ann while I'm recuperating.

                   GEORGE
            (smiles at Ann; into phone)
        Don't worry, Bill, I'm taking good
        care of her -- have no fear...
              (George kisses Ann)
        Hey, Bill. How'd you like to go
        skydiving next weekend?

INTERCUT PHONE CONVERSATION means that the person who is speaking becomes the subject of the shot and the camera would cut back and forth between the two characters as each one speaks.

Of course, all three phone techniques can be combined in one scene, but there is no need to get that intricate. Just write the scene utilizing the phone technique that works best for the situation.

SCREENWRITING TERMINOLOGY

The following is an explanation of the most frequently used screenwriting terms and abbreviations.

> FADE IN: is the term used to indicate an image gradually appearing on a black screen. Of course, FADE OUT: would be the opposite, where an image gradually fades out until the screen goes black.

> DISSOLVE TO/CUT TO: are editing terms some writers like to use between scenes. They are not necessary. An unencumbered screenplay is pleasing to the eye and a much easier read. That is why it is best to stick to the basics: the scene headings, scene descriptions, and character/dialogue segments. That's all you need.

> OFF CAMERA (O.C.) and OFF SCREEN (O.S.) are essentially the same. If a character is off camera when the shot is taken, he or she will be off screen. The choice of which to use is discretionary.

There is a difference, however, between off screen and voice-over. Off screen is best used when someone speaking is in the scene but is not on camera—such as speaking from behind a closed door or from another room. Voice-over is best used for phone conversations when someone is clearly elsewhere. Again, (V.O.) or (O.S.) is placed to the right of the character's name as previously illustrated.

> In the f.g. (foreground) or in the b.g. (background) are terms used to indicate other things happening within a scene. Here's an example:

EXT. STREET - DAY

George walks briskly down the sidewalk. He looks a little uneasy. In the b.g., we see Bill coming up behind him with a two-by-four.

> Scenes utilizing CARS are handled in several basic ways. Again, determine the subject of the camera. Here are two examples and their differences.

EXT. HIGHWAY - MOVING CAR - DAY

In this scene heading, both the car and the highway share equal importance.

EXT. MOVING CAR - DAY

In this scene heading, the car is the focus.

When a car or other vehicle is the subject of the scene heading, you need to indicate INT. or EXT. and whether or not it is moving. Use PARKED CAR if the car is stationary.

By reading *Dead Man's Dance* and other screenplays, you will quickly acquire a sense or feel for screenplay form and the various techniques applied to each.

THE FIRST DRAFT SCREENPLAY

WRITING THE FIRST DRAFT SCREENPLAY

If you have properly completed all the previous exercises and are familiar with screenplay form, techniques, and terminology, you should be well-prepared and very eager to tackle your first draft screenplay.

Don't write your screenplay until you are thoroughly prepared; and once you start, don't stop to polish, correct, or rewrite until the first draft is completed.

The initial draft of my first screenplay, *The 12/20 Club* was absolutely horrible. And while I was tempted, I never stopped or went back to fix anything until after the first draft was completed. Stopping or going back to fix something will only impede your forward motion. If you stop to fix one thing, you could end up in a major rewrite before your project is completed and become totally frustrated trying to perfect what you have already written. Then you can become discouraged and never finish the project.

It's very important not to make any judgments concerning the *quality* of your first draft screenplay as you write it. Just tell your story from beginning to end. Your screenplay will be made better in subsequent rewrites. Writing is rewriting. That's what it's all about.

THE WRITING APPROACH

From setup to resolution, tell your story scene by scene, plot point to plot point. Focus your writing on each ten-page segment.

There's nothing more important than the first ten pages, setting up your story, and the last "x" number of pages covering the resolution.

Within the first ten pages (ten minutes of film time), the audience will decide whether or not they like your story. If you can't grab their attention in the first ten pages, you'll have a tough time maintaining their interest unless your story dramatically improves. In that case, they just might forgive you. More often than not, if the first ten minutes of a film are weak, the rest of the story usually doesn't get any better. That is almost a guarantee. From a weak opening, it's a long, dismal downhill slide into oblivion.

WRITING ACT I - THE SETUP

The purpose of Act I, the first 25 pages, is to set up your story. *In the first ten pages, you must introduce your main character, what the story is about, and the dramatic circumstances surrounding the action.*

Ten pages are more than sufficient to gradually introduce the three primary elements of your story with great care and style. It's possible to set up your story in the very first page or first couple of pages. If you can do it skillfully, without creating the impression of just *throwing* the setup at the audience, then do it.

Every story lends itself to a certain setup which is established from the opening scene. If you were writing an action/adventure film, it would be appropriate to open up with a fast-paced action sequence. If you were writing a mystery, your story might open up at night, in a marsh, where a killer, masked by a swirling fog, murders someone.

In reading screenplays from successful films, you can acquire an instant understanding as to how each story is set up and why it works so well. This analysis can be very helpful in determining the setup of your own story.

Writers spend a great deal of time conceptualizing ideas. In the days before you begin writing your first draft screenplay, define the three primary elements of your story and determine the most effective way to introduce them. Once a smooth opening is established, your story will gradually grow stronger as you develop it.

A good opening sets the *tone* for your story which, in turn, enables you to develop it with far more confidence.

PAGES 11 TO 25

After you have set up your story, your focus and line of development should be aimed at the first major plot point. In the second ten pages, concentrate on the main character while moving your story forward. With a specific objective for each scene, keep moving towards your next goal, the first major plot point. If you have the tendency to write too much, don't worry and don't start counting pages. Just keep writing. Tell your story. You're far better off *overwriting* than not having enough. It's always easier to cut out extra scenes or portions of scenes rather than to create new ones later.

In writing a first draft screenplay, I write continuously without page numbers or separating pages. Only when I'm done and need to print a hard copy will the pages be separated and assigned numbers.

The first major plot point should be significant enough to grab the audience and propel your story forward into high gear. But a word of caution. The first major plot point has to be strong enough to grab the audience, but at the same time, be in balance with the rest of the story. Tell your audience just what they need to know and build from that point. The longer you can hold back critical information, the more curious they will be.

WRITING ACT II - CONFLICT

The focus of Act II, pages 26 to 75, is conflict through confrontations and obstacles with the line of development running from the first major plot point to the second major plot point.

Through rising conflict, you progressively build your story and move towards its resolution. As your main character advances, his or her adversary delivers counter-thrusts or setbacks with the action gradually increasing to the most critical point. Rising human conflict is the primary force behind drama and the most important element in every story. Conflict is also naturally indigenous to every story as well as the internal conflicts created by the main character in attempting to overcome or deal with his or her own personal problems and shortcomings.

While rising human conflict is the primary force behind drama, collectively, all forms of conflict enhance the story and help sustain the audience's attention and interest.

Conflict varies in degrees as well as impact. Some forms of conflict are minor obstacles indigenous to the story or they can be very dramatic confrontations involving the main character and his or her adversary. Conflict is a back and forth motion. The main character advances a step towards achieving his or her goal, then suffers a setback.

CONFLICT IN *DEAD MAN'S DANCE*

Let's look at some examples of conflict from *Dead Man's Dance*.

The story advances when Kerry learns from Sgt. Daily that Lt. Haskins may have been the last person to see her sister alive and that Haskins denies that he ever talked with Elaine. Shortly thereafter, Sgt. Daily is killed and Kerry is *set back* because she now loses his testimony.

At the risk of her life, Kerry enters Lt. Haskins's home to acquire a hair sample for DNA testing and is almost caught. She is later set back when his DNA doesn't match that of Elaine's murderer.

Of course, as she applies more pressure on Lt. Haskins, he retaliates by having a truck run her off the road. And when that fails, he tries to stage another *accident* at the restaurant.

There is *minor human conflict* between Kerry and Mike Burrows in the Black Kettle Restaurant scene (pages 46/47) when he argues with her over going to the State Police or F.B.I. with what she knows. While they are not adversaries, their conflict creates tension and tension creates interest.

There is *major human conflict* when Kerry confronts Lt. Haskins (page 79) with the *Sgt. Daily tape* which, of course, doesn't exist. The fact that she can relate to Haskins what Daily said to her is enough to convince him that she has such a tape. Haskins is now pushed into a corner. That tape, in the hands of the F.B.I., would not only make him a prime suspect in two murders (Elaine's and Sgt. Daily's), but possibly reveal the Mafia relocation program. In either case, his life would be over. For Kerry, she risks getting out of Haskins's office alive or being murdered later. Because of what both characters risk, this scene has considerable tension.

All the various obstacles, confrontations, struggles, and major and minor conflicts strengthen a story and sustain the audience's attention and interest until the very end.

In writing Act II, work from plot point to plot point while maintaining awareness of rising human conflict. Have you accurately treated the conflict within your story? Is it strong enough to sustain the audience's attention and interest? Does rising human conflict gradually increase until the final climax is reached?

While every story is essentially the same in the way the rules of dramatic writing and screenwriting are applied, each story has different requirements in regard to the treatment of all the elements in order to make it work. In executing a premise, it is the writer's job to determine the treatment of every aspect accordingly.

If you see problems within your script as you write it, don't stop or go back, just make *notes* highlighting those areas. This procedure will greatly reduce any anxiety you might have on those days when you are tempted to stop and improve something. You can always fix things later—just keep moving forward.

Writing Act III - The Resolution

Once Act II is completed, you have hit the home stretch. At this point, the writing will become much easier as you work towards your resolution. Within Act III, pages 76 to 90, you follow the remaining plot points connecting the action which leads to your ending.

Story Endings

While beginnings and endings share equal importance, there is one big difference between them.

Because you have ten pages, setting up your story is a lot easier than resolving it. Once the audience knows the ending is near, they get anxious and want a swift, conclusive finale.

This means that once the main character overcomes the last major obstacle and all issues have been resolved, the ending must be as tight as possible. Endings require much greater skill.

In handling your story's resolution, there are a number of important things to keep in mind.

> Endings require careful planning and flawless execution if they are to work properly. If the first ten pages, the setup, establishes the audience's interest in your story, then the ending will determine *how much* they really like it.

> Once it becomes obvious to the audience that your story is soon ending, it should be wrapped up as swiftly and as efficiently as possible—after the final crisis has been overcome. The tighter the ending, the more effective it will be.

> Every issue must be clearly explained with nothing left unanswered.

> Everything must be resolved rationally and logically without resorting to coincidence.

> While today's movie audience wants and expects an upbeat ending, an unpredictable resolution or twist can greatly enhance the final outcome—only if it is logical. This type of treatment applies to every film genre from drama to comedy.

> Until all the facts are revealed, the audience should not be able to guess how (the details) the final outcome will be reached.

One of the most effective twists comes at the end of *The Odessa File*, starring Jon Voight. If you haven't seen this film and would like to, then don't read the next paragraph so you can fully appreciate the surprise.

The Odessa File, set in 1963 Hamburg, Germany, is the story of German journalist, Peter Miller (Voight), on the trail of a Nazi war criminal, SS Captain Eduard Roschmann (Maximillian Schell), who was the commandant of a wartime death camp. In the beginning, it's revealed that Miller's father, a German officer, was killed during World War II. At the end, when Miller confronts Roschmann, the audience believes his only motive for hunting the Nazi down is for his crimes against the Jews. However, as things unfold, it is revealed that Roschmann murdered Miller's father in cold blood while attempting to commandeer a boat. The twist is handled so effectively that it is both believable and comes as a complete surprise.

SCREENPLAY TITLE

In the literary world, the average best-selling book title is 1.8 words, so it is not a bad guideline for determining the title of your screenplay. Creating a title that sounds appealing and is significant to your story is a practical consideration.

For *Dead Man's Dance*, the significance of the title is obvious. Kenneth Hobart, presumed dead, is living and enjoying life under a different name.

A good screenplay title conveys an impression about a film that may be very ambiguous, but sounds appealing or intriguing—and that's what is important.

Will a good title attract people to a film? If they haven't read any negative reviews, a good title—along with a favorite actor—can often prompt people to see it.

I once read an article about films with bad titles. Almost every badly titled film that they listed bombed at the box office. The article also made the point that *The Shawshank Redemption*, which did okay in theaters, might have done more business with a better title. I found that second point interesting because in spite of the positive reviews, I passed on seeing *The Shawshank Redemption* in the theaters. The title just turned me off. Later, at the recommendation of a friend, I saw it on Pay-For-View and liked it. A good title can help and, in some instances, make a big difference.

ADAPTATIONS

Even if you are not immediately involved with this segment of screen-writing, it's important to understand the basic facts about adaptation.

The term adaptation means to adapt, not copy, from one medium to another.

If you're adapting a novel, play, short story, or magazine article, the treatment will be the same as writing an original screenplay.

Sometimes the source material is so well-structured, it lends itself to adaptation without a lot of modification. At other times, an adaptation can be extremely difficult because the story does not lend itself to dramatization. With some novels, you may have to add new characters, additional scenes, and elaborate on the story line in order to make it work. It's not just a matter of copying or transferring the source material into screenplay form.

When you adapt a novel, you are not required to remain true to the original material. However, if the novel is very popular, you would be well-advised to remain as faithful as possible to the original work. If you were given the assignment of adapting a 650-page novel covering the life span of a woman, your approach may be to focus on the most interesting segment of the woman's life, which may only account for a third of the book. In many cases, an adaptation can be more difficult than an original screenplay since the treatment requires a higher level of creativity to make it work.

Most of the adaptation work is controlled by the studios or major production companies. Because they are willing and able to pay top dollar to acquire film rights, they have first access to the best source material.

A $3 million dollar deal was made based upon two chapters of an unfinished novel, *The Horse Whisperer*, by a first-time novelist, Nicholas Evans, because the premise of his story was so appealing.

When a studio acquires the rights to a novel, a producer is assigned to the project who, in turn, hires a writer. After discussing how the material will be developed, the writer scurries off to his or her little burrow and goes to work. After the writer turns over a first draft screenplay, the real work begins through a series of rewrites. As long as the writer stays *on track*, he or she will remain on the project.

Twenty-three years ago, John Mastrobuono, a friend, lent me a book saying it would make a great film. This was before I had any serious

116

interest in screenwriting. The book was *First Blood*. It came out in 1972 and was optioned in 1979 by Columbia Pictures for $90,000. Who knows what that book could have been quietly acquired for by a writer before a major studio started sniffing it out. My guess is that if an unknown writer pursued the film rights to *First Blood* a year or two after the book had been released—and there were no other interested parties—the cost could have been very modest in comparison to what the studio paid.

While all the prime source material—best-sellers, plays, magazine articles, etc.—is usually scooped up by the studios and major production companies, there is still a glut of potential winners out there for the writer who is willing to make a careful search. Remember, every decision concerning what is potentially a commercial property is *subjective*. A studio might pass on a particular source material if they can't envision a treatment that would work as a film. But a creative writer may find a way of approaching the source material and turning it into cinematic gold.

More than likely, there are many books out there that would make great films even though they never made the best-seller's list. They might have been published this year or twenty years ago. *First Blood* was around for seven years before a studio recognized its potential as a film.

Maybe a friend can recommend a book that he or she feels would make a great film story, something that everyone else has overlooked. People who work in bookstores are usually voracious readers, so they could be another great source. Someone might be able to recommend an obscure novel that would adapt well to film, possibly a personal favorite that was panned by critics but may be a real sleeper.

Rummage sales, garage sales, and stores specializing in used books are but a few of the potential sources for finding older novels that might adapt well to film. If you find an interesting book or article that would make a good film story, engage an entertainment attorney to secure, check, and clear the rights for you. Ahead of time, the attorney can advise you as to the cost involved so you would know exactly what your investment might be. By keeping your eyes opened, you might just find a real opportunity out there.

To illustrate this important screenwriting function, the short script you are about to read is an adaptation followed by the original source material.

EXT. PARK - DAY

The park is busy with couples walking hand in hand, parents playing with children, and teenagers tossing Frisbees.

TOM ANDERSON, 25, clean-cut, neatly dressed, holding a red book, gazes towards the fountain. With a slight limp, he moves to a nearby bench and takes a seat.

Sitting next to him, NOREEN, a friendly woman, mid-30s, reading a book, notices his apprehensive behavior.

> NOREEN
> Are you all right?

He gives her a tight nod and quick smile.

> NOREEN (cont'd)
> You seem nervous.

> TOM
> I'm meeting someone for the first time.

> NOREEN
> Obviously a young lady. No need to be nervous.

Tom considers the woman for a moment, then speaks.

> TOM.
> It's a little complicated.

> NOREEN
> How's that?

TOM
I've fallen in love with someone
I've never met.

NOREEN
Sounds intriguing.

TOM
Six months ago, I came to New York
looking for a job. First day here, a
truck runs a red light and broadsides
my car. I ended up in the hospital
with a concussion and two broken legs.

NOREEN
Welcome to New York.

TOM
(smiles; then)
One of my nurses found out I had
no family except an uncle back in
Minnesota -- that's where I'm from
-- so she gave me the name of this
organization. She said if I wrote
to them, someone would write back.
She thought it would be a good way
to help pass the time.

NOREEN
So this young lady answered your
letter?

TOM
She kept in touch with me the
whole time I was in the hospital.
I just got out yesterday.

NOREEN
I take it her letters were very
special.

TOM
Special? I don't know how I
would've survived without them --
dealing with the pain, the
physical therapy, being laid up
all that time. It's amazing how
you can get to know someone from
exchanging letters. After a
while, I found myself falling in
love with her and sense she feels
the same about me.

NOREEN
What do you know about her?

TOM
Only that she's my age, single, and
works for a publishing company.

NOREEN
Do you know what she looks like?

TOM
No. When I asked her to send me a
photo, she wouldn't. She said how
she looked shouldn't matter.

NOREEN
I can understand that.

TOM
I know it's not everything, but
I'd be less than honest if I said
it didn't matter.

NOREEN
What if she doesn't meet your expectations?

TOM
I don't know.

NOREEN
Have you ever spoken to her?

TOM
No. When I asked if I could call
her, she insisted we keep our
communications to just writing.

NOREEN
How'd she leave things with you?

TOM
She said we'd meet after I got out
of the hospital and go from there.

NOREEN
So you're meeting her here?

TOM
By the fountain.

NOREEN
How will you know each other?

TOM
She told me to carry a red book --
and she'd be wearing a red ribbon.

He glances at his watch.

TOM (cont'd)
I'd better get over there.

Tom gets to his feet.

NOREEN
Good luck.

He nods apprehensively, then limps over to the fountain.

Out of the crowd of people heading his way, he sees a
BEAUTIFUL WOMAN, about his age, dressed in a flowered
sundress. To his surprise, she is looking directly at
him and smiling. After she passes, Tom stops and looks
back at her, but she keeps on going.

When he turns and faces the fountain, his heart sinks.
Standing there wearing a red ribbon is a PLUMP WOMAN,
30, not unattractive, but not what he was hoping for.

After a brief pause, he steps forward and addresses her
with a slight stammer in his voice.

> TOM
> Carrie? I'm Tom Anderson. I'm so
> glad we could meet... Would you
> like to go somewhere for a drink?

> PLUMP WOMAN
> I don't know what this is all
> about, but that girl in the
> flowered sundress begged me to
> wear this ribbon, and said that if
> you asked me to go out with you, I
> should tell you she's waiting for
> you in the parking lot. She said
> it was some kind of test.

Tom hugs her, then limps off at a quick pace in the
direction of the Beautiful Woman, shouting joyously.

The script you just read is an adaptation of a wonderful story,
"Appointment with Love," by Sulamith Ish-Kishor from the book, *A
Third Helping of Chicken Soup for the Soul.*

Ms. Ish-Kishor was born in England on November 16, 1896. Her
family moved to the United States when she was in her teens. She
attended high school and college in New York City. While she wrote
poetry, short stories, articles, nonfiction and novels, she is primarily
remembered for her fine children's books.

Among them are *The Master of Miracle*, *A Boy of Old Prague*, *Our Eddie*, and *Carpet of Solomon*. Ms. Ish-Kishor died in 1977.

The following is a reprint of "Appointment with Love."

Six minutes to six said the big clock over the information booth in New York's Grand Central Station. The tall young Army lieutenant lifted his eyes to note the exact time. His heart was pounding with a beat that shocked him. In six minutes, he would see the woman he had never seen, yet whose written words had sustained him unfailingly throughout the war.

Lieutenant Bradford remembered one day in particular, the worst of the fighting, when his plane had been caught in the midst of a pack of enemy planes.

Five minutes to six. In one of his letters, he had confessed to her that he often felt fear, and only a few days before this battle, he had received her answer—"Of course you fear... all brave men do. Next time you doubt yourself, I want you to hear my voice reciting these words to you. 'Yea, though I walk through the Valley of the Shadow of Death, I shall fear no evil, for Thou art with me.'" He had remembered, and it had renewed his strength.

Now he was going to hear her real voice. Four minutes to six. A girl passed close to him and Lieutenant Bradford got excited. She was wearing a flower, but it was not the little red rose they had agreed upon. Besides, this girl was only about eighteen, and Helen Taylor had told him in one of her letters she was thirty. "What of it?" he had answered to himself, "I'm thirty-two." He was twenty-nine.

Three minutes to six. His mind went back to the book he had read in the training camp, *Eternal Love*. Throughout the book were notes in a woman's writing. He had never believed that a woman could see into a man's heart so tenderly, so understandingly. Her name was on the book—Helen Taylor. He had got hold of a New York City telephone book and found her address. He had written—she had answered. Next day he had been shipped out to sea, but they had gone on writing.

For thirteen months she has faithfully replied. Even when his letters did not arrive, she wrote anyway, and now he believed he loved her—and she loved him.

Two minutes to six. But she had refused all his pleas to send him her photograph. She had explained— "If your feeling for me has any reality, what I look like won't matter. Suppose I'm beautiful. I'd always be haunted that you had been taking a chance on just that, and that kind of love would disappoint me. Suppose I'm plain (and you must admit that this is more likely), then I'd always fear that you were only going on writing because you were lonely and had no one else. No, don't ask for my picture. When you come to New York, you shall see me and you shall make your decision."

One minute to six. He swallowed hard. Then Lieutenant Bradford's heart leaped. A young woman was coming toward him, she was beautiful. Her figure was long and slim—her blond hair lay back in curls. Her eyes were blue as flowers, her lips and chin had a gentle firmness. In her pale green suit, she was like springtime come alive.

He started toward her, forgetting to notice that she was not wearing a rose. She moved, a small, provocative smile curved her lips. "Going my way, soldier?" she murmured. He made one step closer to her. Then he saw Helen Taylor. She was standing almost directly behind the girl—a woman well past forty, her graying hair tucked under a worn hat. She was more than plump, her thick-ankled feet were crushed into low-heeled shoes. But she wore a red rose on a rumpled coat. The beautiful girl in the green suit was walking quickly away.

Bradford felt as though he were being split in two. So keen was his desire to follow the pretty girl, yet so deep was his longing for the woman whose spirit had truly companioned and upheld his own through her letters and there she stood. He could see that her pale, plump face was gentle and sensible—her gray eyes had a warm twinkle.

Lieutenant Bradford did not hesitate. His trembling fingers gripped the worn copy of the book, *Eternal Love*, which was to identify him to her. This may not be love, but it would be something precious, a friendship for which he had been and must be grateful.

He squared his shoulders, stepped forward, saluted, and held the book out towards the woman—although even while he spoke he felt the bitterness of his disappointment. "I... I'm Lieutenant Bradford, and you... you are Miss Taylor. I'm so glad you could meet me. May... may I take you to dinner?"

The woman's face broadened in a tolerant smile. "I don't know what this is all about, young man," she answered. "That young lady in the green suit, she begged me to wear this rose on my coat. And she said that if you asked to go out with you, I should tell you she's waiting for you in that restaurant across the street. She said it was some kind of test."

THE ADAPTATION - FINDING THE RIGHT APPROACH

"Appointment with Love" is a well-crafted, poignant love story. Ms. Ish-Kishor creates incredible tension using the ticking clock. As it gets closer and closer to the scheduled meeting time, it makes it very easy for us to feel the Lieutenant's anxiety. Of course, the nice twist at the end is not only unexpected, but very uplifting. Consider the prime elements of "Appointment with Love." It is a period piece, set in Grand Central Station, and has a lot of exposition not carried by dialogue. My goal in doing the adaptation was to capture the essence and spirit of the story.

CHANGING THE STORY'S TIME PERIOD

The short story was set at the end of World War II. This was a great period in American history with G.I.s returning home to their loved ones and to great opportunities with a burgeoning U.S. economy. It is clear that Lt. Bradford was sustained through the most difficult time in his life by a woman he had never met, one who gave him comfort and encouragement which allowed him to do his duty and to return safely home.

My first step in approaching the adaptation was to make "Appointment with Love" a contemporary story using a more feasible location, as if I were shooting it as a short film project. Who wouldn't want to shoot in Grand Central Station? It is one of the most recognizable pieces of architecture in the world. However, think of the complexities of trying to shoot this script during the madness of the rush-hour period (even though the location would intensify the story's built-in tension).

CHANGING THE LOCATION

My selection of a park, the great outdoors, makes this a much easier shoot to control. Having the two key characters—Tom Anderson and (the friendly woman)—sitting on a bench provides a natural situation to prompt their meeting and conversation.

ABOUT THE CHARACTERS

Starting from scratch, I first created Tom Anderson. He's a clean-cut young man from the heartland of America—like the character Timothy Bottoms played in *The Paper Chase*. In one sense, it is a paradox since Lt. Bradford was returning from war while Anderson was moving to a war zone—what some from the Midwest consider New York City to be.

Since "Appointment with Love" is told through exposition, an additional character was needed, the friendly woman, to solve that problem. And with the exception of the Plump Woman's dialogue—which I slightly refined—the rest of the dialogue was created from the story's exposition.

CHANGING THE CIRCUMSTANCES

The circumstances that bring the two characters together needed to be changed. Using a soldier returning from duty today doesn't come close to matching the romantic aspect surrounding the end of World War II. So Tom Anderson's war is the months he spent in a hospital suffering pain and battling loneliness.

CASTING THE ROLES

In shooting this or any film, casting is the single most important element—matching the right actors to the characters. I feel confident that my adaptation would work as a film given the strength of the source material and the uplifting ending. While I enjoy writing original screenplays, it would be nice someday to meet the challenge of doing an adaptation of a novel.

EXERCISE 8: WRITE YOUR FIRST DRAFT SCREENPLAY

Using your list of scene descriptions and narrative treatment as a guideline, write your first draft screenplay. Write continuously without regard for page numbers and page breaks. Focus on your character and your story's plot points. Again, don't stop for any reason; keep writing until your script is finished.

THE REWRITING PROCESS

AFTER WRITING THE FIRST DRAFT SCREENPLAY

After completing your first draft screenplay, take a well-earned rest and get away from your project as long as you possibly can. Don't read it, browse through it, or talk about it. If at all possible, don't even think about it. If you can, get involved with other activities.

The more time you can put between completing your first draft and rewriting it, the better off you will be.

The biggest problem *every writer* has to contend with in writing and rewriting is objectivity. Because we spend so much time with a project, we lose our ability to assess it accurately. After a project is completed, it could take months before you really *see* your work objectively. And for the novice writer, who lacks the skills to identify problems, the situation is exacerbated. How can you make improvements if you don't know what needs improving?

If you're a novice writer, don't panic. A solution to this rewriting problem will be presented shortly.

Waiting as long as you can between rewrites can't be stressed enough. You should, at the very least, wait a week before tackling your first rewrite. And again, that means staying away from the script: no peeking allowed. Doing an immediate rewrite of your first draft is like trying to read in the dark by candlelight. You see things, but not too clearly.

THE REWRITING PROCESS

Many screenplays require constant refinement before the real quality of the work is evident. Therefore, no step in screenwriting is more important than rewriting. It's more important than all the previous steps combined.

A screenplay which might be mediocre is made great through successive rewrites and polishing. You may spend considerably more time completing your rewrites than you did in handling all the previous steps up to that point. You may rewrite your screenplay two, three, or even a dozen times until you are really satisfied. So don't feel compelled to complete the revision as quickly as possible. Give it as much time as it takes.

After you have taken a break from writing the first draft screenplay, the rewriting process looks likes this:

Step One:

Analyze your first draft screenplay, rewrite it, register it (details to follow), and then take a break.

Step Two:

Analyze your second draft, rewrite it, and then take another break.

Step Three:

Analyze your third draft and rewrite it.

Step Four:

Take a break while two trusted readers (to be explained shortly) evaluate your fourth draft screenplay.

Step Five:

Evaluate the feedback from your trusted readers, make those changes which you feel are necessary, and then polish the screenplay—down to the last detail.

Step Six:

Have someone *proofread* your screenplay for spelling, punctuation, and grammatical errors.

Step Seven:

Fine-tune your final draft until you are totally confident in the way it *looks* and *reads*.

The first thing everyone who reads a script in Hollywood does is quickly page through it. They are looking for an initial impression as to whether or not the writer is worthy of their time and consideration. Is the script appealing to the eye? Is it correctly formatted? Is the work neat? Some people may read a few lines of dialogue to quickly appraise the writer's style and skill level. Can a reader accurately assess a writer's ability by just reading a few lines of dialogue? Absolutely. After struggling through hundreds of screenplays, a reader can tell with one quick glance if the writing is competent. This, of course, has nothing to do with whether or not the reader will like your story. But that is not the point here. Your goal is to get someone to read your script and give it serious consideration.

If you happen to miss a few small errors (a misspelled word or a mistake in punctuation) in your final draft, it should not detract from the overall quality of your work. However, handing out a script riddled with errors is altogether different. A sloppy script can create an impression that the writer is unprofessional. And once that opinion has been formed, no matter how strong the story is, the reader may very well pass on it.

Unfortunately, some writers adopt the half-baked attitude of: "Why bother correcting my work now? It'll only have to be rewritten later." Anything less than a full commitment to rewriting is a total waste of time.

If you follow all the procedures outlined for rewriting, you and/or your trusted readers will more than likely see any critical flaws in the treatment of your characters or story. Initially, some problems may be difficult to identify, but through the rewriting process, they will eventually surface. Often other issues within your screenplay may bring those problems to your attention.

You will quickly realize that *minor changes will often significantly enhance your entire screenplay*.

After my script is *polished* and I am satisfied with the results, I no longer desire to read it because it might prompt unwarranted second thoughts about changing certain aspects of the story or inconsequential details. (Making changes at a later date may be necessary and very practical, but this issue will be covered later.)

The number of times someone rewrites a screenplay before showing it to agents or producers will vary. Your *ready script* may be a fifth draft or possibly a tenth.

Screenwriting is an imperfect art form in that most writers never reach a point of total satisfaction with their work. At any later date, when a fresh perspective is acquired, rereading your screenplay always prompts the desire to change (improve) things. Also, there is a natural tendency for writers to *second-guess* their work. That is why it is important to follow the rewriting procedures and make every effort to properly fine-tune your work through the initial phase of rewriting. You don't want to be dealing with major problems *after* you have circulated your script.

Before the details of the rewriting process are covered, a few other issues will be addressed first.

CONSTRUCTIVE FEEDBACK

Because of our inability to see our work objectively, it is next to impossible for a writer to effectively fine-tune his or her work without the assistance of at least one trusted reader, preferably two.

First of all, I don't know of any writer who could not benefit from input coming from an insightful, constructive source. No matter how skilled a writer might be, someone else's perspective can often be extremely helpful—not necessarily in pointing out a problem, but in offering suggestions which might enhance a character or plot issue.

THE TRUSTED READER

Now, who is a trusted reader? It is someone who has the ability to assess creative writing, provide very specific feedback on every element within a story, and propose changes that will improve the work. Obviously, that person would have to be totally honest with you and hold nothing back. Of course, being tactful about it would be nice. However, given the importance of meaningful feedback, I'd be willing to suffer indignities if it meant acquiring information that would help improve my script.

If a reader is the sensitive type, he or she might be reluctant to tell you the truth rather than hurt your feelings—no matter how insistent you may be in stressing your need to know. Keep that in mind when you are trying to find a trusted reader or two.

Even if a reader can't provide you with the solution to a problem, the mere fact that you are made aware of it gives you the opportunity to address it. Whenever you ask someone for feedback on your work, in many instances you will get a lot of subjective comments. In other words—how that person would change your story. If you ask for someone's input, hear the person out even if he or she is totally off base. It's quite possible that you still might come away with a few valid tidbits that could be helpful. With all readers, even those who you consider trusted, you need to dismiss subjective comments. In some cases, the reader might have very strong feelings about the subject matter which may result in unrealistic criticism.

At the same time, that reader might point out a specific flaw in a character. Be grateful, because you are now in a position to address a problem you were probably unaware of. If a reader's suggestion for fixing a problem is not the direction you want to take, then follow your own instincts.

During my first two years of screenwriting, I relied upon the same two readers. In those days, I agreed with ninety percent of their input. Two years ago, while working with one of the original readers, I found myself agreeing with only ten percent of that person's input. Much has to do with my growth as a writer and developing my ability to execute things better and to avoid making the same mistakes over again.

When finishing the second draft of *Dead Man's Dance*, I had no one who could serve as a trusted reader. As pointed out in Chapter 2, I made the fatal mistake of relying only upon the comments of friends who read for entertainment—and then shoved the script out the door in thirty days. My actions can be best described as shooting oneself in the foot. As long as you learn from mistakes and don't repeat them, it's a valuable lesson. In spite of my growth as a writer, I desperately need feedback on my work—especially after spending ten hours or more a day for weeks on end grinding it out. With my objectivity temporarily shot, it is beneficial to have someone else's input—especially if it is a trusted reader.

If a reader likes your story, you will get more objective feedback—if the person doesn't, the feedback will be limited and/or excessively critical.

To reiterate an earlier point—*you should only seek advice on your project during the research stages and after the first draft is completed. Discussing your work while writing can be inhibiting and disruptive.*

The only time a script should be turned over to readers is when it has been fine-tuned to the point where you have *initially* exhausted your rewriting capabilities. If you turn it over prematurely, there may be so many problems that they distract the reader from seeing the real potential of your story, and you end up with a less than positive response.

Are you better off handing readers a script they know nothing about? The answer is a big *YES*. If the readers know you are working on a thriller, when they eventually read the script, they might approach it having certain expectations and possibly compare it to their favorite film in that genre.

If that is the case, your script may come up short unless it is absolutely amazing. You want your readers to be as objective as possible, so say nothing about what you are working on.

If you need advice on your story before you start writing, don't go to your trusted readers even if you know their input could be quite helpful. Find other sources.

If you have any doubts about the way you have treated certain things within your script, say nothing to your readers ahead of time. If there is a problem, they will more than likely see it. Later, when you discuss the readers' findings, you can ask all the questions you want, which might prompt additional insights. If the readers don't comment on those areas of concern, then you can bring them up. They may tell you that it didn't register as a problem with them—or now that you mention it, they may agree that a particular issue could be treated more effectively and make some helpful suggestions. Good readers not only spot problems and offer effective solutions to them, but suggest ways of enhancing the overall material.

REWRITING OLD SCRIPTS

Success as a screenwriter hinges upon having a good story that is properly executed.

In eight years, I've written fourteen feature screenplays and believe ten have good commercial potential. Some can stand as is, while others could use a good rewrite. In regard to the other four scripts, one was absolutely horrible and the other three had good premises but were poorly executed. The poor execution was the result of not finding the right approach to developing the premise.

There is a major advantage to be gained by going back and fixing old scripts, if they have commercial potential today. If you are tackling a rewrite on a screenplay you wrote three years ago, you are approaching the material with a higher degree of skill and a fresh perspective—which are two major advantages. At this point, you might just find the approach to realize a story's full potential. And it may only require a minor adjustment in the way the material is rewritten to turn it into something very special.

While it is my intention to write new screenplays, I will give serious consideration to some of my older scripts. Not too long ago, I approached a development executive at a major production company with *Dead Man's Dance*.

When the exec said he had no interest in that genre, I asked him what type of project he'd like to develop. He said his company is always looking for a music-related story. Hearing that, I gave him a rundown on *The 12/20 Club*, my story about the business executive who puts his old high school rock 'n roll band back together twenty years later. Guess what? He asked to see it. I explained to him that I had other projects in the works that would preclude me from giving this script the good once-over it needs before showing it. He told me that whenever it is ready, he would like to see it.

At some point, going back and rewriting an older script might just turn into a major opportunity.

No Free Rewrites!

If someone tells you, on the production side, that he or she would be interested in your script *if* you made certain changes, you could be falling into a trap. And the trap is this: no matter how many times you rewrite *your script*, you will never get it right and nothing will ever come from all your extra work.

If someone is seriously interested in your screenplay, he or she will at least option it and pay you or some other writer to do rewrites. There may be circumstances when doing a free rewrite could be worthwhile and it is a judgment call. If giving up only four hours of your time curries favor with an actor, director, or producer, it might be a smart move. But before you agree, justify the person's motives. Find out what's in it for you.

While the vast majority of agents are honest, there are always those who will try to exploit the novice writer. One popular scam works like this. An agent will tell the novice that his or her script shows great potential but needs a polishing by a more experienced writer who could smooth out the rough spots for a nominal fee of $3,000. More than likely, the agent will give a small portion of the fee to some hack and nothing will ever happen with the script. Of course, the novice writer will be out $3,000.

How To Evaluate Criticism

A writer must be totally open-minded and receptive to input even from a source that is totally off base.

It's quite possible that someone who knows absolutely nothing about creative writing or screenwriting might provide you with some helpful comments.

At the same time, the trusted reader you have always relied upon may not be helpful at all. In most cases, it could be that the subject matter doesn't appeal to the reader.

How do you evaluate criticism, constructive and otherwise, from anyone who reads your screenplay? The answer is quite simple. *A writer must instinctively know if the criticism is valid or not.*

If someone points out a problem in my script, I usually know if he or she is correct almost instantly or after thinking about it for a short while.

There's nothing wrong with trying to explain your point of view to a reader—why you handled some element within your script a certain way. However, don't waste your time defending your work to someone who is not on the same wave length. If you have asked someone for an opinion, listen respectfully, thank them, and quickly move on. If you later realize that you asked the wrong person for help, find someone else next time.

When it comes to your screenplay, there is only one rule: *heed good advice, ignore frivolous comments, and trust your own instincts.* Ultimately, you must decide what is best for your screenplay.

THE VALUE OF CONSTRUCTIVE CRITICISM

A trusted reader can help a writer regain objectivity and sometimes point out things the writer may never see, even after stepping back from a script for a long time. Also, a trusted reader can offer suggestions that can greatly enhance the material; in other words, take your idea and make it even better. Remember, minor improvements can often significantly improve your entire screenplay.

SHARING YOUR WORK WITH FAMILY AND FRIENDS

It's inevitable that family members and friends may ask to read your work if, in fact, you have made them aware of your writing activities.

When you turn over your work to family and friends, you are often setting yourself up for disappointment.

Don't be surprised if:

1.   They actually don't read it.

2.   They read it but never tell you what they think—even if you prompt them for an opinion.

3.   They don't like it. And if they don't, they will probably say something like "it was interesting" (so as not to hurt your feelings).

4.   They come back with all kinds of worthless criticism such as: "I think Kerry Parker should be a tattooed mortician from Topeka, Kansas, with an orange-colored Mohawk, a spike through her head, and wearing lederhosen."

Think I'm kidding? You'll see.

REWRITING & POLISHING

Before the actual approach to rewriting your first draft screenplay is covered, a distinction should be made between a *rewrite* (or revision) and a *polishing*.

A screenplay is *rewritten* when changes are made affecting more than twenty-five percent of what you have initially written. That applies to structural changes, eliminating or adding scenes, moving scenes, altering the treatment of characters, and so on. For the first screenwriting experience, it's not unusual for a writer to change over fifty percent of the first draft. So if that is the case, don't be alarmed.

Polishing is best described as a *clean-up* step where your activities are confined to tightening up (cutting back) scene descriptions and improving dialogue.

For most writers, once the characters and story structure are sound, the greatest amount of time will be spent improving dialogue. It is the one element in a screenplay most writers feel always needs improving.

If you picked up a screenplay you wrote six months ago and casually read it, I guarantee that you will find segments of dialogue you will want to improve. And those segments would literally jump out at you in such a way that you'd question why you didn't see them in the first place. It all has to do with stepping back from your work long enough to regain your objectivity, as well as the higher skills you have attained even over that short period.

The Rewriting Approach

The most effective way to approach the rewrite of your first draft script is to evaluate the elements separately.

By isolating the various elements, it's much easier to identify problems and the subsequent solutions. If you are using a computer, it's best to work from a hard copy and write your comments in the margin with a red pen. Later, the revisions will be completed at your terminal.

There is one basic rule which applies to rewriting: *don't feel locked into anything*. If something doesn't work, make it better or create something that does. Flexible thinking is a function of good writing. You may write a brilliant scene but it doesn't work within the context of your story. Be ruthless and cut it out. Save discarded scenes in a file for later use. Who knows, you may be able to work a discarded scene into another story.

Here are the steps involved in analyzing your first draft screenplay.

1. Follow your instincts. Read your script through once without paying attention to any details. Mark only those things that cause you to pause and question something. More than likely, the issue that caught your attention requires improvement. Make a note in the margin regarding that issue and continue reading.

    After a long break, reread your script again, only this time, focus on the primary elements as follows.

a. Characters. Are they well-defined? Have your main character's motives and goals been fully explained? Does your main character go through a progressive change in your story? Is he or she sympathetic? Consider every issue which influences character.

b. Dialogue. How well does it read? Does it have a purpose? Does it reveal information about your main character, his or her emotional state, or the plot? Does it move the story forward? Is your dialogue smooth? Does it flow? Is it believable? Do your characters speak in their own voices?

c.   Plot. Is it original enough? Is it well-paced? Are there any sections where it drags? And if so, how can they be fixed? How strong is the opening? How tight is the ending? How can the plot be improved?

d.   Scenes. Does each scene have a purpose? Has each scene been properly developed? Are there any scenes that should be improved, deleted, or moved?

e.   And once all the previous steps have been addressed, have all the spelling, punctuation, and grammatical errors been corrected?

The whole process of analyzing a script is to address every issue, from every angle, in order to identify things that need improving. *Rewriting is the easy part—it's knowing what to rewrite that is difficult.*

PROOFREADING

Screenplays are difficult to proofread because they lack the streamlined uniformity of all other forms of writing. Scene headings, scene descriptions, and dialogue are all separated. You have to work slowly and carefully, and look at every detail. If you don't, you will later notice a multitude of mistakes.

We become so conditioned to reading our own work that we read over the same mistakes, time after time.

A scene heading might be written INT. when you intended it to be EXT. Or you may have used an incorrect location in your scene heading. Sometimes you will designate the wrong character speaking or possibly leave out a word or two in a section of dialogue.

If you're not extremely careful, no matter how many times you reread your script, you will not see every mistake.

Proofreading requires total concentration when you do it, and help from others. Also, try reading your script backwards. Because you won't be following the flow of your story, it makes it easier to catch typos.

Rewriting: Summing It All Up

Take your time when evaluating and rewriting your first draft screenplay. After that phase, wait another week and reread your second draft. More than likely, you will find other mistakes and be grateful for taking the extra precautions. If you evaluate your script in sections as prescribed here, your rewrite will be far more productive. And take as much time as you need.

Like every other screenwriter, you must contend with agents, studios, producers, and readers when you circulate your screenplay. The last thing you want to do is give someone an excuse not to read your work nor give it serious consideration.

Registering Your Work

Before turning over your screenplay to even two trusted readers, it wouldn't be a bad idea to register it first in case the material is accidentally lost. You're better off being safe than sorry later.

You can register your screenplay with either the Writers Guild of America (WGA) or copyright it through the Library of Congress. This evidentiary procedure helps to establish you as the author of the work. This would be important if you ended up taking someone to court over plagiarizing your screenplay. In any plagiarism case, the person making the claim must prove that the other party had *access* to his or her material. As a precaution, maintain a record of *who* has received your submitted screenplays. While most people in the film industry are honest, you never know when you are likely to come in contact with someone who is unscrupulous.

What is the difference between registering your script with the Writer's Guild of America or acquiring a copyright through the Library of Congress? With the Writer's Guild, the registration covers a five-year term and it can be renewed for another five years. With a copyright, the term is for a person's lifetime plus fifty years. The advantage with the Writer's Guild is that it is quicker. It takes at least two to three weeks for The Writer's Guild to respond to requests that come in through the mail and twice that with the Library of Congress. If you live near a Writer's Guild office, you can walk in, register your script in a few minutes, and leave with a registration receipt. You can also register your work online with the Writer's Guild through their web page (www.wgaeast.org). Since the registration procedures might change with either the Library of Congress or the Writers Guild of America, write or call them ahead of time for instructions.

To register your work with The Writers Guild of America, you don't have to be a member. The details can be acquired by contacting either location listed below or their web page address mentioned in the previous paragraph.

> Writers Guild of America, East, Inc.
> 555 West 57th Street, Suite 1230
> New York, NY 10019
>
> (212) 757-4360
>
> Writers Guild of America, West, Inc.
> 7000 West 3rd Street
> Los Angeles, CA 90048
>
> (213) 951-4000

To copyright your screenplay, contact the Library of Congress for instructions. They will provide you with the "PA" (Performing Arts) Form.

> Register of Copyrights
> Library of Congress
> Washington, DC 20559
>
> (202) 707-3000 or (202) 707-5959

To ensure safe arrival, you can ship your script via certified mail with a return receipt. Your receipt will be returned with your regular mail. Later, with either the WGA or Library of Congress, you will receive a certificate with a registration number. When your registration receipt arrives, attach it to the return receipt from the certified mail and file it in a safe place. If you submit your script to a production company, some may require and provide you with a *release form*. On that form there is a space where you fill in your registration number to verify that you have properly registered your work, so keep your registration number handy.

LITERARY RELEASE AGREEMENT

A copy of the standard Literary Release Agreement is outlined on the following pages. It reads as if you are signing away all your rights. Not to worry, it's just a precaution production companies and studios take to reduce the risk of potential lawsuits.

If someone were to use your screenplay or rip off your story, signing this literary release agreement would in no way preclude liability on the violator's part. Quite frankly, there is no need for any production company or studio to steal a writer's work when they can buy it.

In speaking with heads of development who express interest in seeing my work but require a release form, I tell them that I can submit my script with a standard industry form as outlined here. Most find that acceptable; if not, they will either fax or send a copy of their own release form.

With a computer, set up a file using the language in this Literary Release Agreement and print copies as needed.

LITERARY RELEASE AGREEMENT

DATE:

PRODUCTION ENTITY:

Enclosed for your consideration is an original screenplay (herein called "Submitted Material") written by me.

TITLE:

LOG LINE:

GENRE:

FORM:

NUMBER OF PAGES:

WGA REGISTRATION NUMBER:

I understand that you may submit the Submitted Material to third parties, motion picture studios and distributors. I recognize the possibility that the Submitted Material may be identical with or similar to material that has or may come to you from other sources. Such similarity in the past has given rise to litigation so that unless you can obtain adequate protection in advance, you will refuse to consider the Submitted Material. The protection for you must be sufficiently broad to protect you, your related corporations, and your and their employees, agents, licensees and assignees, and all parties to whom you submit material. Therefore, all references to you include each and all of the foregoing parties.

As an inducement to you to examine the Submitted Material, and in consideration of your so doing, I represent, warrant and agree, as follows:

1.   I acknowledge that the Submitted Material is submitted by me voluntarily and not in confidence, and that no confidential relationship is intended or created between us by reason of the submission of the Submitted Material.

Nothing in this Agreement, nor the submission of the Submitted Material, shall be deemed to place you in any different position from any other member of the public with respect to the Submitted Material. Accordingly, any part of the Submitted Material that could be freely used by any member of the public may be used by you without liability to me.

You agree that you will not produce the Submitted Material unless you shall first negotiate with me and agree upon compensation to be paid to me for such use, but I understand and agree that your use of material containing features or elements similar or identical with those contained in the Submitted Material shall not obligate you to negotiate with me nor entitle me to any compensation if you determine that you have an independent legal right to use such other material which is not derived from me (either because such features or elements were not new or novel, or were not originated by me, or were or may hereafter be independently created and submitted by other persons, including your employees).

2.   I represent and warrant that I wrote the Submitted Material.

3.   I agree that no obligation of any kind is assumed or may be implied against you by reason of your review of the Submitted Material or any discussions or negotiations we may have, except pursuant to an express written agreement hereafter executed by you and me which, by its terms, will be the only contract between us.

4.   If there is any dispute arising out of this Agreement, including the substance, validity, operation or breach hereof (including but not limited to: if you should determine that you have the independent legal right to use the material containing features or elements similar or identical to those contained in the Submitted Material without entering into a written agreement for compensation with me, and if you proceed to use the same and if I disagree with your determination), the dispute between us shall be submitted to arbitration in Los Angeles, California, before an arbiter mutually selected by us who is experienced in the field with respect to the use of the material similar to the Submitted Material; or, if we cannot mutually agree, then such arbiter shall be selected in accordance with the Commercial Arbitration Rules of the American Arbitration Association.

The arbitration shall be controlled by the terms of this Agreement, and any award favorable to me shall be limited to the fixing of compensation for your use of the submitted material, which shall bear a reasonable relation to compensation normally paid by you for similar material. Such award will provide for you and me, respectively, to bear his own costs of arbitration and attorneys' fees.

5.   I assume full responsibility for any loss of the Submitted Material, irrespective of whether it is lost, stolen or destroyed in transit, or while in your possession, or otherwise.

6.   Except as otherwise provided in this Agreement, I hereby release you of and from any and all claims, demands, liabilities of every kind whatsoever, known or unknown, that may arise in relation to the Submitted Material or by reason of any claim now or hereafter made by me that you have used or appropriated the Submitted Material, except for fraud or willful injury on your part.

7.   Should any provision of this Agreement be void or unenforceable, such provision shall be deemed omitted, and this Agreement with such provisions omitted shall remain in full force and effect.

8.   This Agreement is entire. No statements or representations have been made except those expressly stated in this Agreement. This Agreement may be modified only by a subsequent written Agreement.

9.   This Agreement will be interpreted in accordance with the laws of the State of California applicable to agreements entered into and fully performed therein.

10.   You may freely assign your rights under this Agreement.

Signature:
Print Name:
Address:
City, State, Zip:
Telephone Number:

AGREED TO AND ACCEPTED BY:
Production Entity:
Name/Title:
Date:

THE SCREENWRITER

Writing a screenplay is something one does not approach casually, even if it is a part-time activity or hobby-related interest. It requires a tremendous commitment and a lot of work. A person must first learn the basic rules of dramatic writing and screenwriting, read and analyze screenplays from successful films, and then, go through the various steps and exercises involved in creating a finished screenplay from a basic story idea.

It is my guess that it takes anywhere from four to eight months, as a rough average, to complete a screenplay. The amount of time involved is influenced by many factors that will vary from writer to writer and project to project. Much depends upon whether or not the writer is experienced with screenwriting, has the basic talent, works full-time or part-time on the project, the level of commitment, how much research is involved, and so on.

If you approach screenwriting as an interest and really dig into your first project, you will quickly acquire a sense of what is involved. You will either press on and finish your project or give up early out of frustration and a lack of commitment.

If you feel strongly motivated and want to make a career out of screenwriting, then the balance of this chapter will be extremely important to you.

EIGHT BASIC QUALITIES OF BEING A SCREENWRITER

There are eight basic qualities or attributes you must have if you are going to be a successful screenwriter. They are: imagination, desire, discipline, confidence, perseverance, the ability to pitch (tell stories), a positive attitude, punctuality, and good follow-through.

IMAGINATION

Imagination is the most important element in writing and a God-given gift that provides a person with the ability to create something from nothing.

When you write an original screenplay, you are doing exactly that—creating something from nothing. We all write from experience, but the process of conceiving and conceptualizing all the basic elements of a story—such a characters, plot, and action—is a direct function of imagination.

Does everyone have imagination? Of course. But it does vary from person to person and that is what determines the edge in writing. A writer's potential is only limited by his or her imagination.

You can be exceptionally bright, have excellent writing skills, an extensive vocabulary, and a total command of the English language—but without imagination, you will not succeed in screenwriting or any form of creative writing. If you possess this important attribute, everything else will take care of itself. Writing skills and techniques, vocabulary, etc., can all be acquired and developed through reading, studying, and experience.

Imagination is also stimulated by the creative process itself. Even people who feel and say they don't have a good imagination learn that it is a hidden attribute. When someone gets involved with a creative project, the thinking process becomes heightened to the point where ideas are forced to the conscious level. Sometimes you even end up surprising yourself. Part of stimulating imagination has to do with understanding the *mechanics* and *techniques* of the creative process.

DESIRE

Desire to create by writing is a strong need in every serious writer. The urge to write can come early or even late in life. So don't prejudge or dismiss any wavering feelings you have concerning your desire to write. If you really want to do it, you will—regardless of any outside influences, whether they are supportive or not.

DISCIPLINE

To ensure progress, writing requires discipline which is established and controlled by setting realistic writing goals and maintaining a regular writing schedule. It is the only way to guarantee that progress is made—even if your writing is a hobby. If you can only pursue screenwriting on a part-time basis, you need to work at least three or four days a week in order to make enough progress to maintain your interest and to stimulate your creative powers.

You may only be able to write two hours a day, but that's fine. Establishing a routine, writing at the same time every day, reinforces discipline. It's also wise to select your writing hours when there are least likely to be any interruptions or distractions and when your productivity is highest. You could be an early bird and work between 5 and 7 a.m., or a night owl working between 11 p.m. and 1 a.m.

What is a realistic writing goal? Two pages a day? Three? You decide. Productivity varies from writer to writer and from project to project. Work at your own pace—what is comfortable for you.

For me, writing is enjoyable so I write almost every day; and, for that reason, I tend to be very flexible with my hours. If I don't feel like writing one day and take off to do something else, there's no guilt here because, on average, my writing schedule exceeds fifty hours per week.

Whenever I start a new screenplay, my sleeping habits and everything else get turned around until the first draft is finished. Even when going to bed between 10 and 11 p.m., I may read a book for a while and not fall asleep for an hour or more. Then, at 2:30 or 3 a.m., I literally bolt out of bed wide awake and within sixty seconds, I'll be at the computer working at full capacity. By the time most people arrive at work, I will have already put in a solid five or six hours. At that point, I exercise and take a three-mile walk. After a hot shower, I go back to work.

At least two days a week, I go out and have lunch with friends who are either writers, musicians, or former business associates. These inexpensive luncheons are local and rarely exceed an hour.

There are some days when I will work twelve to fourteen hours with only meal and personal-needs breaks. I will get out of my chair for a few minutes to stretch or pick up my J40M (Martin guitar) and play a few tunes to clear my mind. By the time the day is over, I literally crawl out of my office, totally spent.

Working hard sparks creative inspiration, and when it happens, it is magical. If my house ever caught on fire while I was writing in one those inspirational moods, the firemen would find my charred body slumped over the remains of my computer terminal.

CONFIDENCE

If you had to find another element of writing that would balance imagination on a seesaw, it is confidence—in yourself and your work. Without confidence, your *hash* will be quickly settled by all those people who will tell you your work stinks or say what is wrong with it without really knowing. Keep reminding yourself that ***very few people can accurately assess any form of creative writing and provide you with effective, constructive criticism***.

Most people are incapable of recognizing writing talent until after it has been proven by someone else. It requires a great deal of self-confidence, integrity, and risk on the part of an agent or producer to take a chance on an unknown and yet unproven writer.

Successful writers have one thing in common. Over whatever period of time, usually years, they are subjected to constant rejection until finally one day, someone recognizes the potential of their work. Until that day happens, you must strive to maintain a high level of unwavering confidence in yourself and your work.

PERSEVERANCE

Most successful screenwriters, on average, have struggled for many years before catching that first break. Most have probably written five, ten, or more screenplays before one is sold or sees production. Therefore, perseverance determines opportunities and influences success. It's every bit as important as those words you type.

How long does it take to break in? One year, five, ten? It's impossible to say. No two people travel the same road in life, nor do two screenwriters break into the film business the same way. Some writers, with little talent, are very lucky and sell their first screenplay for big money; while more talented writers struggle in obscurity. Face it. Life is unfair. It has nothing to do with who deserves recognition.

You may know that you are talented and firmly believe that your work has commercial potential. Now find someone in the film industry who believes in you and will give you the opportunity to prove it.

Over and above confidence, it takes perseverance on the writer's part to find that person who will recognize your talent and see the potential of your work.

The writer's career cycle is one of writing and trying to sell script after script, because you never know which project will be the one that prompts a sale. You can't sit back with three screenplays—no matter how good you feel they are—and assume that any one of them might be saleable. You must continue to develop new projects while trying to sell your scripts or writing services.

Enduring rejection, senseless insults, and frivolous criticism are all part of writing. These comments are not made to discourage, but to enlighten you to the realities of the profession and to reinforce the importance of having confidence and perseverance.

A few comments about luck and timing are appropriate here. Every now and then you will read how a writer, who may not even be talented, sold a first script for $1 million or more; and, at the same time, you hear about a talented writer who is just breaking in after fifteen years of struggling. Again, life is unfair; accept it.

In a situation where two people are equal in every measure that qualifies for success, one may be successful years before the other. That type of luck is purely mystical and impossible to predict. Therefore you have to make your own luck by working hard at every aspect of the writing profession—from writing to persevering in the face of constant rejection.

As success applies to timing, you hear the oft-repeated phrase: "He sure was lucky. He was in the right place at the right time." By persevering, you make yourself lucky by creating more opportunities to be in the right place at the right time.

THE ABILITY TO PITCH

In the film industry, the strength of a writer's pitch can often have more influence over a producer's decision than the quality of the project itself. It may be very difficult to believe, but it's true. How many times have you bought something you really didn't need because the sales person was so persuasive or very enthusiastic?

Pitching is an art, skill, and tool of selling. If you are given the opportunity to pitch your story, here is the approach you should take. *Starting with the title, but using no extraneous details, tell the listener what your story is about. Make your initial presentation no more than a sentence or two.*

You must pitch with confidence and enthusiasm and grab the listener using those elements of your story that are most appealing. You want that person to say, "Great! Tell me more." That is the objective of the initial pitch—to generate interest and to open up the meeting.

People inexperienced with selling or public speaking may be terrified at the thought of pitching their story. Some rate this experience just below having root canal without anesthesia. Not to worry, there are a number of things you can do to reduce your anxiety and bolster your confidence at the same time. Most importantly, be totally prepared. Know exactly what you're going to say because it will fortify your confidence.

Recognize the fact that it's normal to get the jitters and that once you get past the initial pitch, the rest of the meeting will be a lot easier. Pitching the basic premise of your story should take thirty seconds or less, so don't feel forced to blurt it out and race for the door. Ahead of time, practice by pitching to your friends. Soon you will be able to control your anxiety and nervous energy and channel it into enthusiasm.

Here's my pitch. "*Dead Man's Dance* is a thriller about a woman searching for her sister who disappears after supposedly seeing the man their father murdered."

Read that line out loud yourself and you will see that it takes less than *ten seconds* to deliver. If the producer wants to know more about the story, I would then present the information outlined in the sample fax in Chapter 13.

What do you do after making the initial pitch? You shut up and let the other person think. If the pitch is good, the person will, in some way, indicate his or her interest. It could be a simple smile or a comment. If questions are asked, tell the person just what he or she needs to know. Don't elaborate too much. Some like to play their cards close to the vest, as the saying goes, and not indicate their interest one way or the other. They usually sit there stone-faced, staring at you in such a way that it can be very intimidating; that is, if you let them. Another tactic of theirs is remaining silent while they stare at you squirming in your seat. Don't feel rattled and forced to talk incessantly; that is what they expect. Sit there and stare back at them. All they are doing is playing with your head. I only mention this in case you run into one of these *head cases.*

At the end of any meeting, make sure you know where you stand. If it's clear that the person has no interest in your story or stories, then politely thank him or her and be on your way. If you're not sure what the person's reaction is, take this tack: "Where do we go from here?"

No doubt, writers with dynamic personalities who exude charm and project self-confidence have a major advantage over those who don't. If you feel that you don't match that image exactly, don't worry. First, if you have a good story and you know it's good, you can approach any meeting with confidence. If you have a good story and are totally prepared, that will more than compensate for any shortcomings in the *dynamic personality* department.

POSITIVE ATTITUDE

Maintaining a positive attitude—being diplomatic, cooperative, supportive, and willing to work with other people—is a basic survival tactic in every business. Given the close collaborative environment of film and the long, hard days where temperaments tend to be tested to the max, it is even more important in the movie business.

Nobody wants to be around a constant complainer—especially when the working climate is tough to begin with. It's too disruptive and counterproductive.

Writers are, by nature of the trade, in a very precarious position. There would be *no film industry without screenplays* and yet, most writers, even the best of them, are treated as second-class citizens by people who don't have an ounce of creative talent.

The studios, the producers, the directors, actors, etc., all need writers. And yet, the writer can become the most dispensable person. Why? Because any writer can be replaced at any time in the entire filmmaking process. It's no secret that writers are replaced at the whim of a producer or director and that scripts are needlessly rewritten over and above the vast foray of legitimate reasons. And, in many cases, the quality aspects of a screenplay are literally and totally obliterated. Two factors contribute to unnecessary script rewrites. First, *everyone* thinks he or she is a writer and qualified to make changes. Second, people in power, the director or stars, can most easily flex their muscles by insisting upon script changes—warranted or not.

It's impossible for writers to protect the integrity of their work unless they direct the project themselves.

If a writer's project is sold outright, other writers may automatically be brought in to make changes that are totally unnecessary and that may ultimately destroy what was once a great story. If you, as the author of an original screenplay, are given the opportunity to handle the rewrite, there is still no guarantee you can preserve the integrity of your work. But, at least, you are in a position to try. If you're involved in rewriting your own script, take pride in your work and try not to deal with it on an emotional level—which is very hard to do, because *a real writer cares* for his or her work.

There are a number of temperamental writers who feel their work is *sacred* and that nothing should be touched. This is a totally unrealistic and unreasonable attitude since script changes are always required. In preparing a shooting script, there are many legitimate reasons why adjustments are needed, such as: the budget may necessitate cutting scenes, a certain location may not be available so the scene has to be rewritten, awkward dialogue needs improving, etc.

Also, while a writer is usually the most qualified person to change his or her work, the writer is not always right. On occasion, we don't see certain issues objectively because we are far too close to our work. It is a reality of writing and every writer is affected.

From a standpoint of posture, you must be receptive and flexible in dealing with other people who have direct input into your work. *A writer must display good judgment by knowing when to compromise on less important issues but stand firm when proposed changes would obviously cause severe damage to the screenplay.*

Sometimes dialogue is written or phrased in a way that is difficult for an actor to deliver. Or, quite possibly, the dialogue read well on paper but simply doesn't work when played. If an actor wanted certain lines of dialogue rewritten so it would be easier to deliver, I'd do it without argument. My goal would be to rephrase the dialogue without changing its purpose within the context of the scene.

A writer who makes an issue out of every detail will lose credibility and be quickly replaced. And once a writer earns a reputation for being difficult, it could affect future work opportunities.

When meetings get hot, as they sometimes do, try to keep your emotions intact and logically reason with the other party or parties involved. It's easier said than done, but this type of posture, in most instances, can have a far more positive impact than loud bellowing. Don't be too quick to defend your point of view until you have thoroughly listened to the other person. This is a practical consideration as well as a courteous gesture. If you really listen to someone else's ideas, you may ultimately agree and possibly find a way of improving your script—which is what it's all about.

A writer should protect the integrity of his or her work and, at the same time, place equal importance on what is best for the project.

The way you carry yourself and the attitude you project, often influences how receptive other people will be in dealing with you. These points may seem unimportant and unrelated to writing, but they are ultimately more critical in determining opportunities and success.

PUNCTUALITY & FOLLOW-THROUGH

In business, the ultimate measure of professionalism is how punctual people are in showing up for appointments and following through on commitments. Since *time* is our most precious commodity, there is nothing more important than using it wisely.

Unfortunately, a majority of people fail to recognize the value and significance of punctuality and follow-through. When your business brings you in contact with people who understand the importance of these issues, you will either succeed or fail based upon your performance in these areas. Arriving late for a scheduled appointment shows a total lack of respect for the other party, as does the failure to fulfill obligations you make.

The basic rule of punctuality is to allow for extra time in arriving for appointments, and if you know you're going to be more than ten minutes late, call ahead and advise. And when you arrive late for the appointment, apologize for any inconvenience you might have caused.

In regard to follow-through, don't make commitments you cannot keep. If you later realize you're going to run late on meeting a commitment, advise the party involved of the delay and when you most likely can fulfill that obligation. Most people make promises and don't follow through even when fulfilling them is in their best interest. Why? Because they don't understand the importance of it, or they don't make a note to remind themselves and simply forget. Even when people are well-intentioned and run into delays which might be out of their hands, they fail to advise the other party, which then reflects poorly upon them.

If you apply just what I've told you about punctuality and follow-through on commitments to everything in your life, you will eventually be rewarded. People, especially those in positions of power, who know and live by these standards, will respond to you.

COLLABORATION

Filmmaking is a collaborative art form where the final results are influenced by the combined talents and skills of all the artists and technicians involved.

From the standpoint of writing, the choice of working with another person should not be taken lightly. If two people can be more effective working together than alone, a collaborative relationship is worth serious consideration.

What does it take? It takes two people who can complement each other, talent-wise and personality-wise; and at the same time, develop a strong relationship based upon trust and mutual respect.

Collaboration calls for a clear line of communication and compromise where egos have to be parked at the door—whether you actually work together or handle various duties separately.

The biggest problem with most partnerships is that one person usually emerges as the dominant force. If you or your partner have no objection to who leads the way, then the relationship might work. However, if one person believes that the other is contributing less than what was expected and agreed upon, or that the quality of his or her partner's work is not up to par, the relationship can quickly deteriorate. If one person constantly *keeps score* as to who is contributing more to the partnership, the results will be disastrous.

If two people consider working together, it would be wise to sit down and talk about it at great length. Each person has different motives for collaborating and they should be known. One writer may not like writing alone, while the other has a need to find someone who may be strong in an area where he or she may be weak—such as writing dialogue. Or one person may enjoy doing research, while the other is great at creating interesting characters and developing unusual story lines.

With comedy, many writers collaborate and develop material through interaction. One writer has an idea; the other becomes a sounding board or embellishes it.

We all have idiosyncrasies, so bringing those facts to light can be helpful. One person may get hyper if the project is not going well, while the other may withdraw. Talk about those things. This way, each person knows what to expect from the other so there are no surprises.

There is no standard agreement between collaborators except the one you create. If there is potential compatibility and you are willing to try working together, establish goals and working responsibilities that are mutually agreeable. The agreement you reach with your partner should function as a guideline with built-in flexibility. If something doesn't work out as intended, make the necessary adjustments without pointing fingers at each other.

If your partner does something that really irritates you, you must discuss it *only* with that person—and before it reaches a stage where you have an outburst. You must approach problems rationally and tactfully, without showing emotion or anger. If you recognize the benefits of working together but have problems, don't let those problems sink the relationship. Work things out.

Think of this possibility for a moment. Two important issues were stated earlier. First, minor changes can often significantly improve an entire screenplay. Second, a writer needs constructive feedback from a trusted reader. You may elect to have a collaborator work with you *after* the first draft is completed. If that other person can fine-tune your work into a masterpiece, it might be well worth sharing the writing credits and determining an agreeable split of the financial rewards. With the bulk of the work done by you, the other writer may be willing to put his or her magic touch to your project for ten or twenty percent of whatever profits are derived.

What if you wrote a comedy and needed to have some dialogue *punched up*? It would certainly make sense to find a comedy writer who could enhance your material.

Collaboration can be a very productive arrangement when the right people get together and find a way to work. If you're not sure that collaboration appeals to you, talk to some experienced writers for their advice. Most collaborations probably come out of spontaneous situations. If that opportunity knocks on your door, check it out.

David Brown, while in partnership with Richard D. Zanuck, produced some of the finest films in the past three decades including *Jaws*, *The Sting* (which won seven Academy Awards including Best Picture), *The Verdict*, *The Player*, *Patton*, and *Cocoon*.

In the August 26-September 1, 1996 supplementary issue of *Variety*, Mr. Brown presented his views on screenwriters which most accurately describe the position and plight of "The Creators" in the Hollywood hierarchy. Given the importance of his article, it is reprinted here in its entirety.

THE CREATORS BY DAVID BROWN

When old-time mogul Jack Warner derided screenwriters as *schmucks with Underwoods* (Underwoods being the dinosaurs of typewriters), he voiced an opinion that some executives, producers, actors, and directors share to this day. Schmuck, according to the definition in the Unabridged *Random House Dictionary of the English Language*, is an "obnoxious or contemptible person... a penis." In other words, *a prick*.

Obviously, this description is not applied to Michael Crichton, John Grisham, Tom Clancy, or other members of the nuclear club of popular fiction. It refers to screenwriters who adapt their works or create original screenplays only too frequently to see other writers brought on to obliterate or flatten whatever fresh, cutting-edge elements attracted the studio to their work in the first place.

Some executives who can't spell "cat" do violence to scripts by mandating changes in characterization or plot that are the result of committee group-think. I believe it is better to have one voice than a chorus of many. One person's passion and conviction are preferable to the watered-down consensus of a committee. I don't mind executives who can't spell cat as much as Harvard-educated dullards who lack show business savvy and zeal. Warner, Cohn, Zukor, Zanuck, Goldwyn, and other founding fathers were not noted for their spelling, but for their showmanship, passion, and guts. During my early days at Fox, when the head of distribution offered an opinion about a script, Darryl Zanuck retorted, "I didn't know you could read," and forthwith banished all noncreative executives from dailies, rough cuts, and previews. They're only result-players, he reasoned.

BELEAGUERED WRITERS

The antipathy to screenwriters has deep roots in Hollywood history. They have long been the lowest order in the food chain. Critics routinely ignore their contributions and give directors credit for what they have merely transferred from the page to the screen. Screenwriters fare no better socially. Little has changed since Oscar Levant proclaimed that the lowest form of celebrity in Hollywood is the writer's wife.

All this is bizarre, although nothing is really bizarre in Hollywood, where the myth of the place has always been less than the reality. The reality is, of course, that nothing moves without the script. Screenplays, good ones, pay the dividends, attract the multimillion-dollar stars and directors, keep studio executives employed and their ex- and new wives clad in Armani, provide thousands of jobs for technicians and crew and enrich their health and welfare plans, and pay down second mortgages on Brentwood mansions.

I repeat. Nothing moves forward without the script. It is the acorn from which the oak of a movie grows. A screenplay starts the process of budgeting, casting, hiring of key personnel. Offices are redecorated, monster Winnebagos are leased, trucks loaded with equipment roll to locations, artists feverishly create scene sketches. Following the shoot, the post-production crew, the music and sound technicians, and the marketing mavens come aboard. A hundred million dollars may well be spent on 120 pages or so of a screenplay by someone who might not even be invited to the set, the dub, the mix, or the scoring session although the hundreds of men and women, including the director and stars, who have worked on the picture owe their jobs to the culmination of the writer's work.

In all fairness, it must be acknowledged that most screenplays are not very good. Neither are most movies—and there may be a connection. Frankly, it is the despair of studios, actors, and directors that so few scripts are worth their backing. It is unassailable, however, that the writer is the most important element of Hollywood success or failure. Without schmucks with word processors, there would be no motion picture or television industry—just a junkyard of tangled wires, lights, and cameras.

As important as screenwriters are, authors like Michael Crichton may be even more so. The greatest movies ever made have been based on novels, from before *Gone With the Wind* until today. But it must be noted that screenwriters bring these novels to the form from which they can be photographed. I do not derogate the importance of great directors and stars, but without scripts they are without work.

What then are writers' main complaints in today's Hollywood? Lack of fidelity to the script is one. True, many a script acquired in the heat of competitive bidding and read at 35,000 feet or after a Hamptons or Malibu weekend turns out to be less than stellar, and to require layers of other writers in an attempt to restore its virginal promise. More likely, the unborn script invites mindless tampering based on reams of studio "notes," often from anonymous readers. These notes often amount to nothing more than pabulum, rendering the once sought-after script a mishmash of conflicting opinions and conventional plotting.

Perhaps the most common grievance is the alacrity with which writers are replaced. Some directors—they know who they are—dispose of writers like Kleenex. A cursory examination of writers' credits shows that not infrequently, three or more Oscar-caliber writers share credits, and the resulting scripts are consequently dysfunctional. My own belief is that any one of them, properly guided, would have turned out a superior script. There are, of course, instances, particularly in adaptations, where numbers of writers have failed to solve the script problems. A book is not a script. The surviving screenwriter justifiably receives a solo credit and is honored for good work. Obviously, good producers and directors participate in the creative process, and the writer benefits by having his work enriched by their input. Once the script is "locked," some directors will not tolerate the slightest variance from what is written. Hitchcock was one. He used the example of a conductor of a symphony orchestra being asked to change a note. The time to improvise, he said, was when writing the composition.

The best films with which I have been associated were based upon solo or joint screenplays. Examples from films Richard Zanuck and I produced: David Mamet's Oscar-nominated solo screenplay of *The Verdict*, David Ward's Oscar-winning solo screenplay of *The Sting*. Still another is Michael Tolkin's solo Oscar-nominated screenplay of *The Player*, directed by Robert Altman.

What, then, do I recommend to producers and directors for the care and feeding of screenwriters in Hollywood?

1.   Resist that impulse to change for the sake of change. A famous Hollywood writer (whom I decline to mention) received a large writing fee for changing only seventeen words of a musical he was adapting. That reluctance to tamper was well worth his fee.

2.   Read, for God's sake, and don't rely on "coverage." Darryl Zanuck forbade me to include readers' comments on synopses.

3.   When you interview a writer for a project, make certain that you are in accord with the writer's views. Do not throw a curve ball at him or her. When Jay Presson Allen was engaged by Richard Zanuck and me to write a screenplay for *The Verdict*, she said, "Just tell me what you want. I don't like to give or get surprises." Jay delivered what we wanted, although what we finally wanted turned out to be something different, namely David Mamet's original screenplay augmented by suggestions for the ending from the director Sidney Lumet.

4.   Back the writer against the worst instincts of a director or star. Directors and stars tend to be self-serving, although I trust an actor's

instincts more than most directors. You will not win all these battles, but you will win the respect of the writer and perhaps spare him the imposition of another writer or rewrite.

As Shakespeare counseled, "The play's the thing." Get close to those schmucks with word processors. They can make you rich and famous and maybe even happy.

DAVID BROWN INTERVIEW

Given the significance of Mr. Brown's article, "The Creators," I arranged to interview him at his Manhattan offices. With the exception of one brief phone call he had to take, he gave me his complete and undivided attention. He is not only a visionary, but a real gentleman. I know you will find his comments and insights on screenwriting and the film business both highly informative as well as very entertaining.

BERMAN: How did you get your start in film?

BROWN: As I tell film students, I was a journalist and totally disinterested in movies. I was summoned to Los Angeles by the then-mogul, Darryl Zanuck. He had the notion that a studio should be structured like a national magazine with a managing editor. In those days, producers, directors, writers, and actors were all under contract—it was the big-studio era. Zanuck's interest in me was based upon my experience as a managing editor in buying fiction as well as nonfiction, and my knowledge of writers and agents. Inasmuch as I was getting a divorce and wanted to change my personal life, I accepted his offer and left New York for Los Angeles in 1951. I came out as his creative executive—effectively number two in the studio hierarchy.

BERMAN: How did you make contact with Darryl Zanuck?

BROWN: I didn't. In late 1951, he sent word to his eastern scouts that he wanted the best editor in New York. Somebody perhaps lied a little, somebody may have told the truth, and I boarded the Super Chief and the Twentieth Century Limited to California. I arrived in Pasadena and was taken to the Twentieth Century-Fox studios.

BERMAN: How did your relationship with Richard Zanuck evolve?

BROWN: Dick and I worked at Twentieth Century-Fox. On December 29, 1970, we were fired and joined Warner Brothers together as executives.

BERMAN: What lead to you and Richard Zanuck forming your own company?

BROWN: As supervising executives, we had made between us more than two hundred movies without having our names on any of them. We'd taken the blame for some bad films and made millionaires of those who were credited with some highly successful films we actually initiated.

On July 7, 1972, we tore up our contracts with Warner Brothers and formed our own independent movie production company. We were partners until June of 1988 when I formed my own company, the Manhattan Project.

BERMAN: How do you go about selecting projects?

BROWN: Largely by my heart and my gut. If it moves me, if it's something I would want to see, if it has some degree of elegance or style, then I go for it. As a consequence of my elevated taste, I have many forlorn projects that have a difficult time getting made, such as *The Player* which was turned down by forty-two financing entities. However, to atone for my elitism, I also make mega-productions. I am one of the producers of *The Saint*, for example, which Paramount will release in 1997.

BERMAN: How many projects do you have in development at any given moment?

BROWN: No more than eight or nine.

BERMAN: How many of them will become films?

BROWN: Three or four if I'm lucky.

BERMAN: What determines a project going forward?

BROWN: You either have to have a major movie star who can open a picture or a high-concept, cutting-edge film like *Independence Day*.

The studios' aim is to attract a large audience on the first weekend. That's the marketing syndrome. Given the limited number of screens available at any given time and the difficulty of staying on them, the opening weekend frequently decides the fate of the movie. *The First Wives Club* is a phenomenon and like all phenomenons, nobody knows why. It opened in what is considered the worst time of the year, the early fall, competing against the World Series, the play-off games, the Jewish holidays, the weather—all that stuff. And it will do over one hundred million dollars at the box office in the United States. Why? My theory is that it works as a comedy and at the same time strikes a nerve among older women, a lost audience.

BERMAN: So, to get a film under way...?

BROWN: Subject matter is critical but very definitely the directorial and casting auspices. Subject matter can kill a star vehicle, but good subject matter alone will not get a film on without stars in mainstream Hollywood—unless, of course, it is a resoundingly high concept that makes stars unnecessary, like *Twister* and *Independence Day*.

BERMAN: What about attaching a star or director to your project, then taking it to the studios?

BROWN: You can't attach anyone. You are a supplicant. You are Willy Lohman with a sample case. You get to submit your material and decisions are made. Sometimes you get lucky. This happened to Richard Zanuck and me when we acquired *The Sting*. We didn't have to do anything. Both Paul Newman and Robert Redford wanted to do it as hired actors. George Roy Hill wanted to direct. They smelled that *The Sting* was something special.

The same was true of *The Verdict* which Paul Newman did. Everyone wanted to do that movie based upon reading a précis of it in the newspaper reviews of the book on which it was based. When I read material, I don't read as a producer or studio executive but as an actor. I say, "Is this a role that would make an actor—who is also a star—reach for it?" Well, Paul Newman reached for a role in which he was a womanizer, out of shape, alcoholic—all the things he is not. Frank Sinatra wanted to do it and said, "I have no problems with any of those things."

BERMAN: How did you happen to acquire *The Sting*?

BROWN: At the time when Richard Zanuck and I started our company, we didn't have anything but a couple of scripts and *The Sting* was one of them. It came our way because, as studio executives, we had backed a former project, titled *Steelyard Blues*, written by David Ward and produced by Julia and Michael Phillips, then married. We were so protective of that project that when another script by David Ward came along, involving the Phillips, they said we owe you one. They offered us the script and that script started our company.

BERMAN: What is the biggest obstacle you face as a producer?

BROWN: The bureaucracy of large studio organizations and their inability to focus on a given project for very long. They rely on their perception of whether the project will lure this director or that star.

It's difficult to get them to say a subject ought to be made—as was the case for Richard Zanuck and me with a movie titled, *Neighbors*, based on Thomas Berger's book. When Frank Price was head man at Columbia, he said to us, "I want to make this. We'll cast it the best way we can and it'll be our Christmas movie." That doesn't happen anymore.

BERMAN: Doesn't your track record have impact on the studios to support new projects you bring to them?

BROWN: No matter how important you are or how good your track record is, it's an ad hoc business—it's project by project. Some of the biggest producers in the world are turned down—and many of them have gone three and four years without making a picture because they couldn't get studios to agree with their creative judgment. If you're a star director like Steven Spielberg, that's different. Spielberg has earned autonomy from studio interference. The studios are confident his instincts are better than theirs because of his track record. Richard Zanuck and I produced his first two pictures and we're now working with him on a third.

BERMAN: How do you go about selecting a writer?

BROWN: You make a list of the writers you consider best suited to the project and find out their availability. They read the material, come in, we discuss it and get their spin on it. You also have to get your studio to agree to your choice of writers.

BERMAN: Typically, what is the first meeting like when you select a writer?

BROWN: The writer selects you. The kind of writers we go for tell us whether or not they are interested. They come in, spend an hour or so, and tell you how they see the project—realizing, of course, that perspectives may change when the actual writing commences.

BERMAN: Can you be swayed by the writer's point of view if it is different from yours?

BROWN: Oh, sure. If the writer's point of view seems rational and interesting—and better than yours.

BERMAN: How long does a writer have to prepare a first draft screenplay?

BROWN: It's up to the writer. He or she has as much time as needed, unless it stretches out for a year or more. There are fast writers and slow writers.

BERMAN: Can you name a writer who is fast?

BROWN: Michael Tolkin who wrote *The Player* is reasonably fast. Way back in my early days, I remember getting a call from the famous agent, Irving Lazar, whose writer, Romain Gary, wrote a movie titled *Roots of Heaven* based upon his novel. Lazar said, "Romain finished the script over the weekend, but tell me honestly—should I hold it for three months because people will figure it's no good if he writes it that fast?"

I said, "No, send it right over." I was wrong and sent it back for more work. If he had taken three months, it would have had more credibility—that's the cynical view. You don't select a writer for speed, but it's an important thing because if it takes forever, a picture will never be made. Writers today are a lot faster than they were thirty or forty years ago. Although at Fox, we had a number of contract writers, famous ones, like Nunnally Johnson and Sydney Boehm, who could turn out a screenplay in nine weeks, on the dot.

BERMAN: And it was good.

BROWN: It was makeable.

BERMAN: After completing a first draft script, how close is the writer to fulfilling the vision of the project?

BROWN: It varies widely. It's a miracle if the initial writer stays on a project until the end. That was the case with Aaron Sorkin and *A Few Good Men*.

BERMAN: How many rewrites will a writer be allowed before he or she is replaced?

BROWN: That depends upon the director and the producer and whether or not the writer is burned out. You can tell pretty much—and so can the writer. If you read the *New York Review of Books*, John Gregory Dunne stated in his article that he and Joan Didion did twelve drafts of *Up Close and Personal*.

BERMAN: In developing a project, do you find that making subtle changes in the treatment of a character or a plot issue can significantly improve the entire script?

BROWN: Yes. For example, Richard Zanuck and I made an unsuccessful movie called *The Island*, based upon a Peter Benchley book. It was Michael Ritchie's (director) take that the young boy who was kidnapped should be something of a brat, not sympathetic... unlike the child in an old Metro movie *The Champ*, which would have been the conventional way to go. As a result, audiences cheered when the kid was kidnapped and booed when he was rescued.

In *The Verdict*, it was David Mamet's (writer) idea that the story was not about the amount of money that was won in the malpractice case, but about redemption. That's why we never announced the amount of the award. And it was Sidney Lumet's (director) take that Paul Newman's character should never hook up with Charlotte Rampling's character at the end.

If Sidney hadn't had the final cut, the conventional studio wisdom would have required that the foreman of the jury announce an award of three million dollars, which would've ruined the movie.

BERMAN: What would you describe as the most difficult aspects of making a script work?

BROWN: Character. Plot is subservient to character. It's all about creating someone who is memorable and sympathetic or anti-sympathetic to a degree of being fascinating... such as the Hannibal Lecter character in *The Silence of the Lambs*. Dialogue, of course, is very important.

The other thing is freshness, the film not being a clone of something else—which is very difficult to achieve. To have an original permutation on a familiar theme because there are only so many stories, to create verisimilitude, to give the audience a feel that something is real or if not real, then something wonderfully wild. That's the challenge.

BERMAN: In the 60s and 70s, films like *Hud*—with unsympathetic characters and downbeat endings—were acceptable to audiences. Today you really can't make those kinds of movies and expect them to do well.

BROWN: It's hard to say that you never can. *Fatal Attraction* is an interesting example. A focus group did not accept the original downbeat ending and so it was reshot. You can still make a *Bonnie and Clyde* or *Butch Cassidy and the Sundance Kid* which had negative endings. It depends upon how well it is done. *Leaving Las Vegas* is a very bleak movie but it works.

BERMAN: Is there any film out of all those you have made that you wish you would have made differently?

BROWN: Nobody who makes movies that I know, including Woody Allen, looks at his movies again. I suppose, in the case of *The Island*, I wish we had chosen a different route. I think the picture would have been successful had the kid been made sympathetic; someone the audience could have rooted for.

BERMAN: Why didn't you insist upon it?

BROWN: You have to respect the director's take or not use that director. Michael Ritchie is a very fine director, very intelligent. We bought his vision.

BERMAN: What was his reason for having an unsympathetic kid?

BROWN: Most of his films have an edge to them. That's the way he saw it.

BERMAN: In your *Variety* article, "The Creators," you made a point that most screenplays are not very good, hence, neither are most movies. Doesn't the fact that many inexperienced studio readers frequently pass over what are good screenplays significantly add to the problem?

BROWN: Yes, but we read every screenplay—we don't send it out for coverage.

BERMAN: As I understand it, in Hollywood, most screenplays go to readers.

BROWN: Oh, sure. Most scripts do go to readers. They're the ones who should be running the studios. If you read my piece in the *New Yorker*, "Development Hell," readers are the scourge of the industry. And it's not that they are not bright. Quite frequently, they have wonderful takes on things, but when Darryl Zanuck was running Twentieth Century-Fox, he would not permit the story department to put readers' comments on coverage.

BERMAN: Given the importance of the screenplay, I am amazed that the selection process isn't more effective. If an outside reader passes on a script, no one else within a production entity will read it.

BROWN: You're absolutely right and it's sad. Usually, what makes someone pass on coverage is subject matter. Someone says this is the Black Plague of 1230 in London and the response is I'm not interested in that. Based upon subject matter, coverage is useful, but based upon the texture of something, the character development, it's useless.

BERMAN: Is anyone in Hollywood looking at changing the system on how screenplays are covered?

BROWN: I'm not in the loop to tell you that. I think the people who run studios are very smart. Sherry Lansing was a successful producer. You'd have to ask her. She would probably tell you there is simply not enough time. I think all would agree that they'd like to focus more on the process of selecting screenplays, but for some reason, the amount of work has escalated. Zanuck and I used to make twenty-seven pictures a year and run a television operation without any development executives. And if you wanted to make a deal, you came directly to us—you didn't go to a vice president.

We would meet with you, you'd leave whatever material you had, and we'd send it over to the story department. But we had great readers. In fact, frequently, synopses were so good that when we read the full material, having not read it before, we were often disappointed.

BERMAN: Have there been any special projects that you have been unable to make?

BROWN: Many. Zanuck and I made *Jaws* and *Jaws 2* and both were successful. We wanted to make *Jaws 3* as a send-up. We had a script, the National Lampoon people as partners, but Universal wouldn't hear of it. We would've liked to have made the sequel to *Gone with the Wind* and had an excellent take on it, but MGM, which controlled the project, didn't want to go into competition with their existing movie, which is regularly seen on television.

BERMAN: How do you account for the amount of time it takes to get some pictures to the screen? *One Flew Over the Cuckoo's Nest* took eleven years; *Forrest Gump* eight.

BROWN: It's standard. George Stevens, the illustrious director, told me, "All great movies are made over the dead bodies of studio executives." And it's true. I remember meeting George Stevens and his partner, Henry Ginsberg, after he had made a movie called *Shane*, which Paramount thought was unreleasable. Stevens acquired the rights to Edna Ferber's *Giant* and couldn't set it up. I tried to sell it to Fox but they wouldn't hear of it because of Paramount's opinion of *Shane*. He finally made a deal with Warner Brothers. Jack Warner wouldn't put up any money but gave Ferber, Stevens, and Ginsberg a third of the profits. They made more on *Giant* than on all their other pictures. And when *Shane* came out, it was a great movie. But that's how little people know. As Bill Goldman said, "Nobody knows anything."

BERMAN: What was the longest it has taken you to get a project made?

BROWN: It took Zanuck and me almost sixteen years to get *Patton* made. I bought the original book by Ladislas Farago, *Ordeal and Triumph*. Frank McCarthy came on—he was the producer and the film won the Academy Award. Calder Willingham wrote a treatment and Francis Ford Coppola, who knew nothing about the Army, wrote a script. Darryl Zanuck was fixated on the project and came up with the idea of George C. Scott. Scott was the one who asked what was wrong with the Coppola script. He saw it years before. We asked if he would commit to it. He said yes, and by that time, Coppola was off directing a movie, so we got a writer named Edmund North to do some stitches.

In the meantime, previous writers had rewritten the famous speech in front of the American flag. It was my job to undo all the writing that had been done for years at a cost of hundreds of thousands of dollars and restore the original script. Coppola and North met for the first time when they accepted the Academy Award for Best Screenplay.

It was a long process to make *Patton* because at the time, America was violently antimilitary, antiwar, and Patton seemed like an anachronism. But the film was heralded as both an antiwar and pro-war movie. Both the doves and the hawks embraced it, including the Patton family. While it took forever to make, at least the studio always had it in development.

It can take forever to get projects even adopted by a studio. *Forrest Gump* is an example and there are many others. It's almost a badge of honor to have your project rejected over the years.

BERMAN: What was the quickest you have been able to get a picture made?

BROWN: Unfortunately, the quickest was our least successful movie, *The Island*. We had the script, the cast. Everything came about except the picture. *Jaws* came together fairly swiftly but it was helped by the threat of an actors' strike. We had to have the picture in production by a certain time or the studio wouldn't start the movie. Part of getting the green light on *Jaws* was the urgency to get pictures made before the strike deadline.

BERMAN: If you look at the top box-office movies in 1996, almost all are special-effects driven at the expense of good characters and good plots. How do you feel about this trend that seems to be moving away from good stories?

BROWN: I don't think about trends. *The Saint* has real effects, real fire, real danger coming off the screen. There are visual effects, but the film is not dominated by them. *Jaws* utilized real effects, mechanical, but character was important. There were no state-of-the-art computer effects at that time.

Today there are fewer and fewer good stories being made. In the case of *Jaws*, Robert Shaw's eight-to ten-minute monologue about the U.S.S. Indianapolis is one of the great scenes of any film. Today focus groups and research people would probably tell us to take that out because it stopped the story. I'm also convinced that the same focus group would urge the song "Raindrops Keep Fallin' on My Head" be eliminated from *Butch Cassidy and the Sundance Kid* because it stops the story.

Research is another scourge of the business because these self-appointed critics frequently govern the final cut of a movie. Sometimes it works, as in the case of *Fatal Attraction* or with a comedy, because you can tell how an audience feels. Pauline Kael said a long time ago, "One painful truth is bad movies make money." And the studios are in the business of making money. And sometimes one of those big movies is good.

BERMAN: What advice do you have for aspiring screenwriters?

BROWN: Have talent. Nothing takes its place. One would hope that you have the ability to write dramatic works that will attract actors and directors. Writers should think about actors when they write and not about plot-driven pieces.

BERMAN: How do you feel about working opportunities for older actors? (This question was asked to determine the practicality of writing scripts for older actors.)

BROWN: They work. Look at *The First Wives Club*. Not one of the three women could open a picture today, but the ensemble and the subject matter work, brilliantly. They're simpatico personalities... Goldie Hawn, Diane Keaton, and Bette Midler. Paul Newman works consistently and he's been a character actor for years. He's astute. He in *Nobody's Fool* and is doing another picture with Robert Benton. Redford is as successful as he's ever been and works all the time. Jack Nicholson works. Clint Eastwood, who is well into his sixties, is working. The only thing that doesn't work is when you put someone in a role that calls for a younger actor. Then the actor lacks credibility with the audience. But that doesn't happen much any more because there are plenty of jobs for older actors and a definite market, as proven with films like *Cocoon*, *Driving Miss Daisy*, *The Cemetery Club*, and *Grumpy Old Men*.

BERMAN: Any other thoughts on screenwriting or the film business?

BROWN: There were never, in my recollection, going back now over forty years, more than ten or eleven writers who could write a movie and get a sole screenplay credit, like my good friend, Ernest Lehman. It was easier to get a solo screen credit then because the studios had control of the casting and the directors. They said, "This is the script you're gonna shoot, report to stage eleven, two weeks from Monday." Now there are these highly-paid *script doctors* who have never written a successful screenplay from the ground up.

In all the articles I have written, I have made the point that no picture goes forward until a director, who can attract an actor, is acceptable to the financing entity. And that's true of niche companies like October Films or major studios like Paramount or Disney.

A writer has to be careful in the selection of material. If a writer has written a good script, even if it is unproduced, it's a passport to work. We used a writer named David Klass on a movie that we are making called, *Kiss the Girls*, with Morgan Freeman and Ashley Judd. It was his unproduced script, which is now being produced, that got him the job. With Jonathan Hensleigh, our writer on *The Saint*, we read many of his scripts, some of which were unproduced. On *Cocoon*, it was an unproduced script that got us our writer. The right script will be your calling card. Try not to make movies from movies. In the earlier days of Hollywood, writers, as they do in the theater, wrote from life. Today the tendency is to write from other movies; duplicating other successes. That sort of writing doesn't attract good actors and good directors who aspire to quality.

BERMAN: What's your take on the independent film market which has gotten a lot bigger?

BROWN: I like to make independent films. I got the IFP (Independent Film Project) Award many years ago for *The Player*, which was an independent film. Recently I saw *Secrets & Lies* and thought it was wonderful. I haven't seen *Big Night* yet, but I hear it's very good.

BERMAN: How important is it for a screenwriter to live in Los Angeles versus anywhere else in the country?

BROWN: It really doesn't make any difference if you're writing on your own.

BERMAN: What about access to people?

BROWN: If you have a script, you have access to people. I don't know where *The Sting* was written and I don't care. What a writer needs is one of these young agents. They all read and are always looking for new clients. That's a writer's access to Hollywood. You don't have to network when you're a writer, in my opinion. Just write well.

If you would like to know more about David Brown, I highly recommend reading his memoirs, *Let Me Entertain You*. While it is out of print, there are still copies available through bookstores specializing in out-of-print books. A few are listed in the Appendix in the section entitled "Screenplay and Filmbook Sources."

MEETING WILLIAM GOLDMAN

Given his extensive film writing credits and two Academy Awards, William Goldman is one of the most successful screenwriters in the history of Hollywood.

When I started working on the first edition of *Fade In*, I had just finished reading William Goldman's *Adventures in the Screen Trade*—a highly recommended read for every aspiring screenwriter and for anyone who enjoys movies. Having been a longtime fan of his—and since he lived in nearby New York City—I decided to contact him.

I sent a letter to Mr. Goldman at Warner Brothers Books—the publisher of *Adventures*. My letter was very personal and one, I hoped, that would at least prompt a reply. In addition to giving him some background on me, I mentioned that I was working on a screenwriting book and would like to interview him for it. To ensure that he would not be misquoted or taken out of context, I told him he could read the interview before it was published. I also told him that I would not use his name to help promote the book or in any way infer that he was endorsing it.

Four weeks after sending the letter, my phone rang. At the time, I was in my garage—hot, sweaty, and a little distracted having just cut the grass. This is how the conversation went.

> ME
> (into phone)
> Hello.

> MR. GOLDMAN (V.O.)
> Bob Berman?

> ME
> Yes?

> MR. GOLDMAN (V.O.)
> This is Bill Goldman.

> ME
> So?

> MR. GOLDMAN (V.O.)
> (impatiently)
> Didn't you send me a letter?

Since it had been four weeks since I sent the letter and it slipped my mind, and I didn't think of him in terms of "Bill" Goldman, just William Goldman, it didn't register at first. When it did, I felt like an idiot.

After getting past the awkward moment, he was very gracious but not one to bandy words. He said that he didn't like to give interviews. After I told him that his input could be helpful to aspiring screenwriters, he agreed to meet with me.

He checked his appointment book and said he had to go to L.A. for a while and gave me his office number in New York City. Three weeks later, on the exact date he asked me to get in touch, I called. He sounded harried and, at first, had to be reminded who I was. He said he was off to France and that I should contact him in four weeks.

After four weeks passed, I made the call. He answered the phone sounding a bit agitated. Again his schedule precluded us from getting together soon.

For six months, I spoke to Mr. Goldman every three to four weeks until finally one day, he set an appointment.

(While I called him Bill during our phone calls and meeting, I refer to him here as Mr. Goldman to avoid giving the impression that we are good buddies and have stayed in touch over the years. Too many people, after a brief encounter with a celebrity or public figure, like to brag and say that they know so-and-so. I am not one of them, thank you.)

To my surprise, Mr. Goldman had me come to his home just off Park Avenue. On that morning, at precisely 10 a.m., the appointment time, I was giving my name to the doorman at his apartment building.

The elevator took me to his floor, where I was greeted by Mr. Goldman and half expected to see Robin Leech from *Lifestyles of the Rich and Famous*. Now visualize a huge apartment that is both expensively and tastefully furnished. After meeting his lovely wife, I wandered with him into the den which had bookshelves running from the floor to a twelve-foot-high ceiling.

Before we got started, he made it clear that I had forty minutes and that the clock was ticking away. I realized then that I would not have the opportunity to do a real in-depth interview that might lead to some interesting comments from Mr. Goldman.

Not one to waste time, I proceeded to ask questions. My focus, of course, was on how unknown screenwriters break in. He said his advice would not be a major revelation, but a restating of the obvious—live in L.A., write something good, trust your own instincts, and persevere.

The conversation soon shifted to writing novels. When he asked who my favorite authors were, I sat there with a blank expression on my face as if the next word out of my mouth would be, "Duhhh."

As mentioned in the introduction, one of my handicaps was not being a big reader of fiction, so authors' names, at that point, were not rolling off my tongue. As my eyes glazed over coming under his stare, I deftly changed the subject by looking down at his feet and commenting, "Nice shoes." (Not really, but you get the picture.)

Next thing I know, Mr. Goldman and I are in a taxi on our way to his uptown office. I don't remember if he invited me or I invited myself. Anyway, the cab ride gave me a little additional time to ask questions. When we reached the destination, Mr. Goldman shook my hand, wished me well, and disappeared into his office building.

Was I disappointed in the way the meeting turned out? No. As luck would have it, we met the day before I turned over the completed *Fade In* manuscript to Michael Wiese, my publisher. There was not sufficient time to conduct a proper interview, prepare/edit the material, and add it to the book. Remember, it took six months from mailing my letter to Mr. Goldman until the day we actually met. Getting together with him at that point was strictly an opportunity to meet someone I admired, nothing more. Given his busy schedule, I was grateful for the time he gave me and immediately followed up with a letter expressing my thanks.

I think the only reason he finally met with me was because he realized, like in *Fatal Attraction*, I wouldn't go away having called him for six months. I also have to believe that he was impressed by my persistence and punctuality in calling him on those dates when he asked me to.

It can be extremely difficult to meet high-profile people within the film industry without having the benefit of an introduction from someone they know.

My story about William Goldman was told not just to amuse, but to make a point. With the right approach and a lot of perseverance, you can get to and meet *anyone*.

WILLIAM GOLDMAN'S WRITING CREDITS

NOVELS

The Temple of Gold (1957)
Your Turn to Curtsy, My Turn to Bow (1958)
Soldier in the Rain (1960)
Boys and Girls Together (1964)
No Way to Treat a Lady (1964)
The Thing of It Is... (1967)
Father's Day (1971)
The Princess Bride (1973)
Marathon Man (1974)
Magic (1976)
Tinsel (1979)
Control (1982)
The Color of Light (1984)
Heat (1986)
Brothers (1987)

NONFICTION

The Season: A Candid Look at Broadway (1969)
The Making of "A Bridge Too Far" (1977)
*Adventures in the Screen Trade: A Personal
View of Hollywood and Screenwriting* (1982)
Hype & Glory (1992)

MOVIES

*Masquerade** (1965)
Harper (1966)
*Butch Cassidy and the Sundance Kid*** (1969)
The Great Waldo Pepper (1975)
The Stepford Wives (1975)
*All the President's Men*** (1976)
Marathon Man (1976)
A Bridge Too Far (1977)
Magic (1978)
Mr. Horn (1979)
Heat (1987)
The Princess Bride (1987)
Misery (1990)
The Year of the Comet (1992)
*Memoirs of an Invisible Man** (1992)
Maverick (1994)
*The Chamber** (1996)
The Ghost and the Darkness (1996)
Extreme Measures (1996)
Absolute Power (1997)
*Mission: Impossible Sequel****
Script Doctor Work:
Twins, Chaplin, Last Action Hero, Indecent Proposal

* co-writer   ** Academy Award-winning screenplay   *** Current writing assignment

ETHAN WILEY, SCREENWRITER

One day, Jon Sholle, a good friend and very talented guitarist, said to me, "It just came to me that I know this musician who is a screenwriter. His name is Ethan Wiley. He moved here from L.A. Why don't you call him?" Not bashful, I made the call, and we got together.

While Ethan Wiley may not be a household name like Joe Eszterhas, he has been a working screenwriter for twelve years. In 1984, at the age of twenty-four, he sold his first screenplay and it was made into a money-making film, *House*. Two years later, Wiley wrote and directed the sequel, *House II*. From there, he has done his share of work for hire while writing spec scripts, some of which have been optioned or sold.

Since meeting a little over a year ago, we never shared our work. From our discussions, I understood his focus as a writer was in the horror, action, and sci-fi genres. Then one day, he asked me to read one of his scripts, *The Velvet Gentleman*, a period piece about Erik Satie, the French composer. It is a killer script that made me laugh and, at the end, I had to fight back tears. Given Satie's eccentric nature and outlandish behavior—which is well-documented—

The Velvet Gentleman is not your typical slow-moving period piece. In your wildest imagination, you couldn't create a more interesting or colorful character than Satie. Wiley has put together a script that is rich in character, story, and texture. It is a brilliant piece of work which has tremendous commercial possibilities.

In view of his experiences as a screenwriter, I know you will find his comments and observations both enlightening and very helpful.

BERMAN: Where did you grow up?

WILEY: In Marin County which is north of San Francisco.

BERMAN: When did you first develop an interest in film?

WILEY: By the end of my high school years, I was making short, super-eight films with my friends; sort of James Bond spoofs. On the weekends, I'd literally drag them out of bed on a Saturday morning and say, "I've got a convertible and we're going to the beach. On the way there, we're gonna film a spinout when no one is looking." That's how my film career started. When it came time for college, I heard UCLA was the place to be. I went there as an undergrad studying theater, and in my junior year, switched over to a film major.

BERMAN: Why did you make the change?

WILEY: I had always been involved in theater from back in my high school days and got a lot out of it—as an actor and in writing and directing my own shows. But I had a much stronger desire to pursue film.

BERMAN: Any *notable* classmates from your days at UCLA?

WILEY: A number of them. Greg Widen (*Backdraft*), Randall Jahnson (*The Doors*), Fred Dekker (*Robo Cop 3*), Shane Black (*Lethal Weapon*), Chris Matheson (*Bill & Ted's Excellent Adventure*), and Tim Robbins (*Dead Man Walking*). It was a successful class. Part of it had to do with being there at a time when the studios were clearly looking to the film schools for talent.

BERMAN: Did you get a lot out of going to UCLA?

WILEY: Definitely. What is even more important than the courses and the teachers is the relationships you make with other students. Fred Dekker and I were roommates in 1978 and now in 1996 we're working together on a project.

If someone decided on a career in film, it would be very helpful to attend any one of the major film schools like UCLA, USC, NYU, or Columbia. I know that going to UCLA was a good way to be ushered into the town. It's four years of safe sanctuary where you get a lay of the land and a feel for Hollywood.

BERMAN: What did you do after UCLA?

WILEY: Actually, after my third year, I had an opportunity to work at Industrial Light and Magic (ILM), George Lucas's company.

BERMAN: How did that come about?

WILEY: Through a friend of my father's who was a model maker. Shortly after going to work there, I got a job with Chris Walas who was starting his own special effects company after working at ILM for two years.

BERMAN: What did you do for Walas?

WILEY: I started off as his assistant even though I knew nothing about special makeup effects.

BERMAN: Why did he hire you then?

WILEY: I was young, enthusiastic, and he liked my attitude and take on things. I got my first hard-knocks lesson working for Chris. We were hired to do this movie and a year later, we were still waiting for the checks to show up. It was a good lesson to learn. Movie after movie fell through. It was tough, and after a while, I started wondering if I had made a bad decision. I found out that working in the film business meant that most of the time you weren't working.

BERMAN: Did anything good come from working with Walas?

WILEY: Oh, yes. We finally landed the movie *Gremlins*—directed by

Joe Dante and executive-produced by Steven Spielberg. It turned out to be a fantastic project and I worked on that film from the very beginning to the very end. I got experience being on the sets and taking direction from Joe Dante—who is an excellent director. After *Gremlins*, I realized that special effects wasn't my thing. I didn't have the artistic background and expertise to flourish there. I really wanted to write and direct. That was my dream. Having saved some money, I moved to L.A. and wrote my first screenplay, *House*.

BERMAN: How did you come up with the idea?

WILEY: It came from Fred Dekker, my roommate at UCLA. He had an idea for this haunted-house picture, so we cooked up this scheme where I would write it and he would direct. Somehow we'd figure a way to scrape together the money to shoot it ourselves at his parents' old Victorian home in Marin County. I figured I could use my connections to get some special effects done on the cheap.

BERMAN: What happened?

WILEY: Fred got his first writing job and was working for a director named Steve Miner. Miner had worked with Sean Cunningham who had done the *Friday the 13th* movies. When I finished writing the *House* script, I gave it to Fred and he gave it to Steve just to get his reaction. Lo and behold, Miner called me a couple of days later and said he wanted to option it. A year later, it was in production, and it was released in 1985.

BERMAN: What was the story with *House II*?

WILEY: *House* was extremely successful for a low-budget movie in that genre; so suddenly, they needed a sequel. I wrote the script in two weeks and got the job directing based upon my special-effects experience.

BERMAN: How did *House II* do?

WILEY: It was not as successful as the first one but it did make money. The first one was released in February so it had a weekend to itself. *House II* was released in July and had to compete with all the summer blockbuster movies. Two more sequels were made but I was not involved.

BERMAN: What did you do next?

WILEY: I wrote a script called *A Stranger in Leadville*. It was optioned by Steve Tisch (*Risky Business, Forrest Gump, The Long Kiss Goodnight*) and later purchased by Warner Brothers.

BERMAN: What is the premise of *Stranger*?

WILEY: It's about an alien who lands in a Colorado mining town in the late 1800s. I was inspired by H. G. Wells and tried to capture the atmosphere of his novels which, I felt, had never been properly done by Hollywood. *The War of the Worlds* was not made in the same time period as the novel. Essentially my approach to creating *A Stranger in Leadville* was what would it have been like if H. G. Wells had written a western?

BERMAN: What happened to the script?

WILEY: It has come close to production numerous times but the prohibitive expense has been the primary reason it has not been made. Today, budget-wise, it would be among the top movies out there—from forty to one hundred million depending upon the scale of production.

BERMAN: Did you make the deal for *A Stranger in Leadville* or did your agent?

WILEY: I didn't have an agent when *House* went into production, but not too long after it did, the phone started ringing.

BERMAN: Who did you get calls from?

WILEY: A variety of agents. I ended up signing with William Morris. They set up the deal for *Stranger*. A couple of big directors have shown interest in it.

BERMAN: Like who?

WILEY: At one point, Tim Burton (*Batman, Mars Attacks!*) as well as Chuck Russell (*The Mask*). It's still in development at Warner Brothers.

BERMAN: What happened after *A Stranger in Leadville*?

WILEY: I wrote a script with a group of my college buddies called *Urban Legends*. It was basically a comedy about modern urban folklore and was optioned by New Line, actually twice. The first time, I was attached to direct and things didn't work out. The second time, I was to be a producer with someone else attached as director.

BERMAN: What ever happened to *Urban Legends*?

WILEY: It never made it out of development.

BERMAN: This script wasn't bought outright?

WILEY: No, it was only optioned. To have a script bought outright and not go into production is very rare, in my experience. The usual scenario is that a script is optioned for one year with an additional year. Whether or not the second option is picked up is at the discretion of the producer.

What gets complicated is that after a script is optioned, you are paid to rewrite the material and the rewritten material becomes the property of the studio. Later, when the option expires, you own the rights to your original script but not the rewrite. Under these circumstances, it's very difficult to take your script elsewhere because of the possible threat of legal entanglements. The question is: what was in the original script and what was part of the rewrite that the studio paid for and still holds the rights to?

BERMAN: Can't you just return the money you were paid for doing the rewrites and take your script to another studio, as a turnaround deal?

WILEY: Exactly. That's generally what happens. Even if you have no intention of using any of the material you did during the rewrite, you still buy the rights to it so there is no legal questions as to: "Was this joke in the draft you originally wrote or is it a variation of that joke from the rewrite?" *Urban Legends* went through the basic routine of being optioned, then having to go into turnaround.

BERMAN: Do you still have any interest in pushing this script?

WILEY: Over the years, after the battles of trying to get it made, I got burned out on it for a while. But, yes, it is still something I'd like to get going again someday.

BERMAN: What happened after *Urban Legends*?

WILEY: I wrote five spec scripts over a period of a few years and didn't sell any of them.

BERMAN: How did you feed yourself during that period?

WILEY: Doing work-for-hire jobs. I wrote a couple of scripts for various producers. I did a remake of the old movie, *The Enchanted Cottage*, for Steve Miner. I did a comedy for Disney and a couple of different TV scripts.

BERMAN: Did any of them see production?

WILEY: None so far. I occasionally hear that two of them, *The Enchanted Cottage* and *Spider-Man*, are still in the works. James Cameron is now involved in *Spider-Man*, but there are a lot of legal problems over the rights which they're trying to resolve.

BERMAN: What happened in the period after you wrote these spec scripts?

WILEY: Those spec scripts were mostly comedies and they didn't attract any interest. I don't know if it was a problem of trying to change gears from my other movies that were considered in the horror genre. Also, my sense of humor is kind of off-the-wall and perhaps people weren't sure if the scripts were funny or not. When those scripts didn't work out, I moved around agencies a little bit. I went from William Morris to Triad; from Triad to a boutique agency, Richland, Wunsch & Hohman; and from there to my current agent, Rima Greer, at Above the Line Agency.

BERMAN: What happened next?

WILEY: I co-wrote a script with Jim Isaac called *Red Ivory*. It was optioned by Gene Kirkwood and John Hyde. Kirkwood is best known as the producer of *Rocky*.

As a work-for-hire, I wrote a feature script, *Christmas Apocalypse*, a cop-thriller which takes place in New York City. When Fox TV first started, I wrote an original TV pilot for producer Stuart Cornfeld (*The Fly*) and one for director, Joel Schumacher (*A Time to Kill*). I also wrote a *Tales of the Crypt* episode that never made it to the screen.

BERMAN: Did you take a lot of meetings?

WILEY: Yes. And there are so many different kinds of meetings. There are those where you are meeting a producer or development executive to get a sense of who they are and vice versa. Or there are very specific pitch meetings where you have been given material to look over, along with fifty other writers, to present your views. During the period when I was writing all these spec scripts, I spent a lot of time taking meetings.

BERMAN: Were any of those meetings productive?

WILEY: I saw the opposite side of the process as a director auditioning actors. An actor would come in for a part and be totally inappropriate, and you'd wonder why they had been sent over by the casting agent who knew they weren't right. What is important for actors is meeting a director and shaking hands. An actor may meet the same director ten times over a period of ten years and may be appropriate only once for a role. So it's important that they make all those auditions, and the same holds true for writers. It's not necessarily what comes from it now, but later.

BERMAN: How do you access studio executives and producers for meetings?

WILEY: Once you are represented by a good agency and have had some success, meetings can be arranged. You might not be able to spend an hour with Steven Spielberg (*Jaws*) or Bob Zemeckis (*Back to the Future*), but you can have meetings with the people who work for them. If there is someone in the town you really want to meet and have a reason, I have found that if you have a good agent, they can open those doors for you—even if you're not known by this person. That's why having a good agent is so important to taking meetings in Hollywood.

BERMAN: Any funny stories regarding meetings you or any of your friends have taken?

WILEY: All the time, you hear stories about producers falling asleep during the middle of a pitch. Once I had a meeting with a producer who had read one of my scripts and said he really liked it, but felt it was reminiscent of some other recent movies. He told me he was interested in truly original visions that were completely unique and weren't derivative of something else. In the next breath he said, "What I'm looking for is something like *Rosemary's Baby*."

Certain films fall into favor with the studios, ones they want to emulate and for good reasons. It might have been a great film like *Rosemary's Baby*. For a while then, every meeting you'd go into, people would say they are looking for the next *Rosemary's Baby*. And the next year, it's a different movie.

BERMAN: When and why did you move to New York?

WILEY: We moved in 1993. I was getting tired of living in L.A. and felt I was stagnating there, and thought a change of environment would stimulate the creative juices. When an opportunity came along in New York for Kate, my wife, I encouraged her to take it for the sake of her career as well as mine. Moving elsewhere to acquire new inspiration is something you hear writers talk about a lot in Los Angeles.

BERMAN: What was your most recent project?

WILEY: I just finished a story treatment of *Children of the Corn 5* for Miramax. If they approve it and commission me to write the screenplay, then it's a writer-director deal. I'm waiting to hear from them right now.

BERMAN: Let's talk about *The Velvet Gentleman* and how this project about Erik Satie came about.

WILEY: Satie represents a new direction for me as a writer. Part of moving to New York that we already talked about was getting some new inspiration and looking at some different things to write. As a child, my mother would play the music of Erik Satie and told me these interesting stories about this amazing, eccentric man.

At a certain point during the mid-eighties, when I started renewing my interest in music, I realized that I had never been able to connect my love of music with anything I had written. And for a long time, I had been looking for a way to do that.

Somehow I got reconnected to the concept of what an interesting character Satie was and what a great subject he would be for a movie. Slowly I started collecting material on him. I started off by buying his music and doing arrangements for mandolin and guitar. Then, in the late eighties, I made several trips to Paris and fell in love with the city. On one of them, I did research. I went all over Paris hunting for books—in both French and English—and revisited the places where he used to live and frequent, to get a sense of the man and his time—which I found so fascinating.

I came back from Paris with a lot of great material and photographs. Some of these books I could not get in the United States. After uncovering all these interesting facts about Satie's relationships with Ravel and Debussy, the concept and structure of the movie really took shape. There was so much material to draw from, historical facts, that it became difficult to keep things out of the script. It was an embarrassment of riches.

By the time I finished the story treatment for Miramax of *Children of the Corn 5*, I was almost done with *The Velvet Gentleman*. I devoted the past two months to completing it. From its inception, it's taken five years.

When I signed with Rima Greer, she was very enthusiastic about this project but warned me it might not be the easiest sale—doing a historical biography about an obscure French musician. But she was very encouraging and told me that it should be a project I work on in between other projects. So that is exactly what I did. I chipped away at it from time to time.

BERMAN: How did you capture the language of Satie's times? It sounds so real and so lyrical.

WILEY: That is probably the most challenging aspect of writing a period piece. You're trying to strike a balance between accurately portraying the language of the era, yet also creating language that's going to be accessible to a modern audience. It all came from research and reading novels written during his time. I got the voice of Satie from his writing, which is fairly extensive, and from understanding certain traits in his personality that he was famous for... such as his paranoia and acerbic wit.

BERMAN: Do you have any favorite authors?

WILEY: I usually find myself reading the classics because I feel my knowledge of the great books is far too limited. I read authors like Mark Twain, H. G. Wells, Chekhov, and Dostoyevsky. Another big influence is the comic-artist Walt Kelly who wrote and drew the Pogo comic strip.

I was introduced to him as a kid and he did something similar to Mark Twain in that every time you go back and read the material, you get something new from it. I really like the way he combined childlike fantasy and comedy with deeper issues and deeper themes. You could look at a Walt Kelly comic strip and enjoy it purely for the slapstick, purely for the poetry of the language, or for the political and social observations—all simultaneously. With my writing, that approach inspires me to create something that is multi-layered.

As a screenwriter, I find inspiration from sources other than film. Satie was inspired by other artists, people like Picasso who weren't musicians. I can relate to that because I feel I've been inspired by a lot of musicians in their approach to their creativity, craft, and music.

BERMAN: Can you name five favorite films?

WILEY: I prefer to name filmmakers like Hal Ashby, Stanley Kubrick, Howard Hawks, Alfred Hitchcock, Carroll Ballard, John Boorman, and the Monty Python Comedy Group. One of the things I really admire about Hal Ashby is his versatility. He has made an amazing variety of films like *Harold and Maude, Coming Home, Being There, Bound for Glory, Shampoo.* I find him very inspirational.

BERMAN: Where do you get your story ideas from?

WILEY: Anywhere and everywhere. Sometimes it's hearing an anecdotal story or reading a newspaper article. Things just pop into my head like the proverbial light bulb going on. Sometimes I will be able to develop an idea almost immediately while others have to slowly gestate or germinate over a long period of time.

BERMAN: How important is research?

WILEY: For a piece like *A Stranger in Leadville*, it was essential to do research about the town of Leadville and the Colorado Rockies. I actually went there and to the Colorado Heritage Society, which had tons of photographs and invaluable material.

Take the *Red Ivory* script I co-wrote with Jim Isaac. It's a story about an American mercenary hired to train park rangers at an African nature preserve to defend elephants from poachers. This project obviously required knowledge of the subject matter, and since we weren't able to go to Africa, we did extensive research.

Of course, my script on Erik Satie is another example where the subject matter required a lot of research.

BERMAN: In preparing a project, what steps do you take? Do you complete character biographies? Do you outline scene descriptions or complete a narrative treatment?

WILEY: My approach depends upon subject matter. If it's a mystery, I will outline the story in paragraphs with as much detail as possible, and work within the same document that will eventually become the actual screenplay. After outlining the scenes by paragraph, I cut and paste and reorganize everything into a logical sequence. Then I go back and add more details to each paragraph including scene headings and dialogue. This story treatment gradually evolves into a script. The only time I develop character biographies is when I collaborate. Because each writer has different ideas, you need to establish one voice for each character. I don't develop bios when working on my own projects since I have a very clear impression of each character in my head.

BERMAN: What type of work schedule do you keep?

WILEY: Now that I have a son, I don't have any schedule at all. It's whenever I can get to the computer. My ideal schedule is to write in the morning from eight to noon, then from one to five. I usually don't write during the evening, except now that I have a baby. After he goes to sleep, I'll write from nine to eleven. A lot of my writer friends are real night owls and don't get started until around 11 p.m. They write into the wee morning hours and sleep in. I usually write my best rolling out of bed after half-sleeping, half-dreaming about my work.

BERMAN: Do you work on weekends?

WILEY: I never keep track of what day it is. My wife tells this story about how we went out on our first date on Saturday night, which meant to her, date night. And to me, the concept never even crossed my mind. Whether it was a Tuesday or Saturday, it didn't matter to me.

BERMAN: What does Kate think of your writing?

WILEY: She's totally supportive. She's proofreading one of my scripts right now, as we speak.

BERMAN: Are there any areas of your writing you would like to improve?

WILEY: All of them. But that aside, most of my projects are concept-driven and the character is developed out of a given story theme. I want to improve or shift my focus to working from strong characters. Obviously, *The Velvet Gentleman* is character-driven and a major step in the right direction.

BERMAN: How do you feel about collaborating?

WILEY: I have mixed feelings about it. I've always been drawn to it because writing is such a lonely profession and it can be a lot of fun writing with other people. With comedy, it can be especially beneficial because you have someone you can play ideas and jokes off and see if they are funny or not.

I've also had experiences where it has been difficult to strike a democratic balance with the other writer. Ultimately it seems that one has to take the reins and the control and the other has to be willing to acquiesce. Also, collaborating with another writer does you no good unless you plan it as a career. What happens is this. When you go off on your own after writing scripts with someone else, everyone wants to know what you wrote and what the other person wrote. Since there is no way to really determine that, scripts you wrote with someone else do not end up being a calling card for either one of you.

BERMAN: What advice can you give on dealing with rejection?

WILEY: You have to have confidence in yourself or you'll never survive. It takes a big ego to handle all the rejection. Every writer goes through these different stages when rejection hurts, or is frustrating, or it just rolls off your back. You need intestinal fortitude to tune out all those negative comments about your work.

BERMAN: How important is it for a writer to live in Los Angeles?

WILEY: I wouldn't recommend living outside Los Angeles for someone who is starting a career unless they have writing credentials in another writing profession or something that connects to the industry. Novelists or playwrights are in professions that relate to film. For someone young, trying to break in, it's not only important to be out there because of the connections you make, but to get a sense of what the industry is like. Once you're an established feature writer, you can live anywhere given all the modern communication devices available.

For television writers, it's very important to live in Los Angeles because all the work is there. For sitcoms and series writing, you're part of a staff and you have to spend a lot of hours there.

Because I lived in town for years and established some contacts and have a few credits, it was not a big hindrance for me to move.

It's still a bit nerve-racking because I'm no longer running into people at restaurants or at the gym. So there is a sense of isolation, but there are also many benefits like getting more work done. When I lived in Los Angeles, I found myself constantly pulled between writing, taking meetings, and socializing. Some days, it felt like I wasn't getting much work done.

BERMAN: Do you think your career, with its ups and downs, is fairly typical of most writers?

WILEY: Yeah. I think the longer you're in the business you realize that it's a hit and miss kind of profession, unless, of course, you are at the very, very top.

When I was having trouble getting my spec projects off the ground, I found inspiration after reading this article about the top filmmakers, guys like George Lucas and Barry Levinson, who had certain dream projects they couldn't get made. No matter what level you're at, you're always struggling. After that, I no longer felt like I was the only person in town who couldn't get a picture made.

If you're a writer, you have to look at the long term. You can't be concerned with what happened yesterday or today. Embracing that philosophy has allowed me to write my dream project, *The Velvet Gentleman*, and not worry that it was taking me away from bringing in some income.

I've considered opportunities in the developing world of multimedia and interactive entertainment, and have actually done a little work in that field. But in spite of my interest in other creative mediums, I come back to film and screenwriting. It's the only thing I know how to do... and I'm not the first person to say that. I just find that my creative ideas seem to be best expressed as movies—for better, for worse.

BERMAN: Given all the competition out there, it is very difficult getting an agent today. You came through the back door, by having a project made before having an agent. What about the average writer, starting out? How does he or she get an agent?

WILEY: I tell people the best way to get an agent is to have a feature film in production. [Laughs]

It's pounding on the door, being relentless. I recently read a quote from a movie executive who said, "I respond to people who are relentless because I know that's the way I'd be." That's very important.

You go to an agent the first time, then a second time, and a third time. You show him that you're not some fly-by-night and that you're not doing this for a lark. There are a lot of people out there who write one screenplay. So the best way to get an agent is to write a screenplay, then a second one, then a third, then a fourth.

When I was signed by Rima Greer, it was right after the period of these down years, when I had been struggling to sell my scripts. I went to her and said, "You may be wondering what I've been doing for the past few years." I then opened up a bag full of scripts and dumped them on her desk and said, "This is what I've been doing."

Basically I was telling her that while I was not visible in the industry with a bunch of *go* projects, that hasn't meant that my passion has dwindled in any way; and through the ups and downs, I continue to be a hard-working writer with no intention of stopping.

I think it's important for an agent to see that you're a professional... that you're in it for the long term... and that you're not in it for a fast buck and to become a star overnight.

BERMAN: Any advice for aspiring screenwriters?

WILEY: Having an agent and having a good relationship with your agent is very important. When I moved from agency to agency there for a little while, in retrospect, I blamed them for my problems. Now I realize that I take equal blame because I didn't communicate as well with them in terms of who I was and what I wanted to accomplish. And part of that was I really didn't know. I didn't have a clear, concise idea of where I wanted to go and what I wanted to do. And that makes it tough on the agent. You need to be focused in how you deal with them. If you can tell them what you want, they can be far more effective in helping you.

With Rima Greer, she takes more of a managerial approach, which is great because she helps me shape and guide what direction my career should go in.

It's very helpful for a screenwriter to establish an identity in a certain genre. Get people to think of you as a comedy writer, or a thriller writer, or an action writer. Go with your strengths.

In closing this chapter, the following issues are offered as food for thought.

EARLY ENTRY

Early entry in every career field is a major advantage because of the amount of time it takes to develop the job skills and contacts that determine work opportunities. Screenwriting is no different. Also, by starting a career early, before assuming responsibilities like marrying and raising a family, you can take greater risks.

While that is the ideal set of circumstances, if you decide, like me, to pursue screenwriting later in life, then don't let age hold you back. According to the Writers Guild of America, the average age of new members is *thirty-five*. It's an interesting point because most people guess it to be twenty-five. If the average age of new members is thirty-five, you can bet that there are a considerable number of writers forty and older who help make up those statistics. When it comes to writing, it doesn't matter one iota to the audience how old you are or what you look like, if your work is entertaining them. If you can make them laugh, cry, or have the hair on the back of their necks tingle, they wouldn't care if that movie was written by a bowl of soup.

Direct Your Own Script?

Some people want to be just writers. Some want to use writing—with no regard for craft—as a stepping stone to directing. And some want to be writer-directors.

Directing your own script is an option worth considering, especially if your material has been rejected after years of banging on doors and is considered *non-commercial* by agents and producers. Even if you can put the hook into family and friends and raise $25,000, the cost of making *The Brothers McMullen*, you had better understand the risks involved and what it takes to be a director.

This applies to every film. Even with a great script, perfect casting, an unlimited budget, and a great director at the helm, the final results could be a horrendous disaster. Success with film is illusive. After a film bombs, you can look at it and sometimes rationalize why. On the next occasion, you will watch a movie that is equally bad but it does $100 million at the box office. Then again, you may enjoy a well-crafted film that resonates with charm but dies a quick death in the theaters.

If you have an interest in directing, here are the personal traits and characteristics that best qualify a person for the job.

1.   Have a lot of talent. It is a big step moving from screenwriter to director. Film is a visual medium. You are trying to tell a story where the visual aspects are ultimately more important than words of dialogue. You have to create an atmosphere and mood that will allow the actors to give their best performances.

196

2.   You must be a leader who inspires confidence in everyone around you. You must know what your objectives are at all times and show everyone that you are in control—juggling many things at once and making snap decisions.

3.   You have to be a *people person* and recognize the needs of everyone from the actors to the crew. You have to know how much direction to give each actor by treating them as individuals. Some want and require more; others need *space* if you are to get the most out of them.

4.   Making a film is a grueling task—physically and mentally. With fourteen- and sixteen-hour days, you need to have the stamina of a bull. Staying *balanced*—not losing your temper or sense of humor—reduces *set* anxieties. If you're in control, it will be a lot easier for everyone else to do their jobs.

If you're thinking about directing, there are two steps you can take initially to test the waters. You can enroll in a course like the Hollywood Institute's *Two-Day Film School* run by Dov S-S Simens. He offers classes in Los Angeles, New York, and a number of cities between the two coasts. I attended his program two years ago at New York University (NYU) and found it quite helpful. Look in the back of any film magazine like *Premiere, Movieline,* or *Entertainment Weekly* for his ads and those of other filmmakers.

The second step is to make a short film—something like the script I prepared in Chapter 7 to illustrate an adaptation. Can a short film open doors? Some producers say that directing a short film doesn't qualify someone to direct a feature. Others say if a short film is good, the filmmaker will be recognized. If you're serious about directing, this would be a good way to get your feet wet.

ALL ABOUT WRITING

THE EMOTIONAL ASPECTS OF WRITING

Before you begin writing your first screenplay, it is important to understand the emotional aspects of writing—those issues which have the greatest impact on a writer's emotional stability, attitude, and performance. On those days when you struggle with your work, especially the first project, this information will be extremely helpful and very comforting.

Writing is a lonely occupation filled with a broad spectrum of emotional experiences. Most of the time, it is very rewarding, or there wouldn't be any writers. But let's take a look at the two major extremes. At some point, a writer may experience despair, anxiety, apprehension, and confusion. Even when you are thoroughly prepared to write, there are moments when you cannot seem to think clearly. It becomes difficult to concentrate. You force yourself to write and what comes out is awful. Don't worry about it. It's a natural experience every writer contends with from time to time. Sometimes, through pure persistence, you can work your way out of this frame of mind and get back on track. When you are unproductive and feel nothing but frustration, it's time to take a break. You could be over-tired. If that is the case, then take a brief nap or maybe a short walk. Knock off a bag of Fritos or other favorite snack. You'll quickly regain your desire to write and become productive again.

On the other side of the coin, there are those magical moments when you rise above what you believe to be the limits of your own talent and abilities. And as long as the moment lasts, the level of satisfaction you experience will be incredible. If you diligently pursue writing, you will eventually experience this phenomenon yourself.

Here are the key issues affecting a writer's emotional state. Being aware of them makes writing much easier.

1.   ***The more you write, the easier it gets***. This applies to the development of each project and, especially, every project after your first one. Experience sharpens your writing skills and intuitive sense, as well as fortifies your confidence. With experience, you will be able to work much faster and far more efficiently.

2.   ***Writing is rewriting***. This point can't be emphasized enough. Don't make any serious judgments on your first or even second-draft screenplay. Many scripts require constant refinement until the real quality of the work is evident.

3.   ***Since you make every decision concerning the treatment of your characters and your story, you will naturally make mistakes in the process. If you do, know that you have the ability to determine the solution***. It may take time to correct a problem, but you will do it. While mistakes are frustrating, there is a continuous benefit derived from them because they ultimately teach you new skills and new techniques.

4.   ***It can't be repeated enough. Minor changes can often significantly enhance the final results***. You could conceivably spend a few hours fixing a problem that might dramatically improve your entire script. What might have been mediocre, quickly becomes great.

5.   ***Towards the completion of every project, you may reach a point where you are reluctant to finish***. You begin to stall and find reasons not to continue. It's a natural experience. When it happens, accept it, but press on and complete your screenplay.

6.   ***Is there such a thing as writer's block? Yes. And it happens to even the best writers***. However, one distinction should be made. Inexperienced writers often put themselves into a position of writer's block (not being able to write) by not being properly prepared.

If you attempt to write your screenplay without completing the necessary preplanning steps first, you might spend a great deal of time staring at a blank screen. Your story must be outlined, with as much detail as possible, which is the function of completing all the exercises.

7.   Does *creative inspiration* exist? Of course it does. But if you wait around for the mood to strike, it will never happen. ***Creative inspiration is a by-product of working hard—perspiration***. Without

question, it is totally unpredictable and spontaneous. Working at this extraordinary level can last minutes or many hours. *Being prepared, working hard, and following a regular schedule, are the keys to sparking creative inspiration.*

8.   *It's practical to seek advice and opinions on your work during the research stages and after the first draft is written—but not as you write.* Negative comments can be inhibiting, disruptive to your concentration and impede your creative flow.

9.   *A writer's objectivity is greatly diminished because of his or her closeness to the work.* The only guiding light is to follow the structure of your story in order to stay on track. And even so, it may take months after you have finished your script before you really see it objectively.

10.   *If you write full-time or put a lot of hours in at one time, you must learn to pace yourself.* Writing is both mentally and physically exhausting. After two hours or more of sitting in one position, I develop what I call *dead ass*. My butt actually becomes numb from sitting too long. Before that point is reached, I get up, stretch, and walk around for a minute or two. If you reach a point where you are getting very tired but continue pushing without a pause, your work will suffer. Learn to pace yourself and take short breaks.

11.   *Being a writer and having a relationship with other people can be difficult at times. Writers tend to be introspective and somewhat moody—and our attitude is often influenced by the various stages of our work.* When things are going well, we can be happy and delightful to be around. When things take a turn for the worse, as they sometimes do, we tend to sulk and withdraw.

Support from spouses, children, girlfriends, boyfriends, as well as tolerance from close personal friends, is a must. People who are not *creative writers* often find it impossible to understand the needs of those who are.

As interruptions are disruptive to a writer's train of thought and frame of mind, so are a writer's lifestyle and working habits to those close to him or her. Communicate. Talk about it. Reach agreements that come close to satisfying each other's needs. Without support and understanding, a writer cannot be productive.

12.   Working environment. What is it? It's a specific area of space where we write. Most importantly, ***each writer must create a working environment that is conducive to his or her needs***. It is a personal choice and a very important consideration. One writer may seek the security of a comfortable setting surrounded by personal photos and memorabilia, while another may have the need to create a *special mood* attained by effective lighting and soft background music. From day to day, and even hour to hour, my mood shifts as well as my needs. Most of the time, the only sound I hear is the constant hum of my computer. In that case, my primary need is total quiet and solitude. However, there are times when I do listen to music and the decision is purely spontaneous. What do I listen to? Depending upon my mood, it could be light FM, jazz, or thundering rock 'n' roll. When the moment is right, even with my system cranked up and blasting out Buddy Guy's version of "Mustang Sally" with Jeff Beck wailing away on his turbo-charged Strat, it is not distracting—it's stimulating and doesn't interfere with my concentration. Be selective and experimental in determining the needs of your working environment because it often has a great bearing on your productivity and the quality of your work.

13.   ***As in any business, the type of equipment you have is extremely important***. If you decide to pursue a career as a writer, a computer is an absolute must. And today you don't have to spend a lot of money to acquire a good computer and laser jet printer. Can't afford new equipment? Buy used. There are companies who specialize in selling used office equipment, including computers. Shop around until you find something within your budget.

For those who write at night, you might consider a halogen torchiere floor lamp. Since it reflects and even disperses a very soft light off the ceiling, it is especially effective during dark hours. These lamps are not inexpensive but they can diminish eye fatigue caused by poor lighting conditions.

Most writers work sitting down, so fatigue can quickly set in and disrupt your concentration. Find a good chair—one that is comfortable and preferably adjustable so you can alter your sitting position from time to time.

Selecting the right equipment is an important issue, so consider all your options very carefully.

THE EVOLUTION OF BEING A WRITER

I started screenwriting in January of 1987. Discounting the six months it took me to write the first edition of *Fade In*, my thirteen-month hiatus to earn some money via my business career, and a six-month period during which I went into the tank and then didn't write a word, I've been screenwriting for eight years. As mentioned in the introduction, I was at a major disadvantage when starting my screenwriting career because I read very little over the years—a prerequisite for being a fiction writer.

Having said that, I can tell you that if you work hard at writing, or anything for that matter, you will improve. How much is determined by how much natural talent you have and how hard you work. There are many people who succeed on less talent because they work hard.

Since growth is gradual, you may not recognize your progress until suddenly one day it becomes obvious to you and to those who have been following your work.

The first measure of progress is that things come easier. A screenwriting exercise you would agonize over for weeks now only takes days. Your characters come across as being real. Your dialogue becomes more succinct and has a natural cadence that makes reading it enjoyable. Your story line is executed with far greater clarity with each scene smoothly transitioning to the next.

With my own development as a writer, I was able to drop a number of key exercises from the screenwriting process. With my last two projects anyway, I didn't outline the screenplay structure from plot point to plot point, nor the scene descriptions. With the narrative treatment, I only wrote a few pages to get a sense of my characters and the tone of the story. My narrative treatment never went beyond the first act and yet, instinctively, once I had my ending, I knew I could complete my screenplay without the aid of those exercises. The fact that it only took me thirty days to complete a third draft from story concept is a direct benefit of my growth as a writer. However, speed is meaningless unless the script *works*.

As you grow as a writer, one other skill is greatly enhanced—your ability to recognize problems. You will begin to notice things you were previously incapable of seeing until they were pointed out to you by someone else. At the same time, it is important to realize the benefits derived from the input of trusted readers.

One thing which really helped my growth as a writer was reading a lot of classic books and a very diversified selection of authors which includes Fyodor Dostoyevsky, Ernest Hemingway, William Faulkner, John Steinbeck, Ross MacDonald, Dashiell Hammett, Raymond Chandler, Elmore Leonard, James Ellroy (one of my favorites), Cormac McCarthy, Philip K. Dick, and Clive Cussler.

KNOW YOUR OWN WEAKNESSES

Dead Man's Dance was submitted to agents without input from a trusted reader right after it was finished as a third draft in thirty days. Therefore I lost the benefit of someone's keen eye and also never gained the perspective that comes from stepping back from a script long enough. As a result, I didn't make those changes that might have prompted a more positive response from agents. I learned an incredible lesson from writing my last two scripts—a lesson that will most definitely influence the way I handle new scripts from this point on.

THE CREATIVE STEPS BEHIND *DEAD MAN'S DANCE*

The creative process is the stimulation of the imagination and inventive powers to create something—and it begins with a basic idea that is either developed or discarded.

The creative process is an intellectual challenge. Can you, as a writer, create characters and a story that will evoke an emotional response? Can you make people laugh, cry, or learn an important lesson about life?

At the time when my first sci-fi script, *Screechers*, was winding down, I wanted to write another thriller. But having written two previously, I knew I would need an incredibly strong premise to make it work. With the earlier thrillers, one turned out well, while the other was such a stinker I never shared it with anyone.

The thriller that *worked* had a terrific twist in the end that not one of my readers guessed. And in spite of the well-sketched characters and well-paced plot, they all had one major criticism that quelled their enthusiasm. Since I'm referencing my thriller, *Macklin*, some background on it would be helpful so you can appreciate the importance of an original story premise.

Here is the log line: After his brother —a New York City detective— is murdered, an unemployed construction worker and his family are pursued by a ruthless drug dealer.

The story relies upon well-defined characters, solid pacing, and an unpredictable twist in the end. The subplot explores the main character's struggle trying to accept his wife's success as a business executive, and his strained relationship with his fourteen-year-old daughter.

Even though the story does not delve into the seedy side of the drug culture and all the clichés that come with this subject matter, as far as my readers were concerned, the use of *drugs* as the crime driving the plot totally overshadowed everything else. In one respect, they were right. That's why I knew, when developing *Dead Man's Dance*, I had better come up with a crime that was fresh and original if I had any chance of prompting a positive response from my readers.

STARTING THE CREATIVE PROCESS

Five days a week, I exercise for thirty minutes and walk three miles. My most productive conceptualization period comes while walking. Being away from distractions at home allows me to think freely. Sometimes my mind just wanders and then something is brought to the conscious level.

If something comes to mind, it is then extrapolated. And *what if* is the exercise I use to stimulate the creative process. One day I had the following conscious spark: what if a person ran into someone who was supposedly dead?

The next question was: who is the person and who is the someone who is supposedly dead? Initially I couldn't answer either question but with a conscious idea in mind, I now had something to focus on.

Within days, things started to click. What if a woman runs into a man her father supposedly murdered? Now my alter ego gets involved. "Okay, turkey, what next?" I respond confidently, "To make the premise more exciting, what if the woman disappears after seeing this man?"

My alter ego says, "Sounds good. But then what?" I respond, "Hmmmm. Let me think a minute." My alter ego starts tapping his foot. Finally I smile and say, "I've got it! What if the woman's brother looks for her?" My alter ego pauses, then says, "Not bad, but you can do better."

My premise was finally fine-tuned to: when a woman disappears after supposedly seeing the man her father murdered, her sister searches for her.

From that premise, the creative process was in high gear. However, my big concern was: where does the plot go in terms of the payoff? What are all the circumstances around the father supposedly murdering this man—and who is this man? What happens at the end that is spectacular? Something new? Something unexpected?

Before coming up with the Mafia criminal relocation program, I started thinking about my main character. I could have developed the story using a brother in search of his missing sister, but decided that it was far more practical—since more roles are written for men—to make the main character a woman.

Remember the procedure for developing a story by going both *forwards* and *backwards* in creating things you need? This exercise was absolutely critical to developing my main character, Kerry Parker.

To determine a logical age for Kerry, I had to first know how old she was when all these events happened, prior to the story starting. That meant: how old was she when her father was convicted of embezzling money from his clients and of killing his partner?

It's truly a back and forth process where going back to create something you need allows you to advance your story.

Thinking about it now, as I write this, it is next to impossible to recall the exact sequence of when each specific issue was resolved. A question leads to an answer that leads to another question and so on— until your project takes on a very definite shape.

Your goal in the creative process is to surpass what you *think* your creative limits are and surprise yourself. In coming up with the "Mafia Criminal Relocation Program," I felt a real sense of satisfaction. Even my pain-in-the-ass alter ego had to admit it was good. "Go ahead. Pat yourself on the back. You deserve it."

There's no point in elaborating any further on the creative steps applied to developing the story and all the supporting details for *Dead Man's Dance*. From this chapter, you should have a good understanding as to how the creative process works and the confidence to know that it will work for you.

Remember, the creative process is enhanced by the* what if *and* forwards *and* backwards *exercises. Use them.

SUCCESSFUL FILMS & MILLION DOLLAR SCRIPTS

THE QUALITIES OF SUCCESSFUL FILMS

With all the demographic studies Hollywood undertakes to determine *market trends* and what the next potential blockbuster will be, the public continues to make decisions for the industry. Most frequently the public passes on films that the studios feel are contenders for the all-time box office receipts and makes blockbusters out of the most unlikely films. *Driving Miss Daisy, Stand by Me,* and *Four Weddings and a Funeral* are examples of surprise hits. By Hollywood standards, they fall into the low-budget category. Some of these films had an R.O.I. (Return On Investment) that was considerably higher than the biggest box office hits of those respective years.

It is truly impossible for anyone to predict the success of a film. However, when you analyze successful films, there are a few common denominators that can provide the writer with some sense of confidence in creating and developing an original screenplay story. In the first edition of *Fade In*, I said the following:

As a general rule, successful movies have always been well-written, well-acted, well-directed, well-made films dealing with a subject matter that the majority of people can relate to. A film must be entertaining, have a likeable main character for the audience to root for, and an upbeat ending.

My reference really wasn't about successful movies, but about ones that are good *films*—and it was meant as a goal for which every filmmaker should strive. With that point out of the way, then a distinction needs to be made between a successful film and one that is good. A successful film is one which makes money—sometimes a lot—while a good film, on the other hand, can't always be measured by box office receipts. It is a personal choice. A good film is one in which the characters and story hold your interest from beginning to end. And when it is over, your emotions have been stirred and you feel totally satisfied. It is a film that you will enjoy seeing again.

209

Following are the five most successful films in 1996. Excluding *Toy Story*, the other four were, in general, criticized for focusing upon special effects at the expense of good characters and, in some, a good story as well.

SUCCESSFUL FILMS - 1996	WORLD BOX OFFICE	THROUGH
1. *INDEPENDENCE DAY*	$692,000,000	11/18/96
2. *TWISTER*	$462,000,000	10/28/96
3. *TOY STORY*	$357,000,000	9/01/96
4. *MISSION IMPOSSIBLE*	$408,000,000	10/28/96
5. *THE ROCK*	$323,000,000	11/18/96

It is obvious that the majority of successful films in 1996—measured by box office receipts —could not stand up to the criteria for being good movies. Hopefully if someone does make a good movie, it will make money. In talking to friends who are frequent moviegoers, most were hard-pressed to name more than two films they really liked in 1996. That's a pretty sad commentary when you have seen more than forty new ones.

Over the years, all kinds of films have enjoyed box office success in addition to critical acclaim. What does this mean to the writer? It means write what you know about and what you would like to see.

Because Hollywood duplicates successful films, many writers feel compelled to take the same approach. But remember that *every successful film which has been made into a sequel started as a fresh, original idea*.

Death Wish, Rocky, Police Academy, The Naked Gun, Friday the 13th, A Nightmare on Elm Street, Lethal Weapon, The Karate Kid, Die Hard, Beverly Hills Cop, Porky's, Psycho, Halloween, and *Crocodile Dundee* all started as original ideas. It's far more practical for a writer to create and develop new ideas by following and relying upon his or her own instinct, judgment, taste, and intuition.

If you wanted to do a genre piece, say action, come up with a basic story premise that has a slight twist and you could have the ingredients for a successful film. "What if a bomb is set to explode on a bus once its speed drops below fifty miles per hour?" From that basic premise, the movie, *Speed*, was created.

At this writing, *Ransom*, the latest Ron Howard film starring Mel Gibson, is in the theaters. It is a story about a wealthy man whose son is kidnapped. While this film is based upon the 1956 movie of the same title, a new twist has been added to the plot which makes this version very intriguing. Rather then rely upon the police and F.B.I., the father (Gibson) of the kidnapped boy takes matters into his own hands and goes to the media offering a million-dollar bounty on the heads of the kidnappers. That's a terrific hook.

THE WRITER'S PERSPECTIVE

What appears to be *offbeat* subject matter, at least on the surface, might become very appealing through the proper treatment. Any subject matter can be made interesting by the writer who finds the right approach.

Another point, stressed earlier, which ties directly into creating original stories is that **the audience reacts emotionally, not intellectually, to film stories. So if a writer can satisfy the audience's emotional needs and, at the same time, stimulate them intellectually, it is a unique accomplishment worthy of special recognition**.

Ordinary People, On Golden Pond, Stand by Me, Body Heat, Kramer vs. Kramer, Tender Mercies, etc., are appealing/successful films that were made with very modest budgets. These types of stories, focusing on human relationships, are a positive area to pursue and, as proven, are difficult to duplicate into a sequel.

While every actor complains about how bad today's scripts are in terms of *quality stories* with *challenging character roles*, the choices for actresses are even far more dismal. We are still living in a predominantly male-oriented society where the focus, emphasis, and importance of many things are geared towards the male gender. Create an interesting story with a strong female main character and the top actresses will kill for the part.

FILM CATEGORIES

The choices of what to write are very broad when you consider all the categories and subcategories of film: drama, melodrama, action,

action/adventure, war, mystery, film noir, horror, thriller, comedy, romantic comedy, ensemble, fantasy, sci-fi, western, sprawling epic, etc.

Since the marketplace is constantly shifting in regard to what film genres are hot—and it takes two years, on average, for a film to reach the local theater after the story has been hatched—it makes no sense to chase a hot genre. Again, write what you know about and what you'd like to see. Even if a genre is lying cold in a shallow grave, the right script might just bring it back to life.

PRODUCTION CONSIDERATIONS

Eight years of further experience support this edition of *Fade In*. One of the things I learned is that the following view, expressed in the first edition, is not accurate. I said back then: a screenplay's saleability will be greatly diminished if it is burdened by unrealistic and unreasonable production demands—even if the story is very good. In a conversation with an agent, he corrected me by saying, "A script with a high budget wouldn't hinder its saleability, even if it were a piece of junk. If studio execs aren't spending a ton of money on a film, they don't view it as a feature." When I replied, "That doesn't make any sense," the agent said, "Now you're learning."

It's hard to argue against his logic when so many bad films, with high budgets, keep coming out of Hollywood. And most of these films were made from horrible scripts. Just follow the trade publications and magazines covering the film industry. They are constantly doing articles on box-office disasters, making the point that the *deal* was obviously more important than having a good script.

In spite of the agent's opinion, I still feel it is far wiser to *maintain a sensible approach to those aspects of a script which affect production costs. What are they? The number of characters in your story, the locations, the set requirements, the use of special effects, the degree of difficulty involved in executing action sequences and stunts, and so on.*

COMMENTS ON WRITING COMEDY

Comedy is totally subjective. You either like something or you don't. Therefore, it is the most difficult genre to sell. From all the books I have read on film, the vast majority of successful comedies were initially turned down by every studio. And the stories behind making these films is one of bloody wars and battle scars. Unless a studio is dealing with an already proven comedy writer, all newcomers are viewed with even greater skepticism than writers of other genres.

While every film project carries a high risk, comedy is probably perceived as having the highest risk status. It is a lot easier for an audience to identify with a well-written drama than a comedy. Conventional wisdom then dictates that it would be far wiser to write anything but a comedy the first time. However, if you have a real knack and desire for writing comedy, then, by all means, do it. But just be prepared to walk into walls of rejection. Look at the Zucker Brothers and Jim Abrahams, the creators of *Airplane!* It was turned down by every studio until Susan Baerwald, a reader at United Artists, happened upon the script. When her studio passed on it, she recommended it to a friend, Michael Eisner, who was then president of Paramount. *Airplane!* was not only a huge hit that year, but it made the careers of the three participants.

COMEDY - THE BASIC RULE

When it comes to writing comedy, there is only one basic rule: place your characters in situations and let them act and react naturally. If you force things to happen, it won't work. The only difference among comedy writers is how each one views the world. Some see humor in everything, including tragic events and the most inane situations.

MEDIA HYPE!

One thing that really irritates me is the way the film trade publications and the national media publicize and hype the sale of spec scripts. (What is a spec script? It is a screenplay written on speculation with the hope that it might be optioned, sold, or lead to writing assignments.) While these articles are written strictly as hype and to entertain, they also create false hopes and the illusion that the whole process of writing a script and selling it is easy. These articles have another drawback. They influence the submission of many more lousy scripts by writers who are not interested in craft but money and fame, thus making it far more difficult for writers who are seriously committed to the profession.

Two newspaper articles on screenwriting published in the late 80s and early 90s stand out and are representative of the one-sided pieces still being cranked out today.

The first, "Hollywood Needs Good Stories," made the following point. ***Don't blame Hollywood for putting out bad movies when you could be writing good ones.*** The article went on to say that many of the better movies are written by first-time screenwriters (which is true) and that living in L.A. is not important (which is false as I substantiate in Chapter 12).

The second article, "Just Write Something Good and the Rest Will Happen," focused on a very young, talented, and successful screenwriter whose name appears on at least two movies a year as writer or co-writer. This screenwriter was quoted as saying forget about networking and schmoozing, write something good and the world will come to you. In reality, that is more the exception than the rule.

Neither article, nor many others like them, point out the harsh realities of the screenwriting profession. In fact, many screenwriters labor in obscurity for ten years or more before achieving success or deciding to give up out of total frustration.

MILLIONS DOLLAR SCRIPTS

Writing original screenplays on speculation is part of the journeyman process for screenwriters. You do it to develop your writing skills and to provide a sample of your work—and sometimes you may even come up with a script that is very special.

Some people are truly gifted and create a great script the first time out, while others are still struggling to develop their skills after writing ten.

In an interview, Oliver Stone said he wrote *eleven* screenplays before he got his first agent. When asked if he would ever make films out of his older scripts, he said that they will remain on the shelf, where they belong.

Some original screenplays are made into films or lead to other writing assignments, like doing rewrites or adaptations of novels.

If your goal is to write a spec script and sell it for $1 million, try becoming a brain surgeon instead—it would be much easier and make far more sense. Statistically speaking, selling a spec script for big bucks is no different than hitting the lottery.

Over the years, I acquired copies of twenty spec scripts that sold for $1 million and more. In sharing them with other writers and some of my readers, we reached an unanimous conclusion: all but two were horrible. Some were so bad that they were impossible to finish reading. Going one step further, *only one of the twenty spec scripts was made into a film and it bombed. And that film was made from one of the two scripts we liked.*

Why did this film tank? In our collective opinion—one of the key actors overplayed the role and the director used heavy-handed techniques rather than rely upon all the nuances in the script that made the story so charming. Had there been a better choice of actor and director, more in *tune* with the material, the picture *might have been successful.*

What happened to the other nineteen spec scripts that sold for $1 million and more? Sure, some were not made because of timing—not being able to put together the right director and cast to *green light* production. However, the majority of these scripts were not made because, at a later date, under careful scrutiny, studio executives realized what they thought was *cinematic gold* turned out to be pyrite or *fool's gold.* Maybe now you can understand how difficult this business is. If Hollywood is spending a million dollars and more on bad screenplays, then it is logical to assume that they are also passing up on good ones at the same time.

So why do studios pay a ton of money for bad scripts? I believe William Goldman has one of the answers. In his book, *Adventures in the Screen Trade,* he made one of the most astute observations: *no one person in the entire motion picture industry knows for sure what will work.* Thus, he coined one of the most repeated phrases:

Nobody Knows Anything.

The second reason studios buy spec scripts for megabucks is because of all the hype agents create. "You have twenty-four hours to read this script and make an offer." Once one studio makes an offer, the bidding war begins—and out of fear that another studio might be getting the upper hand by buying this *hot script*, sensibilities are lost and the cash drawers are thrown open.

When a spec script goes on the market by a big-name screenwriter, insanity rules, with some deals running as high as $4 million. One of these screenwriters had two such deals in a row and both films bombed. And guess what? That hasn't stopped the studios from continuing to throw millions at him.

THE HOLLYWOOD MERIT SYSTEM OF FAILING UPWARDS

In Hollywood, as in many industries, there are countless tales of people who *fail upwards*. It means that no matter how poorly someone performs with one project, the next one he or she will be given will be significantly greater. If a director makes a flop for $15 million, you can bet the ranch that his next picture deal will be for $25 million. Most of the time, it happens that way.

Any writer who has a film made, whether it is successful or not, obtains one important thing—an identity within the film community, and that is a *BIG PLUS*. Should you write a box office smash, especially if you are the only writer on the picture, you are *made* for quite a while. Your agent will be able to select from countless multimillion dollar deals and line up work for you for possibly the next two to three years.

STUDIO EXECUTIVES

Why do the studios, without batting an eye, automatically give big-name screenwriters multimillion dollar deals? There are two reasons. First, most of these screenwriters are very talented, and second, they have a track record with one or more successful films under their belt.

In a number of cases, hiring a big-name screenwriter who has proven talent for writing certain kinds of stories is a smart move. However, if the most desirable big-name screenwriter is not available, a studio might offer the job to another big name who is available but who may not be ideal for the subject matter. Most studio executives would rather do this than risk giving the opportunity to an unknown screenwriter who has demonstrated talent via an original screenplay but whose skills and appeal have not yet been proven at the box office.

In many instances, studio executives hire big-name writers to cover themselves. I mean, should the film fail, they can always take the position of saying that they hired the best producer, director, screenwriter, actors, and so on. Every time studio executives recommend a script for production, they are literally putting their necks on the chopping block. A few bad calls and they're history.

A studio executive's willingness to fight for a script to be made is based upon two key factors: subjective judgment (really liking something) and having a relationship with the producer, director, or writer involved.

Who has talent as a writer and what is considered good writing are totally in the eye of the beholder. Subjective judgment, therefore, is what makes selling a script in Hollywood a crap shoot and a numbers game.

Stories about it taking someone ten years to get a film made are not unusual. And it's not unusual that many of these films that are difficult to get made, because of subject matter, are often quite successful.

Think of your own reaction to films you have seen and you might have a better understanding as to how difficult it is to find a buyer for your script. I don't know about you, but if I see thirty to forty new movies a year, I may only like five and have reservations about three of them.

If I were a studio executive and you had brought *Forrest Gump* to me, I would have passed on it. Was it a bad film? No. It was a well-crafted film in every respect. It just didn't appeal to me.

After *Forrest Gump* tore up the box office ($330 million) and was the biggest film in the history of Paramount, a number of *enlightened* studio executives were quoted as saying, "We want the next *Forrest Gump* script."

My comments on that: "Hey, numbnuts, that script was available for eight years! Just ask Wendy Finerman who busted her ass to get that picture made."

The fact is: *any one of my screenplays or someone else's could be the next* **Forrest Gump** *in terms of success*.

NOBODY KNOWS ANYTHING.

Selling a script is a numbers game. *You can be rejected by ninety-nine people, then find one person who believes in your screenplay—one who turns it into a box-office hit and wins Academy Awards*.

A question every writer must answer in the face of constant rejection is—do I have the confidence to continue trying to find a buyer for this script, or should I write a new one? My answer—keep writing new scripts and don't give up on those you have confidence in.

If ten people reject your script for the same reason, you may want to seriously consider a rewrite. However, if your instincts tell you that their criticism is not valid, and you have the self-confidence, then by all means, put your head down and keep pushing forward.

Many writers are eventually able to sell scripts that have been rejected for years. But it takes a very hard-nosed, thick-skinned person to stay at it.

Don't even dream about selling a spec script for *mucho dinero*. Just concentrate on writing what you know about and what you would like to see, then find a producer, or director, or actor who shares your vision.

THE L.A. STORY

Before you follow my journey from New York to Los Angeles, a few things need to be said. As presented in Chapter 2, I only recently discovered the *real* inadequacies of my script, *Dead Man's Dance*. Therefore what is presented in this chapter does not reflect this recently acquired knowledge. At this time, I certainly have a better understanding as to why my script was rejected. In spite of a good premise, it was poorly executed. As my script analysis and rewriting strategies point out, it is quite obvious that the real potential of my story was not even closely realized.

THE STORY BEGINS

In May of 1996, I went to Los Angeles to find an agent. The whole process—from planning the trip, to spending a week there, to resolving all the opportunities with agents who were interested in me—took one hundred days. Nothing happens quickly in the film industry.

The first stage of preparing for the trip was contacting fifty agents via my *system*. Once twenty-one agents requested scripts, I worked out the critical details: travel dates, flight schedule, a place to stay, and car rental.

Given my limited financial resources, my trip had to be carefully planned. Not being able to stay with someone while I was out there was a big disadvantage. The most practical option turned out to be the Hilgard House Hotel in Westwood which is near UCLA. At $100 per night, it was very reasonable. Westwood turned out to be the ideal location, central to just about everything in Los Angeles.

Part of what helped me in getting the best hotel and car rental prices was being a member of the Automobile Club of America. Without question, the $50 per year annual dues is money well-spent. The membership provides great road service, major discounts on car

219

rentals and hotels, and access to travel information. As my L.A. story develops, you will understand how invaluable this not-for-profit corporation is to someone on the road.

Back to planning my trip. I was able to save hundreds of dollars on my plane fare by buying a non-refundable ticket two weeks ahead of time. With my plane ticket in hand, a place to stay, and a rental car arranged, I was off to Los Angeles. A week's stay in L.A. cost me $2,000—which in my present financial situation, is a lot of money. Over and above the plane, hotel, and car rental costs, meals and phone calls made up the balance.

What I am about to share with you regarding my week in Los Angeles will be extremely beneficial, in many ways.

Most agents don't arrive at their office until 10 a.m. or later. And if they represent actors, they are busy until noon doing *break-downs*— submitting a list of their clients for various auditions that are announced on a daily basis. It was difficult reaching agents before noon, and for me, that was a real problem. Since I was getting up between 3 and 4 a.m. every day, I had eight hours to kill before I could do anything. During that time, I'd exercise, walk, or work on my laptop.

After my second day in town, I was totally depressed. I was having a hard time reaching people and getting phone calls returned. Since I could not arrange appointments, I had nothing to do but to sit in my hotel room hoping for return calls on messages I'd left with agents. The thought of just showing up at an agent's office crossed my mind but common sense told me it was not a good idea.

One thing I quickly learned—agents will not meet with a writer until after they have read your work and like it. This is unfortunate but logical given the fact that time is such a precious commodity. Why should agents meet with someone they may not want to represent? Some agents, because the timing is right, might be able to get to your script in a week, however most need, on average, sixty days. Since I sent scripts to many agents only two weeks before arriving in L.A., I created a problem for myself.

It might have been far more practical to wait for every agent to respond before going out there. In that case, given the final results, there would have been no need to make the trip. On the positive side, you will now benefit from my first-hand experience.

Some agents who have not read your work might be willing to meet with you. Sometimes it is pure luck—calling at the right moment and having an invitation extended. *But don't count on it.*

Before leaving for L.A., I had an interesting conversation with one agent. He said he was impressed by my fax but, unfortunately, was too busy to read my material.

When I reminded him of the dates I would be in town, he said, "Give me a call when you arrive and we'll take a meeting." And we did. Bottom line on that meeting—we hit it off; he read two scripts, liked the writing but didn't feel the material was commercial enough. Bye, bye.

On the morning of my third day, my fortunes changed with one phone call. I was following up with a *junior agent* at a Beverly Hills agency; he had just finished reading two of my scripts. He was not only complimenting my writing, but enthusiastic over both screenplays. While I was highly elated, I learned a long time ago not to assume anything. It has nothing to do with being pessimistic, but just understanding certain realities.

The junior agent asked me about other scripts. In mentioning my action screenplay, he told me he would read it that night if I could get a copy to him during the day. I told him it was no problem. When I delivered the script to his office a few hours later, he was in a meeting so we didn't have an opportunity to meet. The final outcome from this contact will be revealed later.

During a follow-up call with another agent, I was told to stop by "at my convenience." While the agent did not comment on my script, it was obvious he had read it and wanted to talk. Without any expectations, I jumped into my car and took off.

In approaching his block, I had bad vibes. His office is located in a rather seedy area of Hollywood in a shabby, two-story art deco building. I parked across the street, got out, and locked the car. Putting change into the meter, I realized I had locked the car with the keys in the ignition and the engine running. A bad omen or what? For my own car, I carry an extra set of keys in my wallet and have never had to use them. Of course, with a rental car and only one set of keys, I was cooked.

The car was parked in front of a restaurant so I went inside seeking help. After I asked for the name of a locksmith, an elderly woman—a customer sitting at a table—overheard the conversation and probably saved me $50 by inquiring, "Are you a member of the Automobile Club?" A few minutes later, a service truck from Triple A showed up and within seconds, my car was unlocked—no charge. Remember my comment about the Automobile Club being the best $50 you will ever spend? Anyway, I thanked the service man with a $10 bill and—with the car keys safely resting in the bottom of my pants pocket—I crossed the street.

The agent's assistant led me to a cubbyhole of an office. This dingy space reeked of old Hollywood with pictures and movie posters covering the walls.

On the floor, numerous screenplays rested in three-feet-high stacks. The agent entered with my script in hand, dropped into his seat and said, "Mind if I hurt your feelings?" I responded, "It's been done before." He flashed a tight smile then proceeded to say the same thing over and over. "When you have a crime story, you have to have a good character." No matter how hard I tried to prompt specifics out of him, he kept repeating that same line and the reason was obvious—he hadn't read the script. He might have skimmed over a few pages, but that was it. There was no point in arguing or getting angry, so as quickly as possible, I politely thanked him for his time and went on my way.

Later that afternoon, I called an agent who had read one of my screenplays two years earlier. I asked if we could meet so I could update him on my new scripts. Sounding a bit frazzled, he told me he had a five o'clock appointment at the Beverly-Wilshire Hotel and could meet me at the Tea Room there at four-thirty. I told him I would be there. A firm believer in punctuality, I arrived at the Beverly-Wilshire twenty minutes ahead of time. The only problem was—I couldn't find a parking space no matter how many times I drove around the block.

Finally I found a space on a residential street one block behind the hotel. I went to the Tea Room and waited. Five o'clock passed, no agent, so I called his office only to reach his voice mail. Maybe he was in transit. When he didn't show by five-thirty, I left. Returning to my rental car, I found a ticket on the windshield for $37.50. As it turned out, I had parked in a residential zone that required a permit. No agent and a parking ticket—how's that for a double whammy?

The next morning I called the agent to find out what happened. He told me that our appointment had been for that upcoming evening, not the previous day. Talk about feeling like a dummy. The day before, when we were making the arrangements to meet, I was on an outside pay phone on Sunset Boulevard. There was certainly enough noise and distractions that might have precluded me from hearing him say "tomorrow." Whether it was my mistake or not, it didn't matter anymore because the agent said that meeting today would be out of the question.

During follow-ups with the agents who were sent scripts, two told me they were sending them back, unread, explaining that they didn't have the time to read them, and another ten rejected them without comments.

One agent was exceptionally nice. When I first called him from New York, following up on my contact fax, he told me he doesn't consider new writers unless they are referred by someone he knows.

However, given my concise, well-written fax, he requested one of my scripts. When I contacted him during my week in Los Angeles, he passed on the script but was very complimentary of my writing. He asked how I was doing with other agents. At that point, I told him that two had read one or more scripts and had expressed interest in me. He made an offer I found amazing. He said that if it got to a point where I had to choose between agents and needed advice, I could call him and he would tell me whatever he could about them. While I would like to acknowledge him here, I dare not mention his name or he would be deluged by countless struggling writers hoping he would show them a similar courtesy.

When it was apparent there would be no other opportunities to meet with agents, I decided to make a few production calls. One was to a V.P. of production at Touchstone who is a long-time friend of my new neighbors. Using their name, I contacted the executive. When the V.P.

said he would like to read a couple of scripts to get familiar with my work, I offered to drop them off. He told me his company's policy requires that scripts be submitted by an agent. I explained my representation had yet to be resolved, but had two agencies interested in me.

In mentioning the agency names, he highly recommended the one in Beverly Hills and said if the opportunity presented itself, I should sign with them. He asked me to have that agency send him two of my scripts. After getting off the phone with the V.P. at Touchstone, I called the Beverly Hills agent. Unable to reach him, I gave his assistant a detailed message regarding the request for scripts by the Touchstone executive. This was on Friday—two days before I was to leave.

By the way, the day before calling the executive at Touchstone, the junior agent at the Beverly Hills agency informed me that he liked the action script as much as the first two. He explained to me that other agents in his office would read my scripts and then a decision would be made. Things were looking very promising.

Nothing can better illustrate the importance of networking and knowing someone who can open doors than my second production call. In this case, I was contacting a director whose last two pictures were box-office hits. In calling his office, I reached his voice mail and left a very specific message: I told him my name, mentioned I was a friend of so-and-so's, and said I would appreciate the opportunity to meet. I then left the number where I could be reached. Later that day, to my surprise, the director's assistant called to set up an appointment. Since the director's office was on a studio lot, his assistant told me that a drive-on pass would be waiting for me at the gate.

The appointment was for Friday morning at 10 a.m. This was Wednesday. The assistant called me on Thursday and said there was a problem and could I possibly meet next week. When I told her I was leaving for New York on Sunday, she said she'd call me back. The director's assistant called me four times before finalizing an appointment for Friday afternoon. There is no doubt in my mind that this director made major changes in his schedule to accommodate seeing me. Right then, I realized the importance of mentioning my friend who has spent thirty-five years in publicity working for two major studios and knows everyone—and I mean everyone.

Meeting The Director

Pulling onto the studio lot in my rental car, I gave the guard my name. He smiled and said, "Good afternoon, Mr. Berman, we were expecting you." Of course, in my mind, the next thing I hear is: "Now get the hell out of here! We don't need any more writers!"

How Old Are You?

A little explanation is needed here to make a point about something that happened during my visit to the director's office. Saying that a given writer has talent, it would be hard to argue against experience (age) being an asset, right? With the exception of those screenwriters who have successfully worked their way into their sixties—like Robert Towne and William Goldman—writers forty and over are considered old and passé, because the vast majority of studio executives are under thirty.

It's no secret. I'm fifty-two and what little hair I have left is gray. However, given my physical condition, energy, enthusiasm, and sense of humor, most people guess me to be—for whatever it's worth—in my mid-forties.

Having had a number of phone conversations with the director's assistant, my assessment of her was: mid-twenties, bright, and hard-working. Of course, not having met me or knowing anything about me, my age was probably nothing she even considered. All she knew was she was talking to a writer who wanted to meet with her boss.

When I walked into her office, her jaw went slack as if I looked like some relic from the Cretaceous period or Grandpa Jones from Hee-Haw. She was literally taken aback by my age. It's possible that my physical stature (6' 5") might have triggered that reaction, but I firmly believe that seeing someone my age prompted her response.

Since most writers she comes in contact with are probably in their early twenties or thirties, I can understand her reaction. How do I feel about age? It's a chronological number, that's all. Some people are old at twenty—others are young at ninety. More than anything, it has to do with attitude and how you see life—and, of course, your general health and appearance are significant factors.

Back To Meeting The Director

There is something magical about being on a studio lot—and it has nothing to do with seeing famous actors, which I didn't. It has to do with the atmosphere. I mean, here I was sitting in the director's office, on the second floor, looking out the window at palm trees glistening in the afternoon sunlight.

Whenever a meeting is arranged through a mutual friend with someone who is capable of helping your career, it is difficult to tell if that person is giving you serious consideration or just going through the motions. In one respect, it doesn't matter because it is simply an opportunity that could lead to something. My friend, who made the meeting possible, told me the director was one of the most honorable men he knows in Hollywood. And believe me, that is saying a lot.

Did I have the director's undivided attention? No. He seemed a bit *wired* that day because he had decided to get out of town for several weeks and had a lot of loose ends to wrap up. While our conversation took place during and between a dozen phone calls, I got the impression he could do five things at once with great efficiency.

During our small talk, I asked him what he was working on now. He replied—swear to God—in an almost state of panic, "I'm unemployed." The film business is such that unless you are working, your last job might just be your *last job*.

About the director's phone calls. One was to his agent, another to a studio head, then one to an actress. In one conversation, he was complaining about a famous actor who was interested in a part he might be casting. He was saying, "You know so-and-so, if he's on the picture, the budget'll be inflated with all his add-ons, and I'll be fighting him over who is actually directing." In speaking to someone else, he mentioned a big-name producer who wanted him to direct a script. He said to the other party, "I'd like to work with this producer but the script he wants me to do is a real piece of shit." In my mind I'm saying, "Hey, Mr. Director, how 'bout letting me rewrite that piece of shit for you?"

Overhearing his conversations, it was not difficult to understand what was happening. The director had a lot of irons in the fire regarding different film projects, but nothing firm. One project was dependent upon a actor. Apparently, if the actor said yes, the project would go forward—but the actor, coming off a successful picture, was being noncommittal because he was considering his options. Everyone was jockeying for position.

After explaining to the director that I was in town to meet with agents, he picked up the phone to set up an immediate appointment for me with his agency. It not only happened to be one of the big three, but it was the same agency which was currently looking at two of my scripts. He offered to call the agent I was dealing with to prompt an answer. I thanked him but said it would be better not to force a response at this time.

Seeing my bulging shoulder bag, the director said, "I suppose you have some scripts with you." I gave him two which he said he would take with him and read. He told me to call his assistant in two weeks and she would pass along his feedback. The final outcome—he said he liked the scripts but nothing more. Did he read them? I have no way of knowing for sure, but given my friend's high regard for the man, I would say he probably did. Did he honestly like them? Who knows? It doesn't matter because he didn't option them or make me any kind of offer.

BACK TO NEW YORK

Upon returning from Los Angeles on a Sunday, a number of friends called to find out what happened. I told them I had opportunities pending with two agents, but wouldn't know the final outcome for possibly three weeks. When one friend pressed me for my best guess as to how things would work out, I told him that both opportunities would probably go down in flames. He said, "How can you be so pessimistic?" I explained to him the realities as I perceived them. My opportunities with both agencies were dependent upon the reaction of a number of agents, not just the one who liked my work. I pointed out that it is highly unlikely that "x" number of agents will unanimously agree on any writer's work. Also, with enough declining votes, it's highly unlikely that the agent (referring here to the junior agent at the Beverly Hills agency) who liked my work would remain strong in his convictions and insist upon signing me in the face of so much opposition.

First thing Monday morning, I sent a fax to the Beverly Hills agent to confirm the message I gave his assistant that past Friday regarding the V.P. at Touchstone. Two days later, I attempted to follow up with the agent directly. Only I couldn't reach him, nor did he return my call.

Five days later, I called the V.P. at Touchstone and found out the agent had not sent my scripts over. Over a period of two weeks, I called the Beverly Hills agent three more times and followed up with a fax. Guess what? He was always busy when I called and never returned my phone calls or answered my fax. My instincts, unfortunately, were right. The other agents didn't like my scripts and the junior agent folded up like a cheap camera. While rejection is never easy, being ignored like that is insulting. But guess what? Things like that happen all the time.

WHAT I LEARNED FROM GOING TO LOS ANGELES

After making my trip to the coast and spending $2,000 in only one week, I have come to the conclusion: ***To be a screenwriter, it is absolutely essential to live in Los Angeles.***

Having access to people within the film industry on a daily basis, establishing relationships, and taking meetings are as important as having writing talent.

David Brown said that it is not necessary for a writer to live in Los Angeles and that a good script will provide you with access to people. From Mr. Brown's perspective, as a producer, I couldn't agree with him more. However, as he acknowledged, many good scripts are passed over by inexperienced readers who are, more than likely, the ones who will be making judgments on your work and determining whether or not you will work. Therefore, living in L.A. and *knowing* development people or studio executives can often determine *who* covers your script. More on this in the next chapter.

For an unknown writer, short trips to Los Angeles can be very costly. It's often a hit-or-miss proposition regarding who you have an opportunity to meet. Living there gives you the flexibility of taking meetings anytime.

READERS, AGENTS, AND THE SYSTEM

STUDIO READERS

Screenplays are the foundation of every film, and nothing can happen until a script is chosen. Given the importance of the screenplay, you would think that the selection process would be more efficient. A producer was quoted as saying something like: "Studio readers are all egomaniacs who are nothing more than frustrated writers predisposed to trashing other writers' work." Very few writers will argue against that point.

In every career field, there is a small nucleus (five percent) of top performers—people who clearly exceed all others in ability, performance, and achievements. That means, out of all the doctors, lawyers, athletes, or studio readers, only five percent of the total are true professionals performing at the highest possible standards. From that point down, everyone else functions in lesser degrees.

For the most part, the industry works like this. *Given the sheer volume of screenplays submitted to studios and production companies, it's impossible for two or more people to read the same script unless the first person really likes it.*

Your script will be assigned to a reader, and if that reader pans it, it's highly unlikely that anyone else within that entity will look at it. What agents, producers, and studio executives read is coverage—a two- to three-page critique of your script. Although rare, an agent or producer may find something interesting in negative coverage, such as the story's premise or an unusual character. In that case, he or she might read the script and come to a different conclusion.

A good development executive will selectively assign scripts to readers. It would be a complete waste of time and money to give an ensemble piece to a reader who thinks action scripts are high art. But it happens all the time. Do studio or production executives read scripts? Some do, but the majority of them don't—even if they say they do. Sure, executives will read a screenplay after five other people in their company have given it thumbs up, but it's highly unlikely that they will be the first to read a screenplay by an unknown writer—unless they know the writer personally and like him or her. (See why it's important to live in L.A.?)

So, who are studio readers? They are usually young, single people (writers) who are looking for a way into the biz. They certainly don't do it for the money.

The job can be a great stepping stone if the reader discovers the next *Forrest Gump* script or submits one of his or her own and it is sold or goes into development. While some studio readers are fair in preparing coverage, most are ruthless. Granted, much of what they have to read is absolutely horrible, but even when they find a well-written screenplay, they may pass on it because the subject matter is unappealing *to them* or they simply had a bad day and take it out on the writer.

As it applies to unknown writers, ***no studio or freelance reader looks past the script***. This means that even if it is obvious that a given script, with minor improvements, could possibly have great potential, it doesn't matter—the reader will pass on it. In turn, writers with a successful track record are given special consideration. Part of it has to do with the fact that these writers are proven talents; the other reason has to do with the ego of the reader being in a position to critique them.

Take a good, solid script written by a famous writer and submit it to a studio reader under an unknown writer's name. At the same time, take a poorly-written script by an unknown writer and submit it using a famous writer's name. Ninety-nine out of a hundred times, you can guess what the outcome will be.

Submitting a screenplay to an agent, studio, or production company is like a game of roulette. If the right person reads it, you could be on your way.

Writers have no way of knowing how fairly their scripts are being covered by readers. Therefore you must be totally confident in knowing that you have, at the very least, turned over your best possible work.

Obviously if you know someone or can get a referral from someone who knows a production or studio executive, your script might not be dumped into any reader's hands. You might be given special consideration. In either case, no matter what you are told, you will never know for sure—unless, of course, your script is bought or optioned.

Most writers get little or no feedback on their scripts when they are rejected. And in some cases, knowing why could be extremely helpful because some of the criticism might be very valid. As a matter of policy, agents, producers, and studios don't share coverage with writers.

Here's another little ditty. Many production companies file screenplay coverage in computers under the author's name and title and share this information. Therefore opportunities with other production entities might be lost.

This is obviously totally unfair. Good scripts are often panned because the subject matter may not appeal to the reader, or because most readers tend to be overly critical. There is a way around this problem. If you decide to recirculate a script that was rejected and you don't want to take any chances that *computer coverage* will sink opportunities with different production companies, then **retitle it, assign new names to all the key characters, and change the page count.** With a computer, the amount of work involved in making these changes is minimal— and, in the end, you will have the peace of mind to know that your script will not be rejected based upon previous coverage.

In almost every case, a rejected script is only read by one person. And if that person is an outside reader, you might be able to go back to the same production company. Also, with high industry turnover, the executive you originally had contact with is probably gone.

THE NAKED TRUTH ABOUT COVERAGE

Over the years, I acquired coverage on four of my scripts through a friend, or a friend of a friend, who opened doors for me with different production executives. Up front I will tell you that reading coverage of your own work can be a *gut-wrenching experience*. Out of the four, only one was written with any degree of fairness and objectivity.

My very first screenplay, *The 12/20 Club*—even given my limitations as a writer then—was pretty damn good because I was writing about what I knew and had experienced firsthand. And for that reason alone, this script is better than some written years later with improved skills. As previously mentioned, *The 12/20 Club* is about a thirty-eight-year-old executive who puts together his old high school rock 'n' roll band, twenty years later. The story focuses on the impact the music has on his personal life (a wife and two children) and his career.

In his coverage, the reader was highly critical of the main character's occupation because it wasn't glamorous. The executive works for a food broker representing many brands of food products—which he sells to supermarket chains. The industry is *very conservative*. The waiting rooms at grocery chain store headquarters, where salespeople bide their time waiting to see grocery buyers, have an atmosphere not unlike the city morgue. The point the reader missed was this—the reason the executive wanted (his motivation) to put his old band back together was the need for an outlet from his unexciting career. That's not too hard to comprehend and yet it went right over this reader's head.

From there the reader kept saying how I missed all these golden opportunities to do this and that with the story. The reader was essentially *changing my story*. Based upon the reader's coverage, the production executive passed on my script and most certainly didn't read it.

I have always followed my instincts in regard to what to write. To date, my screenplays include drama, slapstick comedy, romantic comedy, ensemble, film noir, thriller, action, and sci-fi. My desire to write different genres also reflects my broad taste and appreciation for different kinds of films. I can go from watching *Die Hard*—an action movie—to *The Remains of the Day*—an introspective Ivory/Merchant film that is a major yawn for some people.

My next screenplay to come under the harsh scrutiny of a reader was *Hurley's Glide*. It is an ensemble piece which examines the relationships of four childhood friends, age forty, who only see each other once a year vacationing on a lake in New Hampshire. The story explores the changes in their lives since their last vacation and those issues yet to be resolved. Like *The 12/20 Club*, *Hurley's Glide* is based upon personal experience, so the characters are well-sketched, and the plot both seriously and humorously addresses contemporary issues. All things considered, my execution of the story was very good.

In the tradition of the genre, *Hurley's Glide* emphasizes character over plot and evokes a similar tone, feel, and pacing to *The Big Chill, Return of the Secaucus Seven, The Four Seasons, Diner, Peter's Friends, Grand Canyon* and *Indian Summer*. The bottom line with ensemble films is you either like them or you don't. Now to set the record straight. Most friends who read *Hurley's Glide* admitted that they didn't like it because they don't like the genre. It was too slow for them. One said, "I never understood what the big deal was about *The Big Chill*."

When my script, *Hurley's Glide*, was submitted to a production company, it was just my luck that the reader assigned to it didn't like nor understand the genre. This was obvious because of his remarks which a writer-director friend described as the most malicious coverage he had ever read. It wasn't enough for this reader to deep-six my script, he had to go on and attack—in two pages of elaborate notes—every aspect of my writing in the most spiteful tone you could possibly imagine. I was so pissed off after reading his coverage, I wanted to track the bastard down and slap him senseless. Maybe now you can understand why production companies don't want to share coverage with writers. If they did, the homicide rate in L.A. would probably double!

My next experience with coverage wasn't quite as bad, but it was frustrating. This reader, who is also a writer, is someone I know. He's intelligent, insightful, and direct in his comments—and someone with a very specific point of view. Here's a conversation between us that occurred after he read a third draft copy of my romantic comedy screenplay, *Cafe Armadillo*.

The PHONE RINGS -- I grab it.

                    ME
               (into phone)
          Hello.

                    READER (V.O.)
          I finished your script.

                    ME
          Oh, hi Mel.

                    READER (V.O.)
          I finished your script and thought
          I'd give you a call.

                    ME
          So, what'd you think?

                    READER (V.O.)
          It's mediocre at best.

I grab a bottle of Jack Daniels and take a big hit.

                    ME
          What was the problem?

                    READER (V.O.)
          Where do you want me to start?

                    ME
               (to myself in V.O.)
          Here we go.
               (into phone)
          What was the biggest problem you
          had with it?

                    READER (V.O.)
          For one thing, I knew Barry and
          Jill would end up together at the
          end.

                    ME
          So?

                    READER (V.O.)
          It was too predictable.

                    ME
          Lemme ask you this. Were there
          any doubts in your mind about Harry
          and Sally getting together at
          the end of *When Harry Met Sally*?
               (MORE)

ME (cont'd)
Or what about the Tom Hanks and
Meg Ryan characters in *Sleepless in Seattle*?

READER (V.O.)
That's different.

ME
How so?

READER (V.O.)
It's just different, that's all.

ME
What else.

READER (V.O.)
I had a real problem with your Cal character.

ME
I thought I did a pretty good job
in developing all my characters.

READER (V.O.)
Barry and Jill were okay, but I
didn't get a sense of who Cal is.

ME
What if I did this...

(Not to bore you with the details, I listed eight things that would
reveal different aspects of Cal's character.)

ME (cont'd)
So, Mel, if I did all those
things, how would you feel about
the Cal character then?

READER (V.O.)
Now you're on track.

                              ME
                         (pointedly)
             All those things I just mentioned?
             They're already in the script.
                       (on his silence)
             Would you like me to tell you what
             page each one is on?

The silence continues.

How did the reader miss those things? Since many of the character issues were handled very subtly, they could be easily missed, which presents a quandary. Whenever possible, I address the various elements within my scripts with as much subtlety as possible because it adds depth to the work. You then have to ask yourself—if the reader doesn't see it, what good does it do?

Readers often miss subtext because they read quickly. Some even skip reading scene descriptions and follow the story by concentrating on just dialogue. In that case, they will most definitely miss subtext that is treated visually because it is outlined in the scene description. Remember, freelance readers are paid by the script—the more they read, the more money they make.

Studio executives, the noncreative types, are notorious for honing in on certain aspects of a script. They love to talk about the *character's arc* (development/change) and have a real problem with those scenes which rely upon subtext. "I don't think the audience will understand this. Maybe you could be... a little more direct?" The audience is a lot sharper than that studio executive.

Back to the reader, Mel. One other major issue came up in regard to my romantic comedy screenplay which is worth mentioning, because it best exemplifies how a reader's subjective judgment so strongly influences his or her assessment of a writer's work. Mel had a major problem with the three characters abruptly taking off for a road trip to Texas. In discussing this issue with him, it soon became apparent what prompted his criticism. Because he wouldn't do it, he found it impossible to believe anyone else would. No amount of explaining how those character types and their motives were well-established in the script would budge him from his position. In Chapter 8, I mentioned that it's not a good idea to try to defend your point of view with someone who is on a different wave length. My experience with Mel reinforces that point. Readers make those kind of judgments every day. Subsequently, some scripts with real potential are passed over. *IF you can convince a production executive to read your script, as opposed to handing it over to any reader, you will be far better off.*

AGENTS

Today the power in the film industry lies with the agents, because they control the talent.

Agents work long hours under pressure from clients and studios and are saturated with talent they can't keep steadily employed - the nature of the biz. This is why they don't respond to the hordes of aspiring actors, writers, and directors beating on their doors. They don't have the time. However, agents are always interested in new talent and, with the right approach, you can get their attention.

THE AGENT/STUDIO RELATIONSHIP

Through an agreement with licensed agents, studios have access to an endless supply of material and are protected from lawsuits by writers who claim their work has been plagiarized.

THE AGENT/WRITER RELATIONSHIP

To the advantage of the screenwriter who is represented, agents know which studios and producers would be most interested in certain projects and can get to the decision-maker without delay. The biggest gripe agents have about writers is that they are lazy, while writers complain that they almost always find the work themselves and the agent just cuts the deal. Of course, if you're a screenwriter on the studios' *A list*, both agents and studios will cater to you.

In the first edition of *Fade In*, I stressed the importance of having an agent because of the difficulty of getting production companies to read unsolicited material. Through experience, my opinion on this issue has changed for two reasons. First, it is just as difficult to interest an agent in your work as a production company; and second, with the right approach, you can get either agents or production companies to read your script. The ideal situation would be to find an agent first, but if you can't, then pursuing production companies would be the next step. And should you make a sale or have your work optioned, at that point you will need a club to fend off all the agents who will descend upon you.

In this chapter, I will share with you my *system* for approaching production companies and studios which has allowed me, without an agent, to have my screenplays read by more than fifty percent of those people contacted. In many cases, when production companies declined to read my work, it was not based upon a lack of interest, but due to timing. Calling back at a later date, I was able to submit my script. In reality, the success rate with my *system* is actually closer to eighty percent.

If you approach agents and/or production companies in a professional manner and make the right impression, they will read your work. Every writer starting out should take a crack at trying to attract an agent because you could get lucky and find one right away. If you can interest an agent in representing you without having to perform the dance of death through coils of fire, then do it. If you can't, then realize that your time and energy would be best spent pursuing production companies and studios.

FINDING AN AGENT - THE FIRST STEP

Talent aside, *who you know* often determines opportunities. While this statement applies to every industry, it is significantly more important within the movie business, since the nucleus of active players is relatively small in comparison to the masses seeking entry and work.

NETWORKING

The practice of reaching out and contacting people and utilizing them and their contacts is known as networking. Networking is an extremely important activity which, at some point, can lead to opportunity. Some people find it difficult contacting *strangers* and asking for help. If you put those feelings aside, you will find that *when you use the right approach, even someone who is a stranger will often be willing to help you.*

Networking activities include making phone calls, writing letters, sending faxes, socializing, and following up on all leads. It's creating visibility for yourself.

The first step in finding an agent is to make a list of everyone you know in the film industry. Okay, so you don't know anyone. No problem. You may have a friend, an old college roommate, a distant cousin, know of a friend's friend who may be in the industry, or be aware of someone in a peripheral business who can open a door for you.

If you're approaching someone you've remained in contact with, he or she will gladly help you. However, if you're approaching someone you have not seen or had contact with in *many years*, that is another story. In these circumstances, don't *hem* and *haw* and say that you've been meaning to call, especially when it is obvious you are calling for a favor. Be honest and straightforward. Explain what you are trying to do while expressing your gratitude for any assistance he or she may be able to provide.

As you develop contacts, make a directory so you can keep track of everyone you talk to and meet. It's also important to inform those who have tried to help of your progress—even if their lead turned out to be a dead end. Let them know what you are doing and thank them for their help anyway. Your gesture will be greatly appreciated.

The importance of networking can't be stressed enough, especially a *firsthand* referral. As previously illustrated, the mere mention of a name often magically opens doors. The person making the referral doesn't have to be famous or even in the industry, just known by the other party.

INFORMATION SOURCES

The second step in pursuing an agent is to contact the Writers Guild of America for their approved list of agencies—a roster which is updated on a regular basis. It's available to nonmembers for a nominal fee (call [213] 951-4000 for info) and it is a good source of finding reputable agents. The WGA list provides the agency's name, address, and phone number, and also indicates whether or not an agency will accept unsolicited material. The only drawback of their list is that it doesn't provide the names of agents, which is a problem because you should always address correspondence to a person—and not use "To Whom It May Concern" in your cover letter.

Without question, the best source of information on agents is the *Hollywood Agents & Managers Directory*. It has a complete agency listing: address, phone number, fax number, and roster of agents by name and title. You will find information on this directory, as well as the *Hollywood Creative Directory*, in the Appendix under "Section 5: Industry Sources Books." *The Creative Directory* not only lists 1,500 production companies and studios with all the personal information, but also provides their production credits. Both are an absolute *MUST* for the screenwriter.

BASIC RULES FOR MAKING SCREENPLAY SUBMISSIONS

In submitting a script, include a brief cover letter that states: "As requested, enclosed is a copy of my original comedy screenplay, *Dead From the Neck Up*. Thank you for your interest in my work. I look forward to hearing from you at your convenience."

Reminder: It takes anywhere from three to eight weeks for an agent or production company to respond once they have your script. So it wouldn't be a bad idea to check in with them after three weeks as a **soft reminder.**

When it comes to producing copies of your script, a good laserjet printer can save you a lot of money in the long run—especially if you reside in a high-cost-of-living area. At my local print shop, the cost of copies runs $.07 per page in quantities of ten or more screenplays. In Los Angeles, I found a number of copy stores that charge only $.025 per page with no quantity requirements. On top of that, they provide punched paper, covers, and paper fasteners—at no additional cost.

Screenplays should be presented on standard white paper—8-1/2" x 11". If you are having your script copied, make sure it is done on a high-quality machine. Provide a crisp, well-printed original. After you pick up your copies, prepare each set with a standard three-hole punch and secure your screenplay with No. 5 paper fasteners; never submit it loose. Don't use any fancy covers or binders. Pick up some ivory-colored card stock (67#) from any good copy store or stationary supply and use that for your front and back covers. The title page should be as illustrated for *Dead Man's Dance*. The screenplay title is positioned in the center of the page in bold CAPITAL LETTERS surrounded by quotation marks; two single spaces below, type Original Screenplay by; and two spaces below that, your name. In the far-right margin on the bottom of the page, include your complete address, telephone number, and fax number.

In preparing a title page, it's not necessary to indicate what draft it is. Everyone in the industry will assume it has been rewritten many times, so there is no need to tell them how many. However, when a screenplay is going into production, it is essential for a producer and director to know which draft they are reading in order to track the writer's progress.

When you have an opportunity to submit your screenplay to some-one, don't include a *self-addressed stamped envelope* —even if it is requested. First of all, every time I've provided a SASE in order to comply, the script was never returned. That's a waste of three dollars—the cost today of sending a script via First Class mail. Second, a returned script is so *dog-eared*, sending it out to anyone else would reflect poorly upon you. Only a clean, fresh- looking screenplay should be submitted.

If you are an *unknown writer*, the only time you should make contact with anyone in the industry is when you have a screenplay you are confident in and proud of showing. ***Never submit an outline, narrative treatment, or synopsis***. A finished screenplay is the only way a writer's talent can be assessed and a story properly evaluated. Given the limited scope of a synopsis, the real quality aspects of your characters and story may not be apparent.

If someone asks for a synopsis, do your best to convince that person to look at your script. Encountering this situation, I make the point that my script is only "x" number of pages and guarantee it will be a fast read because it is well-written. In most cases, it works. If someone says, "Are you saying that I'm going to like this?" My response is, "I have no way of knowing that. All I'm saying is that it will be an easy read." Given all the horrible screenplays these people are subjected to, it's a comforting factor.

Never forward a script without first having someone agree to look at it. In most cases, an agent, production company, or studio return unsolicited material to the sender unopened and *unread*. Sending an unsolicited screenplay to someone is analogous to showing up at a party when you have not been invited. Besides being real tacky and unprofessional, it's a waste of time and three dollars worth of postage.

Again, never use "To Whom It May Concern" in your correspondence.

When contacting someone by name, using the correct spelling is critical because it personalizes things. That is why the *Hollywood Agents & Managers Directory* and the *Hollywood Creative Directory* are so valuable to writers.

In contacting agents, my correspondence is directed to them personally; with production companies, it is to the development executives' assistants. ***An agent's or production executive's assistant is often helpful if you treat him or her with respect and not like some obstacle you have to navigate around.*** Assistants are in those positions to learn the business and move up the ladder. On top of that, they will probably be the first to read your screenplay. (More comments on assistants to follow.)

THE SYSTEM

After my screenwriting method and advice on punctuality and follow-through, the system will be the third most important benefit of the book.

A big part of the battle is getting agents or producers to read your screenplay because it requires two hours they just don't have or paying an outside reader.

That is what the *system* is all about—getting people to read your work. It is a two-step approach: a fax and follow-up phone call(s). The purpose of your fax is to get to speak with the person and, from there, convince him or her to read your screenplay.

While having an agent like your work is totally out of your hands, at the very least, you want an agent to read your work. Hopefully, out of all those who do, one will respond enthusiastically and want to represent you.

Without having the benefit of an introduction, it's next to impossible for an unknown writer to reach an agent by phone. That is why initial contacts are best handled by written communication and followed up with a phone call. And to that point, a well-written fax is the most effective way of making an introduction.

FAXES ARE TREATED DIFFERENTLY

The fax has a decided advantage over letters and even e-mail. Letters take time to reach their destination and have to be opened and sorted. With e-mail, as a rule, it is only seen by the person it is sent to; and once the message is read, it is usually dumped. With a fax, there is a certain immediacy where people, in my experience, read them almost right away. In most cases, if I fax someone in L.A. early in the morning, EST, by late afternoon, PST, he or she has read it. In the last line of my fax, I tell the agent or production assistant that I will follow up with a phone call. This way, since he or she is expecting to hear from me, it's a lot easier getting through. It's not like a *cold call* where the other person doesn't know what the call is about—which makes them reluctant to take it. I usually make the first follow-up call after 7 p.m. EST (4 p.m., PST), the same day the fax is sent.

PREPARING YOUR FAX

Your goal in preparing a fax is to present yourself, and the screenplay you are offering, in a way that is as unique and interesting as possible. If you do, the agent (or producer) will be very receptive to your follow-up call. And there will be those rare occasions when someone will actually call you first. A one-page fax is best, but definitely use no more than two pages—and no cover page because it's a waste of paper. On the first page of your fax you indicate the number of pages.

You want to write the fax with an approach that makes you and your script stand out from the crowd of wanna-bes deluging agents and production companies with faxes. One development executive told me

243

she receives an average of fifty faxes a day from people outside her normal network of contacts. Does she read them all? No. She scans the pile and picks out those that catch her eye. The fax, like a screenplay page, must be first appealing to the eye in form—neat and well-organized— and well-written so that reading only a line or two creates the impression that the sender is someone worthy of consideration.

The sample faxes presented in this chapter are exact copies of what I send to agents and production companies.

As noted in my fax, I mention everything pertaining to my writing background—from being the author of a book on screenwriting to my previous experiences in writing for national magazines on diversified subject matter. Since the *New York Times* is one of the most important newspapers in the world, faxing a copy of an article on me, as the second page, gives me an edge over other writers. The focus of the article is on my weekly jazz sessions that I run at my home as an outlet from writing. These sessions, attracting noted musicians, are now in their fifth year. With those agents, production execs, and assistants who have an interest in music, it is a great groundbreaker.

In presenting your background, focus on your writing-related experiences. Maybe you were the editor of your high school newspaper or had articles published in a noted science magazine—whatever. In describing your material, present just enough information to make it enticing so the agent will want to know more. Never give the impression that you are sending out a form fax or letter. Write in such a way that it appears to be personalized.

After a computer and printer, a fax machine is the most important piece of equipment for a screenwriter. If you don't own one or have access to a friend's, get one. If that is impossible, then write letters following the guidelines outlined here.

FOLLOW-UP PROCEDURES

When following up with agents by phone, exercise patience because they are under constant pressure from clients and studios and are handicapped by long working hours.

When calling an agent, you will invariably be screened by the switchboard, or the agent's assistant, or get dumped into an oblivion known as *voice mail hell.* If you can't get through on your first call, leave a very specific message: "This is so-and-so. I am following up on my fax. When you have an opportunity, can you please call me at...." Rarely will the agent call back unless your fax really impresses him or her. Sometimes the agent's assistant will call and request your script or tell you that the agency is not considering new clients at this time. If that is the case, you say: "You'll be sorry for passing me up!" Then slam the phone down. *Only kidding!*

If the agent or assistant doesn't respond to your first message after a day or two, call back. You want to strike, as the saying goes, while the iron is hot.

I will usually make five follow-up calls within a week and a half of sending a fax. If I can't get through or have my messages returned after five calls, the agent or production assistant is not interested.

In large production companies where there might be three or more production or development executives, if one has no interest in seeing your script, try another—without mentioning your experience with the first.

Earlier I stressed the importance of treating assistants with respect. Production or development executives' assistants are usually listed by name in the *Hollywood Creative Directory.* However, agents' assistants are not always listed in the *Hollywood Agents & Managers Directory.* In making your first follow-up phone call to an agent, make a point of getting the assistant's name and asking for his or her help in getting through to the agent. Assistants are usually inundated with work, so on those days when he or she sounds harried, be polite, not pushy, and keep the conversation short. You might say, "Things sound a little crazy right now, tell me when it is convenient and I'll call back." This goes a long way in winning someone over, and in most cases, they will tell you when it's best to call back. And when you do make that second call, you will find someone who is far more receptive and interested in helping you. On those days when it is obvious that the assistant sounds relaxed and not distracted by pressing matters, making small talk can be very beneficial. It can help you establish a positive identity with that person and possibly be the starting point of a long-term business relationship. Today's assistant could be tomorrow's agent or studio executive.

POSITIVE ATTITUDE

Being upbeat, cheerful, and positive tends to prompt a more favorable response from those you are calling. Stay away from negative impulses. Don't say, "I know you're busy and probably don't have time to talk to me." The minute you make that remark, the other person is likely to say you're right, and the next thing you know, you're listening to a dial tone.

My sample faxes are outlined on the next pages, followed by some very specific comments regarding their use.

ROBERT A. BERMAN
Street, City, State Zip Code
Telephone/Fax Numbers

TRANSMISSION: 2 Pages

DATE: November 14, 1996

MEMO TO: Steve Morse
                   Agency For Crazed Writers
                   Fax (310) XXX-XXXX

FROM: Bob Berman

I am a screenwriter and author of the book, *Fade In: The Screenwriting Process*, published by Michael Wiese Productions. My writing credits also include articles in national magazines on wine, business, music, fishing, and humor. The second page of this transmission is an article about me from the *New York Times*. Below are descriptions of two original screenplays which I am offering as samples of my writing.

Title: *DEAD MAN'S DANCE*
Genre: Thriller
Form: Original screenplay - 100 pages
Log Line: When a woman disappears after supposedly seeing the man her father murdered, her sister searches for her.

Overview: When Kerry Parker's sister is found murdered outside a small New England town, a trail leads to a police Lieutenant. In pursuing him, the plot takes a number of unexpected turns and uncovers a conspiracy involving a Mafia Criminal Relocation Program.

Title: *SCREECHERS*
Genre: Sci-fi Thriller
Form: Original Screenplay - 97 pages
Log Line: A weekend in rural Pennsylvania turns into a nightmare for eight friends. (*Big Chill* meets *Alien*)

Overview: Eight friends arrive at a farm house late one night. The next morning they discover blotches of earth stained with congealed blood and no signs of human or animal life. Running for their lives, they are killed off, one by one, by *unseen* predators. Will any of them survive to reach safety?

I will follow up with a phone call and, at your request, forward both scripts or one of your choice.

ROBERT A. BERMAN
Street, City, State Zip Code
Telephone/Fax Numbers

TRANSMISSION: 2 Pages

DATE: November 14, 1996

MEMO TO: Jason Taylor, Assistant
Danger Zone Productions
Fax (310) XXX-XXXX

FROM: Bob Berman

I am a screenwriter and author of the book, *Fade In: The Screenwriting Process*, published by Michael Wiese Productions. My writing credits also include articles in national magazines on wine, business, music, fishing, and humor. The second page of this transmission is an article about me from the *New York Times*. The following original screenplay might be of interest to you.

Title: *DEAD MAN'S DANCE*
Genre: Thriller
Form: Original screenplay - 100 pages
Log Line: A woman mysteriously disappears after supposedly seeing the man her father murdered.

Overview: Going to work one morning, Kerry Parker had no idea how much her life would soon change. Later that day, her troubled sister, Elaine, calls in a state of panic from Massachusetts and tells her that she saw Kenneth Hobart, the man their father supposedly murdered. When Elaine disappears, Kerry flies from California to Massachusetts to look for her. After Elaine's body is discovered outside a picturesque New England town, the likely suspect turns out to be a local police lieutenant. As Kerry pursues him in a deadly game of cat and mouse, the plot takes a number of unexpected turns and eventually uncovers a conspiracy involving a Mafia Criminal Relocation Program.

I will follow up with a phone call and, at your request, forward a copy of the script.

COMMENTS ON FAXES

You need to be flexible when creating and using faxes. Customizing remarks to an agent, production executive, or assistant can often initiate a positive response. With my faxes, I stress my writing background and often modify them. On the agent fax, I outline the most enticing details of two screenplays to give the agent a choice. To reinforce that opportunity, on the bottom of that fax, I close using a very positive sales technique—I will follow up with a phone call and, at your request, forward both scripts or one of your choice. On the production fax, I only offer one screenplay but have the luxury of additional space to provide more enticing details about my story. The most sensible approach is to develop a standard form that you can modify for different situations.

STORY OVERVIEWS: THOSE *TV GUIDE*-LIKE BLURBS

Writing those short descriptive *overviews* of your screenplay stories is not easy, and it takes time until each one has been properly refined. Your objective is to prompt the readers' curiosity by capturing, as concisely as possible, the essence of your story. This includes the characters, plot, tone, and hook. You want your story to stand out from all the others in that genre. Do it well and they will want to read your screenplay.

TARGETING PRODUCTION COMPANIES

Don't assume that companies producing action pictures or comedies are interested in only those genres. Sure, some specialize in genre pieces while others may be looking for an opportunity to try something else. Your script could be their next project.

MARKET STRATEGY

When you first start sending your script out—to either agents or production companies—it's best not to shotgun the market. Send out five. This means you may have to contact ten or possibly fifteen agents or production companies to accomplish that goal, but that's fine. The purpose of sending out just five is to get reactions. If your script is really good, your phone will be ringing. If it's rejected, then try to get some feedback. Your approach could be, "I really appreciate your looking at my script. Can you give me any advice as to how I can make it better?" If you have a minor problem that is turning people off to your script, but it can be easily fixed, and that feedback comes from your first five submissions, you'll be glad you held off sending more scripts out. Implementing those minor changes in a rewrite may make all the difference in the world with your next submissions.

AGENTS: GETTING SIGNED

While I don't have an agent, my advice on this subject is based upon the input of friends who do, what I have read, and what common sense dictates.

If you find an agent who is interested in representing you, you will be asked to sign a contract not to exceed a term of two years. Without going into a lot of detail, a writer can, after giving notice, terminate the agreement if he or she has not been employed during a period of ninety consecutive days.

Since everything in this world is subject to timing, you'd be well-advised to maintain patience—especially if you know your agent is hustling for you but has yet to make a sale or acquire work. If the timing isn't right, going to another agent might not make any difference. And granted, every agent has his or her own contacts and, sometimes, another agent's contacts might be more receptive to your work. But you don't know that for sure. After working with an agent a while, you will know whether or not the agent is working in your behalf.

Given the nature of the business, a writer would be wise to pursue production contacts even if he or she has an agent. I wouldn't care if my getting work were the result of only my efforts as long as the agent responds promptly to my requests to arrange meetings, forward scripts, and is a shrewd negotiator in my behalf.

Calling your agent to find out if he or she has found you work or calling without a specific purpose is a waste of everyone's time. If you want to call with a lead or follow up on a lead you previously gave your agent, fine.

Having an agent is also a form of status because it means that at least one person has confidence in you as a writer.

CLOSE, BUT NO CIGAR

While nothing short of getting signed by an agent or having a production company buy or at least option your script counts, getting close can be encouraging and very frustrating at the same time. With that in mind, there are three stories worth relating. Two involve this author—the other a writer-director friend.

First my friend. He acquired the rights to a television series that was very popular in the late 60s, early 70s. For the sake of this story, I'll call it *D Block*.

Given the success of other TV shows turned into features such as *Superman*, *The Addams Family*, *Batman*, and *Maverick*, he's holding a potential winner. Since *D Block* is widely seen today on major cable networks, there are two built-in audiences—the generation that grew up watching it and now some of their children.

After writing a feature script of *D Block*, my friend went to a major studio and met with a development executive he knows. The executive, being a big fan of the show was, of course, salivating over the prospect. My friend left his script and went on his merry way. Within days, he met with the executive and his boss. Contracts were signed, and my friend was to be paid to rewrite his script, and D Block was now in development.

A week after he turned in the revised screenplay, the exec called. "I've got great news! The president has given us the green light and you'll direct." Needless to say, my friend was highly elated. The next day, however, brought different news. The development executive called my friend and said very sheepishly, "We've got a problem. Last night, the president went home and said to his kids, 'Guess what? We're gonna make a feature film of *D Block*.' His kids replied, 'What's *D Block*?' "

D Block is now wallowing in development hell, with another studio interested in the project, but without my friend directing. Nice, huh? It happens all the time. In my opinion, that studio president was gutless because his decision to change his position was based upon the reaction of his children. Every project a studio president *green lights* is a high risk; but to my way of thinking, *D Block* would be a much safer call... safer than most.

THE PRODUCER

Shortly after writing a comedy screenplay, I was introduced to a woman producer who is probably ten years older than me. I only mention her age because she read my script and was only one of a few who found it funny. How do I know *she* actually read it? When we met for lunch in Manhattan, off the top of her head, she referenced a dozen scenes and quoted various segments of dialogue, word for word. She knew my script as well as I did. By the way, prior to sending her the script, I checked out her credentials (names she dropped, films she worked on, etc.) since I was unfamiliar with her name. Verifying three of many, I was satisfied that she was legit.

During our meeting, she said she would like to speak with my agent. I was honest and told her I didn't have one, but would by tomorrow. She smiled and said fine. Upon returning home, I immediately called the William Morris Agency in New York City. In asking to speak with an agent, the receptionist said I would have to send a letter to the agency. I explained the urgency of the situation. I am a writer, I have a script a producer (gave her the name) is interested in, and need an agent to represent me. The receptionist repeated herself: send the agency a letter. In asking for the name of an agent or executive, the receptionist wouldn't give me one. All this happened within my second year of screenwriting when I knew nothing about the industry and how things worked.

After striking out with William Morris, I called the producer and explained my situation. She was very understanding and said that we would deal with that later. She told me she was off to Europe to meet with a major director and that I would be contacted by an associate from her office regarding my script.

The next day, the Associate called. In a condescending tone, he told me his background in the film industry—which I didn't ask to hear, and it was more like his life story. Very politely, I listened as he rambled on about how he was a former television executive, a producer, a director, a writer, blah, blah, blah. Before he finished, I was ready to pull an *Ernest Hemingway* and wrap my lips around the barrel of a shotgun. The conversation finally shifted to my script and it went something like this.

                    ASSOCIATE
I read your script. It needs
work.

                        ME
I'm sure it does.

                    ASSOCIATE
I've prepared some notes.

                        ME
Fine. I've got a pencil and paper
-- anytime you're ready.

                    ASSOCIATE
Actually, it would take too long
to go over all my comments. Why
don't I just send them to you and
you can start rewriting.

                        ME
Aren't we gonna discuss it first?

                    ASSOCIATE
No point. Everything you need to
do is clearly spelled out.

                        ME
I may have some questions--

                    ASSOCIATE
                (rudely interrupting)
You're not listening: everything
you need to do is outlined in <u>my</u>
notes.

                        ME
Don't we go to contract first, and
then I do the rewrites?

                    ASSOCIATE
                (impatiently)
You do the rewrites first.

> ME
> (evenly)
> Look. I've already written this
> script on spec and am more than
> willing to do whatever rewrites
> you need, but--

> ASSOCIATE
> (interrupting again)
> There's no way that we're gonna
> buy your script unless it's right.

Right then and there, I remembered my writer-director friend's advice about not doing a rewrite for free, no matter how enticing the opportunity seems. Very politely, I told the Associate I would talk to the producer when she returned from Europe and go from there. For weeks, I called the producer's office, left messages, sent letters, etc. Guess what? She never responded. Do I have any regrets about not doing the rewrite for free? Absolutely none. I could tell by the Associate's attitude that no matter what, even if I followed his instructions explicitly, he would have found reasons to reject all my rewrites.

THE AGENT

I wrote a film noir screenplay titled *Sunset Palms*—sort of a *Chinatown* redux. An agent in L.A. read the script and called to tell me she really liked it. After thanking her for the compliment, she asked me for three more copies so she could send them out to production companies for *feedback*.

Hearing that, I made the point that it's a little unfair to make a judgment on the script based upon the feedback of only three production companies—knowing full well that the results would ultimately determine her interest to represent me. She ignored my point and said that if I sent her the scripts, she would make the submissions. I sent the scripts and followed up with her. All three production companies passed on *Sunset Palms*, therefore she had no interest in me or in even reading another script.

It's frustrating when you find someone who responds favorably to your work but backs off when meeting the slightest resistance. As pointed out, many screenplays take years before they are sold.

Final Comments

The following is a summary of the most important issues regarding screenwriting.

> Write what you know about and what you'd like to see.

> Don't start writing your screenplay until you are thoroughly prepared; and once you start, don't stop for any reason until you have finished.

> Constantly remind yourself that very few people can accurately assess any form of creative writing and provide you with helpful constructive criticism.

> Step back from your script between drafts for as long as possible, and don't rush the rewrite process.

> Find two trusted readers who can evaluate your work and provide you with helpful suggestions to improve it. In the end, however, trust and rely upon your own instincts.

> Remember that minor changes can often significantly improve your entire screenplay.

> Don't take rejection personally—it comes with the territory and *everyone* is subjected to it.

> When things aren't going well, as will happen from time to time, maintain a good sense of humor. Try running naked down the street yelling, "I'm mad as hell and I'm not gonna take it anymore!"

> If you're really committed to screenwriting, move to Los Angeles. It will be to your advantage.

> Use the fax and follow-up phone call *system*. It is clearly the best method of approaching agents, production companies, and studios and getting them to read your screenplays.

> Want to be successful? Then don't forget the importance of punctuality and follow-through.

> Writing is a sedentary occupation, so get plenty of regular exercise.

> When you have an opportunity to help others—even if there's nothing in it for you—do so. It'll make you feel good.

> If you become successful and my book was of any help, send me a nice check in appreciation. Otherwise, a note of thanks would be nice.

FINAL COMMENTS

One of the most exciting moments for every writer is discovering an idea for a story. This experience has often been preceded by weeks or even months of futility and agony.

Step by step, the writer begins to fill in the details until all the key elements have been defined, but, at this point, not developed, nor fully explored.

Once the basic premise of your story takes shape, the unique creative process moves into high gear—constantly building momentum.

Writing and rewriting, the process continues. Without realizing it, many months of *your life* pass by. On any given day, you will stop and reflect upon what you are doing. It could be at a high point in the writing or at some moment as you struggle with a problem.

Like conflict in your story, this is what writing is all about. You make advances—then suffer a setback. But you keep moving forward towards your ultimate goal—a completed screenplay of which you will be proud.

As you follow each procedure in screenwriting, keep in mind that you now have a solid understanding of the entire process so you can work from a position of confidence. Through sheer determination, you can and will overcome every obstacle in your path until your goal is achieved.

Completing an original screenplay is a wondrous experience and a tremendous accomplishment. You may be capable of writing an Academy Award-winning film that everyone will enjoy and remember for a long, long time. So what are you waiting for?

Appendix

Recommended Reading

When you're not writing, you should read as much as you possibly can: books (fiction and nonfiction), screenplays, magazines, newspapers, trade publications, etc. This Appendix is organized into seven sections:

1. Trade Publications
2. Screenwriting Books
3. Writing/Reference Books
4. Film Industry Books
5. Industry Sources Books
6. Screenplay and Filmbook Sources
7. Information on Screenwriting Software

Section 1: Trade Publications

VARIETY
Subscription Department
P. O. Box 6400
Torrance, CA 90504-9867
(800) 323-4345

Variety is *the* industry publication everyone reads. It will keep you well-informed regarding every aspect of the film and television industries.

HOLLYWOOD SCRIPTWRITER
P.O.Box 10277
Burbank, CA 91510
Phone: (818) 845-5525
Fax: (818) 709-7540

This monthly newsletter features interviews of writers, advice on writing, information on the industry, etc.

CREATIVE SCREENWRITING
6404 Hollywood Blvd., Suite 415
Los Angeles, CA 90028
Phone: (213) 957-1405
Fax: (213) 957-1406

Creative Screenwriting is a quarterly publication which presents feature articles that analyze films, script reviews, interviews with top screenwriters, and news columns.

SCENARIO
Circulation Offices
3200 Tower Oaks Blvd.
Rockville, MD 20852
(301) 770-2900

Scenario is a quarterly magazine featuring four full-length screenplays and interviews with their creators.

THE WRITER'S NETWORK
289 S. Robertson Blvd., Suite 465
Beverly Hills, CA 90211
(800) 646-3896

The Writer's Network is an organization created to assist new writers with their film careers. In addition to their quarterly newsletter, *Fade In*, which features interviews with filmmakers, they offer a unique phone support line.

SECTION 2: SCREENWRITING BOOKS

Since there are deviations in teaching methods from one screenwriting book to another, reading more than one can be very helpful for someone just starting out. Sometimes another author's point of view or way of addressing a certain issue makes it easier to understand.

SCREENPLAY AND SCREENWRITER'S WORKBOOK
Syd Field
ISBN: 0-440-57647-4 and ISBN: 0-440-58225-3
Dell Publishing Co., Inc
1540 Broadway
New York, NY 10036

Syd Field is one of the leading screenwriting teachers whose approach to screenwriting is very well-defined. His books cover everything from the technical aspects of screenwriting to detailed analysis of screenplays of successful films. Excellent reading.

FILM SCRIPTWRITING
Dwight V. Swain
Focal Press
ISBN: 0-240-511980

Butterworth-Heinemann
225 Wildwood Ave.
Woburn, MA 01801

This well-structured book addresses the documentary, the factual film, and the feature film. It utilizes sample scripts as well as illustrates everything from dramatic writing techniques to the intricacies of creating scenes.

THE TV SCRIPTWRITER'S HANDBOOK
Alfred Brenner
Writer's Digest Books
ISBN: 0-89879-178-2

Writer's Digest Books
1507 Dana
Cincinnati, Ohio 45207

An Emmy-winning writer and scriptwriting teacher at UCLA, Brenner has written a book which provides much insight beyond TV scriptwriting. There is tremendous depth in this book covering many diversified areas. He takes you through the progressive steps covering both the business side as well as the writing aspects of being a writer who is developing a project. His book contains many helpful details.

WRITING TELEVISION & MOTION PICTURE SCRIPTS THAT SELL
Evelyn Goodman
Westbourne Enterprises
ISBN: 0-9613885-8-7

Westbourne Enterprises
P. O. Box 3263
Hollywood, CA 90028

Evelyn Goodman is a professional writer with many produced scripts to her credit. Her experience also includes teaching television and motion picture writing classes at UCLA. Her book provides excellent focus and depth on dramatic writing from the treatment of characters to developing a strong line of rising conflict within a story. Her book also uses a complete television script to illustrate the various points.

HOW TO WRITE A MOVIE IN 21 DAYS
Viki King
Harper Collins
ISBN: 0-06-27-3066-5

Harper Collins Publishers, Inc.
10 East 53rd Street
New York, NY 10022

Viki King is a writer with television credits, as well as a script consultant and lecturer. Focusing on key screenwriting and storytelling techniques, she leads the writer through all the steps from story idea to completing a screenplay.

MAKING A GOOD SCRIPT GREAT
Linda Seger
Samuel French Trade
ISBN: 0-573-60690-0

Samuel French Trade
7623 Sunset Blvd.
Hollywood, CA 90046

Since 1983, Linda Seger has been a script consultant who has worked with many well-known writers, producers, and production companies.

Her book is broken down into four parts: Story Structure, Idea Development, Character Development, and a Case Study of the Rewrite of *Witness*. Through her method, a writer is able to identify the subtle problems within a script, which allows for an effective rewrite.

SCREENWRITING 434
Lew Hunter
Perigee Books
ISBN: 0-399-51838-X

Putnam Publishing Group
200 Madison Avenue
New York, NY 10016

Lew Hunter has worked as a writer, producer, and executive for both major studios and television networks. Combining writing techniques with references to films and other writers, Hunter's book presents screenwriting in an easy-to-understand, step-by-step method.

SUCCESSFUL SCRIPT WRITING
Jurgen Wolff & Kerry Cox
Writer's Digest Books
ISBN: 0-89879-325-4

F&W Publications, Inc.
1507 Dana Avenue
Cincinnati, Ohio 45207

Jurgen Wolff is a screenwriter, educator, and author who has written for many top television shows. Kerry Cox is a screenwriter with television credits and editor of the aforementioned *Hollywood Scriptwriter*.

Since the focus of their book balances both writing and pitching scripts for all the various film and television markets, it will be exceptionally helpful to those writers who are interested in the selling aspects of the screenwriting profession.

THE TOOLS OF SCREENWRITING
David Howard & Edward Mabley
St. Martin's Press
ISBN: 0-312-09405-1

St. Martin's Press
175 Fifth Avenue
New York, NY 10010

David Howard is a screenwriter, script doctor, and founding director of the Graduate Screenwriting Program at USC. In addition to writing and directing radio and television plays, Edward Mabley is the author of *Dramatic Construction*, a book on playwriting.

By analyzing sixteen notable films, the authors point out the common elements which makes them compelling stories, and outline the steps to write a screenplay that will be saleable.

SELLING YOUR SCREENPLAY
Cynthia Whitcomb
Crown Publishers
ISBN: 0-517-57008-4

Crown Publishers, Inc.
201 E. 50th St.
New York, NY 10022

With an impressive track record—having sold thirty feature-length screenplays, of which ten have been produced—Cynthia Whitcomb provides a real insider's view of the movie business. Because she addresses every aspect of selling a script with specific advice, it allows the reader to approach this important facet of screenwriting with confidence.

SECTION 3: WRITING/REFERENCE BOOKS

The following list of writing and reference books can be helpful to every writer, regardless of skill level. Some, like *The Art of Dramatic Writing*, are essential reading.

THE ART OF DRAMATIC WRITING
Lajos Egri
Touchstone Books
ISBN: 0-671-21332-6

Simon & Schuster, Inc.
Rockefeller Center
1230 Avenue of the Americas
New York, NY 10020

For anyone seriously interested in screenwriting and unfamiliar with dramatic writing, this book is an absolute must. It thoroughly illustrates the treatment of character, creating conflict within your story, as well as many intricate details concerning dramatic writing in easy-to-understand language.

FICTION WRITER'S HANDBOOK
Hallie & Whit Burnett
Harper Collins
ISBN: 0-06-27-31696

Harper Collins Publishers, Inc.
10 East 53rd Street
New York, NY 10022

As co-editors of *Story Magazine*, the Burnetts published the first work of many noted writers. They have also taught creative writing. Their book succinctly offers practical advice on fiction writing that is, at the same time, inspirational.

THE ELEMENTS OF STYLE
William Strunk, Jr. & E. B. White
Macmillan Publishing Co.
ISBN: 0-02-418200-1

Macmillan Publishing Co.
1633 Broadway
New York, NY 10019

In eighty-five pages, *The Elements of Style* provides the writer with the rules and principles of English. If you're not sure how to punctuate a sentence or form the possessive singular of a noun, this book answers those questions.

THE NEW YORK TIMES MANUAL OF STYLE AND USAGE
Revised and Edited by Lewis Jordan
Times Books
ISBN: 0-8129-6316-4

Times Books
New York, New York 10022

Without question, this is the most comprehensive book on punctuation that also includes information on foreign spellings, abbreviations, abstract expressionism, etc.

A POCKET GUIDE TO CORRECT PUNCTUATION
Robert Briton
Barron's
ISBN: 0-8120-2599-7

Barron's Educational Series, Inc.
250 Wireless Boulevard
Hauppauge, NY 11788

Using simple illustrations, this book shows you how to punctuate your writing.

PUNCTUATE IT RIGHT!
Harry Shaw
Harper Collins
ISBN: 0-06-46-1045-4

Harpers Collins Publishers, Inc.
10 East 53rd Street
New York, NY 10022

This quick-reference guide not only illustrates punctuation, but explains the use of numerals, contains a list of standard abbreviations, a glossary of terms, etc.

THE PROFESSIONAL WRITER'S PHRASE BOOK
Jean Kent
Perigee Books
ISBN: 0-399-51338-8

Putnam Publishing Group
200 Madison Avenue
New York, NY 10016

Looking for a way to better express a character's actions or describe the landscape in your scene description? Look no further. This book contains 3,500 descriptive phrases.

HANDBOOK OF COMMONLY USED AMERICAN IDIOMS
Adam Makkai, Maxine T. Boatner, and John E. Gates
Barron's Education Series, Inc.
ISBN: 0-8120-2816-3

Barron's Education Series, Inc.
250 Wireless Boulevard
Hauppauge, NY 11788

This book offers 1,500 colorful American slang expressions, colloquialisms, clichés, expletives, etc.

THE POCKET BOOK OF QUOTATIONS
Edited by Henry Davidoff
Pocket Books
Book Number: 50240

Pocket Books
A Division of Simon & Schuster, Inc.
1230 Avenue of the Americas
New York, NY 10020

Using this book, you can select an appropriate quotation on almost any subject.

SECTION 4: FILM INDUSTRY BOOKS

If you're seriously considering a career in film, you should read as many of the following books as possible. In certain respects, the film industry is unlike any other because the basic commodity is *talent*— and talent, as we all know, is a very subjective thing. ***The decision-making process is not driven by what is logical or right, but by who has the power.*** Understanding how the industry works can at least prepare you for the hardships you will undoubtedly be facing... trying to break in; and after that, trying to sustain a career.

If you're the sensitive type, you may prefer a more passive career field such as full-contact karate with no protective gear. If you're a talented person who is willing to persevere, or a sly, sneaky back-stabbing S.O.B., you will probably succeed in film.

ADVENTURES IN THE SCREEN TRADE
William Goldman
Warner Books
ISBN: 0-446-38385-6

Warner Books
1271 6th Avenue
New York, NY 10020

A two-time Academy-Award-winning screenwriter, Goldman relates his experiences in the industry over a long and successful career starting back in 1965. This book is very helpful to someone considering or pursuing a career as a screenwriter.

Even writers with his talent and stature in the industry suffer indignities and abuse, as his experience has proven. Goldman approaches this book with bold honesty and a strong sense of humor. Like his screenplays and his novels, this book is a great read. (The expanded edition contains the complete screenplay, *Butch Cassidy and the Sundance Kid*.)

REEL POWER
Mark Litwak
Plume Books
ISBN: 0-452-25990-8

Penguin U.S.A.
375 Hudson Street
New York, NY 10014

This book presents the most intelligent and perceptive overview of the entire film industry. If you want to understand how the political machinery of Hollywood really functions, read this book. Litwak addresses the various areas of film in separate chapters (on agents, writers, directors, producers, actors, etc.), relating well-known incidents, as well as quoting those people who were brave enough to step forward and speak out.

THE MOVIE BUSINESS
Edited by Jason E. Squire
A Fireside Book
ISBN: 0-671-75095-X

Simon & Schuster, Inc.
Rockefeller Center
1230 Avenue of the Americas
New York, NY 10020

This book is not an exposé on Hollywood but a microscopic view of the industry's segmented areas through the eyes of forty professionals from the various fields of expertise. Every subject is treated in a separate chapter addressed by one expert, so it is easy to read and comprehend.

MAKING IT IN HOLLYWOOD
Gail O'Donnell & Michele Travolta
Sourcebooks, Inc.
ISBN: 1-57071-015-5

Sourcebooks, Inc.
P. O. Box 372
Naperville, Illinois 60566

If you want a *firsthand look* at making it in Hollywood, this is a terrific book. The authors interview famous writers, directors, producers, and actors—each with their own story to tell on breaking in. The focus of the book is on the single most important ingredient for success and the most innovative ideas for getting your foot in the door.

WORKING IN HOLLYWOOD
Alexandra Brouwer & Thomas Lee Wright
Avon Books
ISBN: 0-380-71500-7

Avon Books
1350 Avenue of the Americas
New York, NY 10019

Here is another *inside look* at the film industry with comments and advice from sixty-four men and women from every career field.

HOW TO MAKE IT IN HOLLYWOOD
Linda Buzzell
Harper Collins
ISBN: 0-06-096596-7

Harper Collins Publishers, Inc.
10 East 53rd Street
New York, NY 10022

Linda Buzzell worked as a production executive at major studios and is a highly respected psychotherapist and career counselor within the film community. Given her background, her book provides a unique look at the industry with advice on breaking in, on surviving rejection, and dealing with all the other negative aspects of the movie business.

HELLO, HE LIED AND OTHER TRUTHS FROM THE HOLLYWOOD TRENCHES
Lynda Obst
Little, Brown and Company
ISBN: 0-316-62211-7

Little, Brown and Company
1271 Avenue of the Americas
New York, NY 10020

Lynda Obst, producer of *The Fisher King* and *Sleepless in Seattle*, shares what she has learned in more than twenty years of experience in the film business. Her book addresses every facet of the industry with incredible honesty and humor. It is not only informative, but a great read!

LET ME ENTERTAIN YOU
David Brown
William Morrow and Company, Inc.
ISBN: 0-688-08048-0

William Morrow and Company, Inc.
1315 6th Avenue
New York, NY 10019

Let Me Entertain You is one of the most interesting and entertaining memoirs you will ever read. Producer David Brown's book shifts from his vast career experiences to amazing and often hilarious stories about Hollywood through his encounters with celebrities and world figures.

THE CRAFT OF THE SCREENWRITER
John Brady
Touchstone Books
ISBN: 0-671-25230-5

Simon & Schuster, Inc.
Rockefeller Center
1230 Avenue of the Americas
New York, NY 10020

Brady, author of *The Craft of Interviewing*, applies his expertise to six famous screenwriters including Paddy Chayesfsky, William Goldman, Ernest Lehman, Paul Schrader, Neil Simon, and Robert Towne. A great read filled with insightful information.

AMERICAN SCREENWRITERS
Karl Schanzer & Thomas Lee Wright
Avon Books
ISBN: 0-380-76727-9

Avon Books
1350 Avenue of the Americas
New York, NY 10019

Sixteen of the most successful screenwriters in Hollywood share their experience and thoughts on breaking in, pitching, writing, and succeeding. Some of the writers include: Ron Bass, Shane Black, Richard Price, Callie Khouri, and Joe Eszterhas.

THE NEW AMERICAN SCREENWRITERS
William Froug
Silman-James Press
ISBN: 1-879505-04-5

Samuel French Trade
7623 Sunset Blvd.
Hollywood, CA 90046

A dozen top screenwriters talk about their craft. Some of the writers include: Dan O'Bannon, Jeffrey Boam, Anna Hamilton Phelan, Jack Epps, Jr. and Jim Cash, etc.

Section 5: Industry Sources Books

Knowing how to contact an agent, producer, or studio executive is essential to creating career opportunities. The following two directories are the best sources of that information.

HOLLYWOOD AGENTS & MANAGERS DIRECTORY
Linda Thurman, Managing Editor

Hollywood Creative Directory
3000 W. Olympic Blvd., Suite 2525
Santa Monica, CA 90404
(310) 315-4815
(800) 815-0503 (Outside California)

For those seeking an agent, this book is an absolute *MUST*. It is a complete list of agencies that includes addresses, phone and fax numbers, the agents' names and their area of responsibility—so you can target those who handle writers. The directory is updated twice a year: February and August.

HOLLYWOOD CREATIVE DIRECTORY
Linda Thurman, Managing Editor

Hollywood Creative Directory
3000 W. Olympic Blvd., Suite 2525
Santa Monica, CA 90404
(310) 315-4815
(800) 815-0503 (Outside California)

When you are ready to contact production companies and studios, look no further. Unequivocally, *The Hollywood Creative Directory* is the best source available. This directory lists, by production company, the addresses, phone and fax numbers, and all personnel by title. It also lists production credits and indicates those companies with studio deals.

The companies and studios are indexed by type (animation, documentary, direct to video, infomercials, interactive multimedia, motion pictures, and so on) so you know where to focus your attention. Most importantly, if someone gives you a lead, just a person's name, you can locate anyone through the cross-reference of names. The directory offers another nice feature—a source guide with information on the various guilds, unions, and major libraries. The directory is updated three times a year: March, July, and November.

Section 6: Screenplay And Filmbook Sources

Coliseum Books
1751 Broadway
New York, NY 10019
(212) 757-8381
(212) 586-5607 Fax
(800) 833-1543

Filmbooks, published screenplays, and handles special orders. Has in-store Muze for Books computer to search for books in print.

Richard Stoddard, Performing Art Books
18 E. 16th Street, Room 305
New York, NY 10003
(212) 645-9576

Specializes in out-of-print filmbooks.

Drama Book Shop
723 7th Avenue
New York, NY 10019
(212) 944-0595
(212) 921-2013 Fax
(800) 322-0595

Filmbooks, theatrical and stage books, published screenplays, East
and West Coast film magazines, biographies, and journals.

Gotham Book Mart
41 West 47th Street
New York, NY 10036
(212) 719-4448

Filmbooks, published screenplays, has library of film magazines back
to the 1950s, and conducts searches for out-of-print books.

Larry Edmunds
Cinema Bookshop, Inc.
6644 Hollywood Blvd.
Hollywood, CA 90028
(213) 463-3273
(213) 463-4245 Fax

Filmbooks, screenplays, and movie posters.

Samuel French's Theater & Film Bookshop
7623 Sunset Blvd.
Hollywood, CA 90046
(213) 876-0570
(213) 876-6822 Fax

Filmbooks, books on the motion picture industry, theater, plus *the
world's largest selection of plays*.

Hollywood Book & Poster
6562 Hollywood Blvd.
Hollywood, CA 90028
(213) 465-8764

Filmbooks, screenplays, and movie posters.

Script City
(mail order only)
8033 Sunset Blvd., Suite 1500
Hollywood, CA 90046
(213) 871-0707
(800) 676-2522 (orders only)

Filmbooks, screenplays, and movie posters.

SECTION 7: INFORMATION ON SCREENWRITING SOFTWARE

The following is a list of the most popular screenwriting software programs outlining the unique features each one offers. All programs include screenplay, sitcom, and stage play formats, plus spelling check and thesaurus.

Final Draft: The only program currently available which offers a Macintosh version. Authors are capable of passing data between platforms without importing or converting files. That is a very valuable feature in a production setting or for those working with a collaborator. Also, as of this writing, *Final Draft* is the only program offering a true 32-bit Windows 95 version.

MovieMagic Screenwriter: Feature-rich and very customizable, this program offers a special format for interactive scriptwriting. Production report can be exported into *MovieMagic Scheduling* program.

MovieMaster: The Windows version has just been released; not much data is available. A sneak preview revealed that DOS users will be able to call up their DOS files without importation. Also, the same function key schema can be used by those familiar with the *MovieMaster* DOS version.

ScriptThing: An extremely customizable scriptwriting program. Settings such as automatically opening the last document the writer worked on, leading (*cheating* on the line height to squeeze more lines onto a script page), and many more features. It contains the special feature for interactive scriptwriting.

Scriptware: The first actual Windows-based screenwriting software, *Scriptware* is very easy to use. It is also the only scripting software which includes the Audio/Visual (A/V) format used for documentaries and commercials. The software review recently conducted by the *Writers Guild of America, West* selected it as their favorite program.

(In talking to friends, in doing research, and based upon my own experience, *Scriptware* is the most user-friendly screenwriting software on the market today. Ninety percent of the program functions off of the Tab and Enter keys. With one simple command, you can convert an entire screenplay into a shooting script. *Scriptware* offers every feature imaginable; and because it is easy to use, it will make you more efficient in screenwriting.)

Scriptware can be ordered directly from:

Cinovation, Inc.
1750 30th Street, Suite 350
Boulder, CO 80301-1005
(800) 788-7090

Script Wizard: An add-on to *Microsoft Word for Windows 6/7*, this feature-rich program offers a format for any type of script ever thought of: all of the ones mentioned so far (sans the interactive format), *plus* variety show, daytime (soap) TV, various ways of tackling the complicated issue of numbering sitcoms, etc. Can do anything *Microsoft Word* can do (foreign characters, etc.). (Note: when *Word* comes out with a new release, the user needs to upgrade both pieces of software.)

STORY DEVELOPMENT SOFTWARE

Should you decide to check out *story development software*, which many feel is an anathema for writers, the most popular programs are *Collaborator, StoryBuilder, Storyline Pro* and *Dramatica*.

Another popular program is *Storyboard Quick* which allows writers to spike their scripts with *storyboard pictures* to put forth their personal image of a scene setting. While this might be *fun* to play with, I would not use this program in a script you are planning to submit to any Hollywood agent, studio, or production company.

SOURCES: COMPUTER SOFTWARE

The Writers' Computer Store
11317 Santa Monica Blvd.
Los Angeles, CA 90025-3118
(310) 479-7774
(310) 477-5314 Fax
(800) 272-8927 Phone Orders Only
(800) 486-4006 Fax Orders Only

The Writers' Computer Store
2631 Bridgeway Avenue
Sausalito, CA 94965-1495
(415) 332-7005
(415) 322-7037 Fax
(800) 272-8927 Phone Orders Only
(800) 486-4006 Fax Orders Only

Web Address: http://writerscomputer.com.

Both stores carry a large selection of software for screenwriting; story development; organizers and multimedia; production, supplies and storyboarding; plus a specialized library of books and tapes for all aspects of writing.

INDEX

"DEAD MAN'S DANCE"

Original Screenplay by

Robert A. Berman

(The following would be filled in
on an actually submitted script.)
Street Address
City, State Zip Code
Phone Number
Fax Number

"DEAD MAN'S DANCE"

FADE IN:

EXT. SUNSET CATERING - DAY

KERRY PARKER, 28, helps two employees, TODD SMITH and
JIMMY NOLIN, both 20, load food trays into a VAN
decorated with the SUNSET CATERING (Palm Tree) LOGO.
The location is obviously California.

> KERRY
> (to Todd)
> If Gordon isn't there when you
> arrive, call me right away.

> TODD
> Gotcha.

Jimmy comes out the door carrying food trays.

> TODD (cont'd)
> C'mon, dude, let's go.

Seeing Jimmy wearing shorts —

> KERRY
> Where are your pants?

> JIMMY
> In my car.

Jimmy slides the food trays into the van.

> KERRY
> Put 'em on.

> JIMMY
> (teasing)
> What's the matter? Don't like my
> legs?

> KERRY
> (giving it back)
> Actually they're nicer than mine,
> but put your pants on.

> JIMMY
> (feigns hurt)
> I want my mommy.

> TODD
> (to Jimmy)
> C'mon, moron. We're running late.

Jimmy runs to his car taking his shorts off at the same
time. Kerry smiles, shakes her head and goes inside.

INT. SUNSET CATERING - KITCHEN - DAY

MEGAN COMBS, 23, approaches Kerry with a list. In the
b.g., three young people are preparing other food trays.

                    MEGAN
          We'll be done with the Holden
          party in forty-five minutes.
          Who's handling the delivery?

                    KERRY
          David and Renny.

                    MEGAN
              (nods; then)
          Have you made out the schedule for
          tomorrow?

                    KERRY
          Didn't Dan?

                    MEGAN
          I don't think so.

                    KERRY
          I'll take care of it now.

Kerry exits the kitchen.

INT. CORRIDOR - DAY

The walls are covered with scenic posters of California.
Heading for her office, Kerry passes JOHN MATHEWS, 40.

                    KERRY
          Hi, John.

                    JOHN
          Kerry, a mistake's been made.

She stops. He approaches and shows her his paycheck.

                    JOHN (cont'd)
          You forgot to deduct all the time
          I took off when Mark was in the
          hospital.

                    KERRY
          I didn't forget.

John smiles gratefully.

                    JOHN
          Thanks.

TRISH MOTT, 22, steps out of an office. Seeing Kerry:

                    TRISH
          Oh, there you are. Elaine's on
          the phone and she sounds very
          upset.

INT. KERRY'S OFFICE - DAY

Kerry enters and closes the door. She stands behind her
desk. It is covered with file folders and menus. On
the wall, framed/signed photos of celebrity clients.

                    KERRY
               (into phone)
          Elaine?

EXT. OUTDOOR PAY PHONE - NIGHT

Teenagers wearing shorts walk past ELAINE PARKER, 30.
She appears to be extremely anxious.

                    ELAINE
               (into phone)
          I saw him! He's here!

INTERCUT PHONE CONVERSATION

                    KERRY
          Who?

                    ELAINE
          Kenneth Hobart!

Hearing that name, Kerry is stunned for a moment.

                    KERRY
          It can't be — he's dead.

                    ELAINE
          I'm telling you — it was him!

                    KERRY
          Where are you?

                    ELAINE
          Westbridge, Massachusetts.

                    KERRY
          What are you doing there?

                    ELAINE
          I told you last week I was going
          to visit Kathy Marks after my
          company's sales meeting.

                    KERRY
          Sorry, Elaine. I forgot.

                              ELAINE
          I'm telling you — it was Hobart!

Kerry is highly concerned for her sister and yet,
extremely frustrated at the same time.

                              KERRY
          It was obviously someone who looks
          like him.

                              ELAINE
                      (desperately)
          You don't believe me, do you?

                              KERRY
                      (sincerely)
          I know you believe it was him.

A KNOCK — Kerry's door opens and DAN WALLACE, 29, her
partner, appears. She waves him in.

                              ELAINE
          I'm going to the police.

                              KERRY
                      (gingerly)
          Maybe you should think about it
          first?

                              ELAINE
                      (pointedly)
          Kerry. I'm going to the police.

                              KERRY
          Call me after you do, okay?
                      (on Elaine's silence)
          Elaine. I love you.

EXT. OUTDOOR PAY PHONE - NIGHT

Looking distraught and on the verge of tears, Elaine
hangs up abruptly.

INT. SUNSET CATERING - OFFICE - DAY

                              KERRY
          Elaine?

Kerry hangs up — clearly upset. Dan looks at her with
concern.

                              DAN
          Are you all right?

                              KERRY
          No.

                    DAN
          What's the matter?

                    KERRY
          That was Elaine. She's in
          Massachusetts. She said she just
          saw Kenneth Hobart.

Knowing who Hobart is, Dan reacts.

                    DAN
          Jesus...

Kerry sinks into her chair and looks at Dan.

                    KERRY
          She really believes it was him.

                    DAN
          Why don't you get out of here.

                    KERRY
          I've got to get tomorrow's
          schedule done.

                    DAN
          I'll do it — go on, go home.

Kerry pauses a moment, then stands.

                    KERRY
          Thanks, Dan.

Sh exits — closing the door quietly behind her.

A   w moments later, Trish KNOCKS and enters.

                    TRISH
          I've never seen Kerry so upset.
          Did something happen to Elaine?

ı — reluctant to discuss it — pauses for a beat.

                    DAN
          You know about her father?

                    TRISH
          Wasn't he convicted of embezzling
          millions from his clients — then
          murdering his partner after he
          found out?
                    (on Dan's nod)
          Didn't he die in prison — a heart
          attack or something?
                    (Dan nods again)
          So?

6.

                    DAN
          Elaine's in Massachusetts. She
          told Kerry she saw the man her
          father supposedly murdered.

                    TRISH
          No wonder she's so upset.

INT. KERRY'S APARTMENT - LIVING ROOM - NIGHT

An exhausted-looking Kerry sits on her couch watching
the telephone expectantly. She gazes at the wall clock
— it's 11:37. Soon, she starts nodding off.

EXT. SUNSET CATERING - LATE MORNING

Dan unlocks the front door and goes inside.

INT. SUNSET CATERING - CORRIDOR - LATE MORNING

The corridor is dark with the exception of light coming
from Kerry's office. Dan turns the corridor lights on.

INT. KERRY'S OFFICE - LATE MORNING

Dan stands in the doorway as Kerry, looking frustrated,
hangs up the phone. Dan walks in.

                    DAN
          What's up?

                    KERRY
          Elaine never got back to me. The
          Westbridge police said she didn't
          contact them. I tried calling her
          friend, Kathy Marks, who she was
          planning to visit there, but can't
          get her phone number because I
          can't remember her married name.

                    DAN
          Don't you know someone who does?

                    KERRY
          I thought I did — but everyone
          I've called hasn't had contact
          with her since grammar school.

                    DAN
          I'm sure Elaine's all right.
          She's probably with Kathy right
          now, having a good time.

Kerry forces a thin smile — then turns serious.

                    KERRY
          If I don't hear from her today,
          would you mind if I took off for
          three or four days?

                    DAN
          To go to Massachusetts?

                    KERRY
               (nods)
          Only if she doesn't call.

                    DAN
          No problem.

Dan picks up a file folder from Kerry's desk.

                    DAN (cont'd)
          Do you have time to discuss the
          Kruger party?

                    KERRY
          Sure.

Dan pulls up a chair and spreads out the contents of the
file folder on top of her cluttered desk.

EXT. LOGAN AIRPORT - BOSTON, MA - LATE AFTERNOON

A jet glides to a landing on the runway.

INT. MOVING RENTAL CAR - LATE AFTERNOON

As Kerry drives, her anxiety is evident as she keeps
flexing her fingers on the steering wheel.

She looks out at the MASS TURNPIKE heading WEST.

EXT. WESTBRIDGE POLICE STATION - NIGHT

Kerry gets out of her car and goes inside.

INT. POLICE STATION - FRONT DESK - NIGHT

Kerry approaches the desk and SERGEANT JIM QUILL, 35.

                    SGT. QUILL
          Yes, miss?

                    KERRY
               (eyeing name badge)
          I'm Kerry Parker. I spoke to you
          Friday night regarding my sister,
          Elaine.

                    SGT. QUILL
        You're the one who called from
        California.

                    KERRY
                (nods; then)
        Have you heard from her since?

                    SGT. QUILL
        I haven't — but let me check.
                (checks blotter)
        I see no entry under her name.

Kerry looks at the Sergeant, highly concerned.

                    KERRY
        Friday night she called from town
        and told me she was going to the
        police. I asked her to call me
        afterwards. Since I haven't heard
        from her, I'm concerned.

                    SGT. QUILL
        Why was she coming here?

                    KERRY
                (hesitantly)
        She thought she saw a man in town
        — someone who supposedly had been
        murdered.

Sgt. Quill looks at Kerry curiously.

                    SGT. QUILL
        Care to tell me about it?

Kerry is not interested in rehashing the past.

                    KERRY
        I really don't want to go into it.
        My uh... my sister's been under a
        great deal of emotional strain.

The desk PHONE RINGS.

                    SGT. QUILL
        Excuse me.
                (into phone)
        Police Department, Sergeant Quill.
                (listening)
        Yes, Mrs. Redfield?.. No... I'll
        give him the message. Goodnight.

                    KERRY
          I'm trying to find a friend of my
          sister's who lives here, but don't
          know her married name.

                    SGT. QUILL
          What's her maiden name?

                    KERRY
          Marks. Kathy Marks.

                    SGT. QUILL
          Know what she or her husband does
          for a living?

                    KERRY
          No.

                    SGT. QUILL
          Tomorrow you might check with Lee
          Beldon at Town Hall — he knows
          just about everyone.

                    KERRY
          Thanks, Sergeant. Can you
          recommend a place to stay?

                    SGT. QUILL
          There's Toomey's Bed and
          Breakfast.

                    KERRY
          How do I get there?

INT. TOOMEY'S BED & BREAKFAST - GUEST ROOM - NIGHT

Kerry, lugging her suitcase, enters looking spent from
the long day. She falls back onto the bed. As tired as
she is, she looks up at the ceiling, transfixed.

EXT. TOWN HALL - EARLY MORNING

A MAN, about 50, walks briskly inside.

INT. TOWN HALL - CORRIDOR - EARLY MORNING

The MAN enters an office. Stenciled on the door: "Lee
Beldon — Assessor."

INT. ASSESSOR'S OFFICE - EARLY MORNING

The MAN stands behind Kerry at the counter while she
talks with LEE BELDON, 60s.

                    BELDON
          That's all you can tell me?

                    KERRY
          I'm afraid so.

                    BELDON
          Sorry I can't help you, but try
          some of the shops on Main Street.
          Someone may know her.

                    KERRY
          That's a good idea. Thanks.

As Kerry walks out, Beldon addresses the MAN.

                    BELDON
          Larry. What can I do for you?

EXT. MAIN STREET - DAY

Kerry walks out of one shop, then into another.

INT. CAFE - NOONTIME

The cafe is crowded with shop clerks and tradesmen.
With conversations running from table to table, it is
apparent that they all know each other.

Kerry sits at a table, picking at a salad. Next thing
she knows, LINDA RUSSO, 20, is standing over her.

                    LINDA
          Remember me?

                    KERRY
          You work in the card shop.

                    LINDA
                (nods; then)
          Any luck?

                    KERRY
          No.

Linda gives out with a shrieking WHISTLE that startles
everyone. With all eyes on Linda:

                    LINDA
          This lady needs help.

                    1ST MAN (O.S.)
          Hey, Linda! You're the one who
          needs help!

A bunch of workmen clap and cheer their buddy.

                    LINDA
          All right! All right!

As the cafe quiets down —

> LINDA (cont'd)
> This lady is looking for a friend.

> 2ND MAN (O.S.)
> (suggestively)
> I'll be her friend!

More hoots and catcalls. Linda addresses the crowd.

> LINDA
> (re: 2ND MAN)
> Peter's the only person I know who
> can give a dog fleas!

The young women cheer Linda — the men boo her.

Highly amused by Linda's brazen demeanor, Kerry cracks a
smile. Linda raises her arms to quiet everyone down.

> LINDA (cont'd)
> Listen up. She's looking for a
> Kathy who's from California, about
> thirty. Her maiden name is—

Having forgotten, she looks at Kerry.

> KERRY
> Marks.

> LINDA
> (loudly)
> Marks.

Looks and shrugs are exchanged. RUSSELL WORTH, 33,
dressed in working clothes, approaches Kerry's table.

> LINDA (cont'd)
> Think you can help her, Russ?

> RUSS
> I'm not sure, but I think Mike
> Burrows' wife is originally from
> California and her name is Kathy.

> KERRY
> How old is she?

> RUSS
> Late twenties, early thirties.

Kerry reaches into her pocketbook for pen and paper.

> KERRY
> Could be. Know the address?

                         RUSS
          Sure. Twenty-six Chestnut Street.

Kerry writes it down, then looks at Linda and Russ.

                         KERRY
          Thanks.

EXT. RESIDENTIAL STREET - DAY

Kerry's car cruises down the street and stops in front
of #26 — a neat, two-story house.

EXT. BURROWS' HOUSE - DAY

The front yard is littered with toys. Kerry goes to the
front door and RINGS the DOORBELL.

KATHY BURROWS, 30, attractive but disheveled-looking,
comes to the screen door. Seeing Kerry, her bloodshot
eyes reveal a faint sign of recognition.

                         KERRY
          Kathy? Kathy Marks?

                         KATHY
          I... I know you.

                         KERRY
          Kerry Parker. Elaine's sister.

                         KATHY
          What a surprise! Come in.

Kathy opens the screen door.

INT. BURROWS' HOUSE - LIVING ROOM - DAY

Kerry follows Kathy inside. The room is messy with toys
everywhere and — on the coffee table — dirty dishes.
Seeing Kerry eye the mess, Kathy starts to pick up.

                         KATHY
          You live in California, too.

                         KERRY
          In Los Angeles.

                         KATHY
          Then what are you doing here?

                         KERRY
          On Friday, Elaine called me from
          here and said she was going to
          visit you.

Kathy stops picking up and looks at Kerry, excitedly.

> KATHY
> She's here?

> KERRY
> Then you didn't hear from her.

> KATHY
> No.
> (on Kerry's concerned look)
> Is something wrong?

> KERRY
> I'm not sure.

> KATHY
> Can I get you something to drink?

> KERRY
> No, thanks.

> KATHY
> I'll be right back.

Kathy disappears into the kitchen. Kerry can see her pick up a 1.5 liter bottle of gin from the counter.

From behind Kerry, JAKE, 7, and TOMMY, 5, explode into the house. Tommy is wiping tears from his eyes.

> TOMMY
> I'm telling Mommy on you!

> JAKE
> Shut up you little crybaby!

Kathy appears in the doorway. Tommy runs to her. She gives Jake an accusatory look.

> KATHY
> What'd you do to him now?

> JAKE
> Nothing!

> TOMMY
> Liar!
> (to Kathy)
> He punched me.

Kathy releases Tommy and goes after Jake. As Jake races for the front door, his father, MIKE BURROWS, 31, enters. He is a carpenter.

                        MIKE
                 (scooping Jake up)
            Hey, big guy, where're you goin'
            in such a hurry?

There is obvious tension between Kathy and Mike.

                       KATHY
            I'll tell you where he's goin' —
            right to his room.

Mike puts Jake down. Jake stands behind Mike. Tommy
runs to his father and clings to him.

Mike sees Kerry standing there, looking a little
uncomfortable being in the midst of this family dispute.

                        MIKE
                 (to Kathy)
            Calm down.

Kathy finally remembers that Kerry is standing there.

                       KATHY
            This is my ex-husband, Mike.
                 (to Mike)
            This is Kerry Parker. Elaine's
            sister.

Mike nods politely to Kerry then addresses Kathy.

                        MIKE
            I finished early so I thought I'd
            take the boys for a while.

Kathy kisses Tommy goodbye, then Jake.

                       KATHY
                 (to Jake; sternly)
            Stop teasing your brother.

                        MIKE
            C'mon, guys.
                 (to Kerry)
            Nice meeting you.
                 (to Kathy)
            I'll have them back by eight.

Mike leads his sons out the front door.

INT. KITCHEN - DAY

Kerry, watching Kathy pour herself a stiff drink, is
unable to hide her disapproval. Kathy notices this.

                    KATHY
          You disapprove?

                    KERRY
          It's not my place to judge you.

                    KATHY
          Then why'd you look at me the way
          you did?

                    KERRY
          Sorry.

Kathy sips her drink.

                    KATHY
          I hope Elaine shows up. I'd
          really like to see her.

                    KERRY
          So would I.

                    KATHY
          You're sure she called from here?

                    KERRY
          She said Westbridge.

                    KATHY
          Would you like to stay for dinner?
          It'd just be the two of us.

                    KERRY
          Sure. Thanks.

EXT. TOOMEY'S - DAY

Kerry's car is parked out front.

INT. TOOMEY'S - KERRY'S ROOM - DAY

Kerry sits on the bed talking on the phone.

                    DAN (V.O.)
          Did you catch up with Elaine?

                    KERRY
                 (into phone)
          No. Did she call?

                    DAN (V.O.)
          I didn't hear from her. What
          about the police?

                         KERRY
          She never contacted them. I found
          her friend, Kathy, and she hasn't
          heard from her either. I'm really
          worried and don't know what to do.

                         DAN (V.O.)
          Think her disappearance has
          anything to do with Hobart?

                         KERRY
                    (pointedly)
          No.

                         DAN (V.O.)
          How can you be so sure?

                         KERRY
          First of all, he's dead — and
          since Dad died, Elaine has seen
          him four other times.

                         DAN (V.O.)
          Jesus... How come you never told
          me that?

                         KERRY
          I just didn't want to discuss it.

There's a long silence; then —

                         DAN (V.O.)
          Elaine's been missing for more
          than twenty-four hours, so why not
          file a report with the police and
          have them look into it?

Kerry notices a note being slipped under her door.

                         KERRY
          Hang on a minute, Dan.

                         DAN (V.O.)
          Sure.

Kerry puts the phone down, picks up the note and reads
it. She grabs the phone, hurriedly.

                         KERRY
                    (into phone)
          Dan — I've got to go. I just got
          a message to contact the police.

                         DAN (V.O.)
          I hope it's good news. Let me
          know.

                    KERRY
     Thanks.

Kerry hangs up, grabs her pocketbook and exits her room.

INT. POLICE DEPARTMENT - FRONT DESK - DAY

Kerry approaches the desk manned by Sgt. Quill.

                    KERRY
          I got your message.

                    SGT. QUILL
          We found an abandoned rental car
          in the woods. We checked with the
          rental company and confirmed it
          was leased to your sister.

                    KERRY
          What about Elaine?

                    SGT. QUILL
          Nothing.

                    KERRY
          Did you search the car and the
          area where it was found?

                    SGT. QUILL
          No. There was no sign of a
          struggle in or around the car, if
          that's what you mean.

                    KERRY
          Fine, but did you search the area?

                    SGT. QUILL
          No. We're guessing it was stolen,
          then abandoned.

                    KERRY
          Then where is she? Why hasn't she
          reported it stolen?

LT. WILLIAM HASKINS, 45, enters from an office.

                    SGT. QUILL
          Lieutenant. This is Kerry Parker.
          The car we found was leased to her
          sister.

                    KERRY
                (to Haskins)
          The Sergeant told me you have no
          intention of searching the area
          where her car was found.

                    LT. HASKINS
          That's right. We have no reason
          to suspect foul play.

                    KERRY
          I don't believe this!
                    (pointedly)
          My sister was coming to this
          police station last Friday, then
          visiting a friend in town. She
          never made it here or to her
          friend's. Her rental car is found
          abandoned in the woods, she can't
          be found, and you're telling me
          you don't think anything's wrong?

Haskins addresses Kerry but flashes an angry look at the
Sergeant.

                    LT. HASKINS
          I wasn't aware of the rest of it.

                    SGT. QUILL
          Sorry, sir, I meant to fill you
          in.

                    LT. HASKINS
                    (to Kerry)
          We'll search the area.

                    KERRY
          When?

                    LT. HASKINS
          We have three hours of daylight
          left.
                    (to Sgt. Quill)
          Call Toby — he should be at the
          fire house — ask him to put
          together a bunch of volunteers.

Sgt. Quill nods, then grabs the phone.

EXT. WOODS - DUSK

About twenty men are walking abreast, five yards apart,
through the woods. Kerry walks between NED WIDGRIN, 28,
wearing a baseball cap — and a uniformed policeman,
SERGEANT THOMAS DAILY, 31.

                    SGT. DAILY
                    (into portable)
          Anything, Jimmy?

                    JIMMY (V.O.)
          Nothing, Tom.

                        SGT. DAILY
                     (into portable)
            Toby! How 'bout you?

                          TOBY (V.O.)
            Likewise.

                        SGT. DAILY
            Sorry, Miss Parker. It'll be dark
            soon — we're gonna have to turn
            back.

A worried-looking Kerry nods her understanding.

                        SGT. DAILY (cont'd)
                     (into portable)
            Attention all units. The search
            is over — head back.
                     (to men nearby)
            We're heading back!

EXT. POLICE STATION - NIGHT

A police car drops Kerry off. She waves her thanks,
gets into her car and drives off.

EXT. TOOMEY'S BOARDING HOUSE - NIGHT

All the rooms are dark save one.

INT. TOOMEY'S - KERRY'S ROOM - NIGHT

Kerry looks both emotionally and physically drained.

                        DAN (V.O.)
            What now?

                          KERRY
                     (into phone)
            Until I find out what happened to
            her, I'm not leaving.

                        DAN (V.O.)
            I understand.
                     (jesting with her)
            Of course, I'll have to hire three
            people to do your work.

As tired as she is, Kerry forces a smile.

                          KERRY
            Maybe four.

                        DAN (V.O.)
            We can't afford four.

                    KERRY
        Did we get that party in Bel Air?

                    DAN (V.O.)
        Four thousand dollars worth.

                    KERRY
        That's terrific.

                    DAN (V.O.)
        By the way, where did you put the
        file on the Studio City function?

                    KERRY
        It's not on my desk?

                    DAN (V.O.)
        Nope.

                    KERRY
        Then try the bottom drawer.

                    DAN (V.O.)
        I hope Elaine shows up.

                    KERRY
        Thanks, Dan — talk to you later.

EXT. CAFE - MAIN STREET - EARLY MORNING

People are hurriedly entering and exiting the cafe.

INT. CAFE - EARLY MORNING

Kerry, at a booth, turns and sees Mike Burrows sitting
behind her, by himself. He sees her and comes over.

                    MIKE
        Sorry about yesterday.

                    KERRY
        No problem. By yourself?
            (on his nod)
        Why don't you join me.

Mike goes to his table and carries his breakfast over.

                    KERRY (cont'd)
            (as he sits down)
        You have two nice-looking boys.

                    MIKE
        Thanks. But since the divorce,
        Jake has become a handful and of
        course, with Kathy's problem—
            (MORE)

                         MIKE (cont'd)
                    (catches himself;
                    looks embarrassed)
          I'm sorry. I don't even know you
          and here I am, dumping my problems
          on you.

                         KERRY
                    (smiles)
          That's all right.

                         MIKE
          Kathy talks about your sister all
          the time. Said she's one of the
          few people from her past who still
          keeps in touch.

                         KERRY
          Elaine's good that way.

                         MIKE
          What are you doing here?

                         KERRY
          Looking for Elaine.

                         MIKE
          She's in town?

                         KERRY
          She was Friday night.

                         MIKE
          I'm surprised Kathy didn't say
          something about that.

                         KERRY
          That's just it — she never
          contacted Kathy. She's missing
          —and yesterday, the police found
          her rental car in the woods.

                         MIKE
          That was her car?
                    (on Kerry's nod)
          I spoke to one of the guys who was
          on the search. If I can help in
          any way, let me know.

Kerry nods. Mike checks his watch. Stands up.

                         MIKE (cont'd)
          You can usually find me here every
          morning 'bout this time.
                    (to Waitress O.S.)
          Millie. Check please.

EXT. CAFE - MAIN STREET - EARLY MORNING

Kerry stands by her car, glancing at her watch, looking
unsure of what to do next.

EXT. WOODS - DAY

Kerry follows a dirt road through the woods into an open
field. She stands on the spot where her sister's rental
car had obviously been found.

She looks at the tire marks, then glances around at the
woods on the opposite side of the open field. She looks
off contemplatively. Then, after a moment, heads back.

EXT. RURAL ROAD BORDERING WOODS - DAY

When Kerry reaches the road, she sees a police car and
Sgt. Daily standing behind her car.

                    SGT. DAILY
          I was wondering whose car this
          was.

                    KERRY
          Just looking around.

                    SGT. DAILY
          Is there anything you can tell me
          about your sister that might aid
          our investigation?

Kerry looks at Daily with both surprise and respect.

                    KERRY
          Since she's disappeared, you're
          the only one who's shown any real
          interest.

                    SGT. DAILY
          Just doing my job.

                    KERRY
               (reluctantly)
          My sister has emotional problems.

                    SGT. DAILY
          She's disappeared before?

                    KERRY
          Yes, but never more than a few
          days without contacting me.

                    SGT. DAILY
          Anything else?

                         CENTRAL (V.O.)
                Central to three-oh-eight.

Daily grabs the portable unit on his belt.

                         SGT. DAILY
                      (into portable)
                This is three-oh-eight. Go ahead,
                Central.

                         CENTRAL (V.O.)
                The body of an unidentified woman
                has been found behind Hillside
                Cemetery.

Kerry is jolted and mutters, "Oh my God."

                         SGT. DAILY
                      (into portable)
                I'm on my way. Three-oh-eight,
                out.
                      (to Kerry)
                It could be someone else.

                         KERRY
                      (convinced)
                No, it's her. I know it.

                         SGT. DAILY
                Why don't you follow me.

Kerry walks to her car with a terrible sinking feeling.

EXT. HILLSIDE CEMETERY - DAY

The coroner's wagon is parked on a dirt road behind the
cemetery. Investigators are walking the perimeter. The
coroner, DR. ANN COMPTON, 40s, stands over the covered
body. She turns as Kerry and Sgt. Daily approach.

                         DR. COMPTON
                Sergeant.

                         SGT. DAILY
                Dr. Compton. This is Kerry
                Parker. Her sister is missing.

Dr. Compton pulls the cover back revealing the nude,
lifeless body of Elaine. Kerry turns away and weeps.

Dr. Compton puts her arms around Kerry. At first, Kerry
tries to push away, then accepts the doctor's comfort.

INT. POLICE STATION - OFFICE - EVENING

Lt. Haskins sits behind his desk. Across from him,
Kerry sits in a trance while Sgt. Daily stands over her.

                    LT. HASKINS
                  (into phone)
          Thanks, Doctor.

Haskins hangs up — then addresses Kerry.

                    LT. HASKINS (cont'd)
          According to the preliminary,
          death was caused by strangulation.

Half-dazed, Kerry looks at Haskins.

                    KERRY
          Was she raped?

Haskins nods. Kerry breaks down again.

EXT. POLICE STATION - EVENING

A grief-stricken Kerry walks out of the police station
accompanied by Sgt. Daily. At her car —

                    SGT. DAILY
          Can I give you a ride somewhere?

Kerry shakes her head. Mike Burrows' pickup truck pulls
up next to them and stops. Mike jumps out.

                    SGT. DAILY (cont'd)
          Hi, Mike.

                    MIKE
          Tom.   .
                  (to Kerry)
          I'm sorry about your sister.

Kerry just stares at Mike with a blank expression.

                    SGT. DAILY
                  (to Kerry)
          Is there anything I can do?

                    KERRY
                  (low but hard)
          You can catch the bastard who
          raped and murdered her.

Daily nods then heads back into the police station.

                    MIKE
                (to Kerry)
        I stopped off and told Kathy. She
        took it hard.

Kerry leans against her car, still reeling.

                    MIKE (cont'd)
        I know you're probably not hungry,
        but why don't you come with me. I
        need to get something to eat. I
        can at least keep you company.
                (on her blank look)
        C'mon.

Mike gently leads her to his pickup truck.

INT. FAMILY-STYLE RESTAURANT - NIGHT

Kerry watches Mike finish his dinner.

                    KERRY
        All of a sudden, I'm hungry. I
        haven't eaten since breakfast.

                    MIKE
        Good. Waitress!

INT. FAMILY-STYLE RESTAURANT - LATER THAT NIGHT

It's now Mike's turn to watch Kerry finish her dinner.

                    MIKE
        I think you ate more than me.

Kerry forces a weary smile.

                    MIKE (cont'd)
        What are your plans?

                    KERRY
                (confused)
        Plans?

                    MIKE
        Regarding Elaine.

                    KERRY
        Her wish was to be cremated.

                    MIKE
        What about your parents?

                    KERRY
        My father's dead and my mother...
        she's... she's in an institution.

                    MIKE
        Sounds like you've had it rough.

Not wishing to discuss it further, Kerry gets anxious.

                    KERRY
        Can we get out of here?

                    MIKE
        Sure.

EXT. POLICE STATION - NIGHT

Mike stands next to Kerry who is sitting in her car.

                    MIKE
        When are you going back to
        California?

                    KERRY
        As soon as I make the arrangements
        for Elaine.

                    MIKE
        Are you flying from Logan?
              (on her nod)
        Why don't you turn in your rental
        here and I'll drive you.

                    KERRY
        No, that's okay.

                    MIKE
        Kerry. You shouldn't be driving;
        you could have an accident. Let
        me drive you to wherever you're
        staying and to the airport later.

Ever stubborn, Kerry responds firmly —

                    KERRY
        I'll be all right.

Mike gives her a chewed-up business card.

                    MIKE
        If you need to reach me, my beeper
        number's on there. Be careful
        driving.

She backs her car out of the space and drives away while
Mike looks after her, concerned.

INT. TOOMEY'S - KERRY'S ROOM - NIGHT

The night table light is on. Kerry is in bed, under the
covers, lying on her side, looking off into space.

EXT. MAIN STREET - EARLY MORNING

Kerry is walking down the sidewalk, half-dazed. A car
pulls up to the curb and a man calls out, "Miss Parker."

Dressed in civilian clothes, she doesn't recognize Sgt.
Daily right away. She approaches his car.

                    KERRY
          Sgt. Daily?

                    SGT. DAILY
          I'd like to talk to you.

                    KERRY
          Sure.

                    SGT. DAILY
          But not here — hop in.

Kerry slides into the passenger seat.

INT. DAILY'S MOVING CAR - EARLY MORNING

Driving down Main Street, a police car passes them from
the opposite direction. The policeman waves to Daily.
His concerned expression does not go unnoticed by Kerry.

EXT. SIDE STREET - ABANDONED FACTORY - EARLY MORNING

Daily's car pulls in and stops near an abandoned factory
— well hidden from view on the street.

INT. DAILY'S PARKED CAR - EARLY MORNING

Daily's cautious behavior sparks Kerry's curiosity.

                    KERRY
          Why'd you pull in here?

                    SGT. DAILY
          I don't want anyone to see us
          together.

Unlike before, Daily is not the calm professional — and
Kerry is no longer out of focus, but highly alert.

                    SGT. DAILY (cont'd)
          I'm going to tell you something,
          but you've got to promise you
          won't repeat it to anyone.

                    KERRY
        This obviously has something to do
        with my sister, so I can't make
        that promise.

                    SGT. DAILY
                  (adamantly)
        If I tell you what I know, it
        could mean my job — and I've got a
        family to support.

Kerry waits. When it is obvious he won't say more —

                    KERRY
                  (opening door)
        Then I'm going to Lt. Haskins and
        tell him about this.

EXT. DAILY'S CAR - EARLY MORNING

Kerry gets out. Daily gets out and blocks her retreat.

                    SGT. DAILY
        Wait a minute!

He agonizes, then after a beat —

                    SGT. DAILY (cont'd)
        It has something to do with him.

                    KERRY
        I'll make a deal with you. Tell
        me what you know and I promise — I
        won't reveal you as my source.

                    SGT. DAILY
        The problem is — if he is
        confronted with this by anyone, he
        will know it came from me.

                    KERRY
        Sergeant. You've been very nice
        to me. Trust me. I'll find a way
        to keep you out of it.

Daily looks off in frustration — torn between keeping
silent and telling what he knows. Finally —

                    SGT. DAILY
        Last night, photos of your sister
        were delivered by the coroner's
        office. Looking at them, I
        realized I'd seen her before.

                    KERRY
        Where?

                    SGT. DAILY
          Outside the station last Friday
          night, talking to Lt. Haskins.

                    KERRY
          She didn't go inside?

                    SGT. DAILY
          I don't think so. Look, I was off
          Friday. When I stopped by to see
          Jim Quill — he was on the desk —I
          saw the Lieutenant and your sister
          talking on the front steps. When
          I came out, they were gone.

His expression convinces Kerry he is holding back.

                    KERRY
          What else?

                    SGT. DAILY
          When I was looking at the photos,
          the Lieutenant showed up. And
          when I told him she was the woman
          I saw him talking with last
          Friday, he said I was mistaken.
          When I told him I was absolutely
          sure, he became angry, said I was
          wrong and told me never to mention
          it again — to him or anyone else.

                    KERRY
          Why would he do that unless he had
          something to hide?
                    (beat)
          Could he have raped and murdered
          my sister?

Daily — sorry he told Kerry anything — is agitated.

                    SGT. DAILY
          I don't know!

                    KERRY
          What do you know about him?

                    SGT. DAILY
          Not much. He's been with the
          department ten years. Before
          that, he was on the job in New
          York City. He keeps to himself.

There's a pause as Kerry thinks about something.

                    KERRY
          What about DNA evidence?

                    SGT. DAILY
          You mean — matching his to your
          sister's murderer?

                    KERRY
          Exactly.

                    SGT. DAILY
          To get a sample from him, he'd
          have to be a suspect — and that
          means I'd have to come forward.

                    KERRY
          So? What if it matched?

                    SGT. DAILY
          What if it didn't? I'd be out of
          a job.

                    KERRY
          Can't you go to the chief? Maybe
          he could help.

                    SGT. DAILY
          Chief Lavery's six weeks away from
          retiring. Forget him. For the
          past year, he's let the Lieutenant
          run the department.

                    KERRY
          What about the F.B.I.?

                    SGT. DAILY
          Same problem. I'd have to come
          forward.
                    (beat)
          There is one thing. I know a
          detective with the State Police.
          Without tipping my hand, I might
          be able to get advice from him.

                    KERRY
          All right. I won't do anything
          until I hear from you.

Daily looks greatly relieved.

                    KERRY (cont'd)
          I'm staying at Toomey's. If I
          need to, how do I contact you?

                    SGT. DAILY
          I'll give you my home number.

Kerry retrieves a pen and paper from her pocketbook.
Using the roof of his car, he writes down his number.

                    SGT. DAILY
          Would you mind walking back?

                    KERRY
          No. Do you know where the
          coroner's office is?

                    SGT. DAILY
          It's in Pittsfield.

                    KERRY
          I'll wait to hear from you.

Daily hops into his car — Kerry walks off.

EXT. MAIN STREET - EARLY MORNING

Kerry is focused and walking with much deliberation.

INT. TOOMEY'S - KERRY'S ROOM - EARLY MORNING

Kerry sits at the little table with pen and paper
scribbling notes, thinking.

INT. DAN WALLACE'S APARTMENT - BEDROOM - NIGHT

The room is in TOTAL DARKNESS except the face of a
DIGITAL CLOCK on the night table. It's 4:45 a.m. The
RINGING PHONE prompts an ANGRY GROAN.

The night table light goes on. Dan looks at the clock
in disbelief and picks up the phone.

                    DAN
                (into phone)
          This better be important.

                    KERRY (V.O.)
          Dan, it's me.

                    DAN
          Do you realize what time it is
          here? We did the Halifax party; I
          just got in two hours ago.

                    KERRY (V.O.)
          I'm sorry — but I wanted to tell
          you I won't be coming back right
          away.

Dan sits up wiping the cobwebs away from his eyes.

                    DAN
          What's right away mean?

                         KERRY (V.O.)
          It means I don't know when —
          Elaine was raped and murdered.

                         DAN
          Jesus...
                    (beat; then)
          Oh, Kerry. I'm so sorry.

                         KERRY (V.O.)
          Make whatever arrangements you
          have to, to cover me.

                         DAN
          Sure. Anything on the murderer?

                         KERRY (V.O.)
          One possible lead.

                         DAN
          Is there anything I can do for
          you?

                         KERRY (V.O.)
          Just keep the business going 'til
          I come back. I'll be in touch.

INT. DR. COMPTON'S OFFICE - DAY

A highly-impatient Dr. Compton vents into the phone.

                         DR. COMPTON
                    (into phone)
          The last bunch of samples I sent
          over came back three weeks late.
          It's inexcusable... I don't care.
          That's your problem, not mine. If
          you can't straighten this out
          immediately, there are plenty of
          other labs eager for my business.

After Dr. Compton hangs up abruptly, she instantly
changes her demeanor and smiles pleasantly at Kerry.

                         DR. COMPTON (cont'd)
          Now. How are you doing?

                         KERRY
          A little better than yesterday.

                         DR. COMPTON
          Are you here regarding the
          disposition of your sister's body?

                         KERRY
          That — and I had a question.

                         DR. COMPTON
          Fire away.

                            KERRY
          What would happen if you ran a DNA
          test on someone — who was not a
          suspect — and it matched the
          evidence in a murder case?

Dr. Compton studies Kerry curiously.

                         DR. COMPTON
          Somehow I have the feeling you're
          not talking hypothetically.
                    (on Kerry's silence)
          My work is strictly forensic —
          preparing evidence. I leave
          matters of the law to the
          prosecutors and the courts.

                            KERRY
                    (nods; then)
          What about my sister's body?

                         DR. COMPTON
          You can make your arrangements.

Thinking about it, Kerry has to fight back tears.

EXT. BURROWS' HOUSE - DAY

Kerry calls inside through the screen door.

                            KERRY
          Kathy?

                         KATHY (O.S.)
          Just a minute!

Kathy appears — her face flushed with alcohol.

INT. BURROWS' HOUSE - FOYER - DAY

Kerry and Kathy hold each other tightly, weeping.

                            KATHY
          I just can't believe it.

Kathy is even more devastated than Kerry, so Kerry gives
her comfort. After a long moment, they separate and
Kerry leads Kathy into the living room.

INT. LIVING ROOM - DAY

Kerry sits across from a teary-eyed Kathy who is
sentimental and reminiscent.

                              KATHY
                    Elaine was my only real friend.
                    The last time we saw each other
                    was at my wedding. She always
                    remembered my birthday with a
                    card and phone call — and at
                    Christmas, she'd send a card and
                    fill out every inch of space with
                    notes about when we were kids.

A CAR DOOR SHUTS. A few moments later — Mike, Jake, and
Tommy enter.

                              TOMMY
                    Mommy!

He races to her. His shirt and face are smeared with
the remnants of chocolate. Jake is not much better.

                              KATHY
                         (pulling Tommy's
                         shirt over his head)
                    This was a brand new shirt! Now
                    look at it.

                              MIKE
                         (evenly)
                    It's only ice cream. It'll wash
                    out.

                              KATHY
                    Easy for you to say — you're not
                    the one who has to do the wash.
                         (to Tommy)
                    Go put another shirt on.

Tommy races out of the room making like an airplane —
arms out, shoulder high, sound effects and all.

Jake looks at Kerry and smiles. She smiles back at him.

                         KATHY (cont'd)
                    Jake. C'mere.

He goes to his mother. She strips his shirt off.

                         KATHY (cont'd)
                    You, too. Put a clean shirt on.

He races out of the room. Mike looks at Kerry.

                              MIKE
                    How are you doing?

                              KERRY
                    All right.

                    TOMMY (O.S.)
        Mom! Jake took my shirt!

Kathy exits. From the stairs —

                    KATHY (O.S.)
        Jake! If you took Tommy's shirt,
        so help me — you're gonna spend
        the night sleeping in a tree.

Kerry smiles — Mike shakes his head.

                    KERRY
        With Kathy's problem, aren't you
        concerned for the boys' safety?

                    MIKE
        I've been to court on that. And
        the funny thing is — there's never
        been an incident. Even on bad
        days she somehow functions. As
        long as there are no problems and
        she goes to counseling twice a
        week, she has custody.

                    KERRY
        Does she drive?

                    MIKE
        She's not allowed to. One of the
        neighbors helps out — takes her
        shopping, drops her off for
        counseling and watches the boys.
        I'm around as much as I can be.

Kathy returns to her drink in the kitchen. Kerry stands
in the doorway, poised to leave.

                    KERRY
        I have to go.

                    KATHY
        How long will you be in town?

                    KERRY
        A while longer.

Hearing that, Kathy looks a bit relieved.

                    KATHY
        I'd like to see you again.

                    KERRY
        I'll be back.

Kathy smiles gratefully through an alcoholic haze.

EXT. BURROWS' HOUSE - DAY

Mike walks Kerry to her car.

>   MIKE
>   I'm tired of having to apologize
>   for my wife.

>   KERRY
>   You mean _ex_-wife, don't you?

>   MIKE
>   Yeah.

>   KERRY
>   Why do I have the feeling you
>   still love her?

>   MIKE
>   She wasn't always this way.

>   KERRY
>   What made her change?

>   MIKE
>   Who knows? We went through two
>   years of counseling together — and
>   not once would she open up.

>   KERRY
>   (nods; then)
>   See you for breakfast tomorrow?

>   MIKE
>   I'll be there.

INT. CAFE - EARLY MORNING

Kerry sits in a booth facing the front door, sipping
coffee, waiting for Mike. Unlike other mornings, the
crowd seems hushed, even somber.

Mike, despondent, enters and slides into the booth.

>   KERRY
>   What's wrong?

>   MIKE
>   Tom Daily was killed last night.

>   KERRY
>   (shocked)
>   Oh, no...

MILLIE HALE, 30s, the waitress, appears at their booth.

                    MILLIE
          Coffee, Mike?

Mike nods — Millie walks off.

                    KERRY
          Do you know how it happened?

                    MIKE
          I heard it was just a routine
          traffic stop — you know, he pulled
          over a car with a busted
          taillight. Next thing, he's shot.

                    KERRY
          Do the police have any leads?

                    MIKE
          No. He supposedly made the stop
          without calling in.

Mike looks at Kerry in total disbelief.

                    MIKE (cont'd)
          We grew up together. He was like
          a brother to me.

EXT. CAFE - EARLY MORNING

They walk out together and say goodbye. Mike heads for
his pickup truck — Kerry walks along Main Street.

EXT. MASSACHUSETTS TURNPIKE - DAY

Kerry's car gets off at the "Route 91 South" exit
heading for Springfield.

EXT. MAIN STREET - SPRINGFIELD, MA - DAY

Kerry parks her car outside an office building.

INT. OFFICE BUILDING - CORRIDOR - DAY

She approaches an office and goes inside. Stenciled on
the door — "C.H. HIBBS - PRIVATE INQUIRY AGENCY"

INT. C.H. HIBBS - PRIVATE OFFICE - DAY

C.H. HIBBS, 50s, stocky, wearing a well-tailored, neatly
pressed suit, sits behind his highly polished oak desk.
Like him, the room, down to every detail, is immaculate.

Kerry, sitting across from him, is obviously impressed.
Hibbs, an Englishman, has a very formal way of speaking.

                    HIBBS
          Now, Miss Parker, who may I ask
          referred you to me?

                    KERRY
          I saw your ad in the Yellow Pages.

                    HIBBS
                 (amused; he smiles)
          How can I be of service to you?

                    KERRY
          Since I've never hired a private
          investigator, can you tell me how
          much you charge?

                    HIBBS
          The daily rate is six hundred
          dollars plus expenses.
                 (on her startled look)
          I'm sure you can retain someone
          for less.

                    KERRY
          But not better?

Hibbs smiles. Handing Hibbs a piece of paper from her
pocketbook, a piece of lint drops on his desk.

                    KERRY (cont'd)
          I would like you to investigate
          this man.

With a whisk of his hand, Hibbs wipes the lint off his
desk. He reads the paper, then looks at Kerry.

                    HIBBS
          May I ask why?

                    KERRY
          Does it matter?

                    HIBBS
          Since he is a law enforcement
          officer, knowing why would
          determine how I would proceed.
                 (on her silence)
          As a client, you can be assured of
          my strictest confidence.

                    KERRY
          I believe he raped and murdered my
          sister.

                    HIBBS
          Why don't you go to the police?

                         KERRY
          At some point I will.

                         HIBBS
          Regarding his tenure with the New
          York City Police Department, some
          of the information can be obtained
          by computer, but in this case,
          going to New York would be more
          effective. I bring this to your
          attention because it would require
          additional travel expenditures.

                         KERRY
          How much?

                         HIBBS
          At least five hundred dollars per
          day. But with any luck, it should
          only take a day or two.

                         KERRY
          Fine.

INT. MOVING POLICE CAR - DAY

Lt. Haskins follows a long driveway to a beautiful house
sitting on five manicured acres. Nearing the house, he
sees DENNIS LUDLOW, 50, coming out the front door.

EXT. HOUSE - DAY

Haskins gets out of his cruiser and approaches Ludlow.

                         LT. HASKINS
                    (nods respectfully)
          Mr. Ludlow.

                         LUDLOW
          What can I do for you, Lieutenant?

EXT. CEMETERY - DAY

Uniformed policemen from all over New England stand
witness to the burial of one of their own.

The casket is positioned over the open grave site.
Linda Daily weeps and comforts her two sons as the
MINISTER reads an appropriate passage from the Bible.

Kerry stands with Mike and Kathy Burrows. Across from
them is Lt. Haskins. At one point, he looks over and
sees Kerry staring at him. Their eyes lock for a long
moment until finally, Haskins looks away. Mike watches
Kerry as she continues staring at Haskins in a most
unnerving manner.

EXT. STREET - OUTSIDE CEMETERY - DAY

People are walking to their cars from the grave site.
Kerry walks with Mike and Kathy.

                    MIKE
               (to Kerry)
          Are you gonna join us at Linda's?

                    KERRY
          I'm really not up to. it.

Mike nods. Kerry looks at Kathy — who appears numb —
then walks to her car.

INT. TOOMEY'S - KERRY'S ROOM - NIGHT

Kerry stands by the window looking outside, transfixed.
After a moment, she goes to the night table, retrieves
the phone directory and takes it to the small desk.

She pages through the directory, then stops. She grabs
a pen and pad from her pocketbook and writes.

CLOSE ON PAD as she writes "Haskins, 123 Elm Street."

EXT. ELM STREET - NIGHT

Kerry's car proceeds slowly up the block passing modest
but well-kept houses and stops outside #123.

INT. KERRY'S SLOW MOVING CAR - NIGHT

Kerry looks at Haskins' house curiously.

EXT. CAFE - EARLY MORNING

Kerry heads inside. Mike's pickup is parked out front.

INT. CAFE - EARLY MORNING

The place is busy. Kerry slides into Mike's booth. He
is a bit subdued — still not himself.

                    KERRY
          Mornin'.

Kerry follows Mike's gaze over to a table where three
young women look their way in obvious speculation.

                    KERRY (cont'd)
          Fan club?

                    MIKE
          I can just imagine what they're
          saying.

                    KERRY
          Maybe we shouldn't keep meeting
          like this.

Mike smiles. Millie brings over a cup.

                    MILLIE
          Coffee, miss?

                    KERRY
          Please.

Millie pours her. Mike gestures at his cup for a
refill. After Millie pours his and moves off —

                    MIKE
          What was that all about yesterday?

                    KERRY
          What?

                    MIKE
          You and Haskins.

                    KERRY
               (evenly)
          I don't know what you mean.

                    MIKE
          You kept staring at him.

                    KERRY
          I must've been in a fog.

Mike sips his coffee. After a beat —

                    MIKE
          Kathy told me she really likes
          you. I guess it has something to
          do with you being Elaine's sister.

                    KERRY
          That's funny, because we're total
          opposites.

                    MIKE
          How's that?

                    KERRY
          Elaine lived in the past and had a
          hard time dealing with the
          present. Her marriage went bad
          after a year, she got divorced and
          sort of... retreated from life.

Thinking about Elaine, Kerry gets teary-eyed.

She is overcome with both pain and regret.

> KERRY (cont'd)
> I wish I'd spent more time with
> her.

Mike nods his understanding. After a long silence —

> MIKE
> I take it you're not married.

> KERRY
> I broke off my engagement last
> year — to my business partner. It
> got to be too much — you know,
> spending sixteen hours a day
> together. We both realized we had
> a better chance of making our
> partnership work than a marriage.

> MIKE
> I'd find it hard workin' with
> someone I used to be engaged to.

> KERRY
> It's worked out well. Dan's a
> very sensitive person and in spite
> of the problems we've had, we're
> still quite close.

> MIKE
> What kind of business are you in?

> KERRY
> Catering.

Millie steps up with her order pad.

INT. TOOMEY'S - KERRY'S ROOM - DAY

> SGT. QUILL (V.O.)
> Police department. Sgt. Quill.

> KERRY
> (into phone)
> Lt. Haskins, please.

> SGT. QUILL (V.O.)
> Who's calling?

Kerry hangs up looking pleased.

EXT. ELM STREET - DAY

Kerry's car cruises down the street and stops in front
of Haskins' house.

EXT. HASKINS' HOUSE - DAY

Kerry looks inside the house through the screen door.
She HEARS someone MOVING ABOUT. She RINGS the DOORBELL.

GAIL HASKINS, late 30s, cautiously approaches the door
and stands some distance back from it. Her head is
cocked to the right as to obscure that side of her face.

                    KERRY
          I'm looking for a Sarah Miller.

                    GAIL
          Don't know her.

Gail turns enough so Kerry can see her right black eye.

                    KERRY
          Thanks anyway.

Kerry walks back to her car looking a little disturbed
and mutters under her breath, "That son of a bitch."

EXT. HASKINS' HOUSE - DAY

Kerry gets into her car and sits there.

INT. KERRY'S PARKED CAR - DAY

Kerry is looking at the front page of the newspaper.

CLOSE ON headline: "COP KILLED IN LINE OF DUTY" Then:

CLOSE ON article reading: "According to Esther Pratt, at
148 Orchard Hill Road, the incident occurred at eleven
p.m. when she heard two shots and called the police."

BACK TO SCENE as Kerry is startled by a voice.

                    MIKE (O.S.)
          What are you doing here?

Kerry looks out her window and sees Mike in his pickup
truck, passenger window down, gazing at her curiously.
The back of his truck is loaded with lumber.

                    KERRY
               (caught off guard)
          I... uh... got lost.

Mike looks at her skeptically.

                    MIKE
          Haskins lives here. What the
          hell's going on?

Kerry expels a breath in resignation. She then happens
to glance at the house and sees Gail looking their way.

                    KERRY
          I'll explain later.

                    MIKE
          When?

                    KERRY
          I can meet you for dinner.

                    MIKE
          It'll have to be late, I'm picking
          the boys up around five.

                    KERRY
          You tell me then.

                    MIKE
          Nine o'clock at the Black Kettle.
          Follow Main Street — it's just
          north of town.

With that, Mike drives off. Kerry keys the ignition and
pulls away under the watchful eye of Gail Haskins.

EXT. ORCHARD HILL ROAD - DAY

Kerry's car pulls into a driveway past a mailbox: PRATT.

EXT. PRATT HOUSE - DAY

The house is well-kept. Along the side, a beautiful
garden is being tended by a cheerful ESTHER PRATT, 70s.

Kerry, clutching the newspaper, approaches her.

                    ESTHER
          Are you here to pick up the
          clothing for the Women's League?

                    KERRY
          No. Kerry Parker.
               (showing newspaper)
          I wanted to talk to you about the
          night Sgt. Daily was killed.

                    ESTHER
          What a tragedy. Are you a
          reporter?

                    KERRY
          Freelance writer. Would you mind
          answering a few questions?

> ESTHER
> No.

> KERRY
> Where did it happen?

> ESTHER
> (pointing)
> Just up the road a ways.

> KERRY
> After you heard the shots, you
> called the police. Then what?

> ESTHER
> I went to the front window and
> looked outside.

> KERRY
> Did you see anything?

> ESTHER
> No. But before I got there, I
> heard a car racing down the hill.

Kerry thinks a moment, then—

> KERRY
> Did it make any distinct sounds?

> ESTHER
> They all sound the same to me. If
> my husband were alive, he could
> tell the difference. He was a
> mechanic.

> KERRY
> (looking disappointed)
> Thanks, Mrs. Pratt.

Kerry heads for her car. Esther turns. Seeing her own
car prompts a sudden realization.

> ESTHER
> Miss!
> (as Kerry walks back)
> That car — it had a fan belt that
> squealed.

Kerry nods thoughtfully and smiles at Esther.

> KERRY
> Thank you, Mrs. Pratt.

Kerry walks back to her car.

EXT. MAIN STREET - NIGHT

Kerry exits a store. Deep in thought, she crosses in
the middle of the block without looking in either
direction. A speeding van races by. Just as it is
about to hit her, a MAN, 40, pulls her back.

                    MAN
               (looking after van)
          Damn fool.

Realizing how close she came to being hit, Kerry stands
there trembling and collecting herself.

                    MAN (cont'd)
          Are you all right, miss?

                    KERRY
               (nods gratefully)
          Thanks.

EXT. BLACK KETTLE RESTAURANT - NIGHT

Patrons are exiting — heading for their cars.

INT. BLACK KETTLE RESTAURANT - DINING ROOM - NIGHT

Given the lateness of the dinner hour, Kerry and Mike
are sitting off by themselves.

                    KERRY
          And that's it.

Mike takes a moment to digest what he has been told.

                    MIKE
          I think you should go to the State
          Police — or maybe even the F.B.I.
          and tell them everything.

                    KERRY
          No — not yet.

                    MIKE
          Why not?

                    KERRY
          If it isn't handled properly, he
          could walk.

                    MIKE
          You think you can do a better job
          than the police?
               (on her silence)
          What about what Tom Daily told
          you?

                    KERRY
He could deny it, then what?
I want to get a sample from
Haskins without him knowing it,
have it tested, then compared to
the DNA from Elaine's murder.

                    MIKE
How the hell you gonna do that?

                    KERRY
I'll get a hair from a jacket or
his car, something.

                    MIKE
Let's say you get a sample and
have it tested. How will you get
it compared to the evidence?

                    KERRY
I'll go to the prosecutor.

                    MIKE
And say what?

                    KERRY
I have DNA test results that may
match the DNA evidence from my
sister's murder.

                    MIKE
They won't test it without knowing
whose it is.

                    KERRY
                (adamantly)
I'll find a way.

                    MIKE
I wish you'd just go to the State
Police and let them handle it. I
think you're asking for trouble.

                    KERRY
                (angrily)
It was my sister who was raped and
murdered, not yours!

Annoyed that she made an outburst, Kerry addresses Mike
in a far more pleasant tone, yet is still very firm.

                    KERRY (cont'd)
Mike. I appreciate your concern,
but I know what I'm doing.

Mike looks at Kerry as she retreats into silence.

EXT. BLACK KETTLE RESTAURANT - NIGHT

Mike stands next to Kerry as she unlocks her car.

> KERRY
> I hired a private investigator to
> check out Haskins.

Mike looks at Kerry in amazement.

> MIKE
> You're really serious about this.

> KERRY
> I must've been a bull terrier in
> another life.

> MIKE
> (smiles; then)
> If I can help — without ending up
> in court or jail — I will.

She kisses him on the cheek and quickly slides into the
front seat of her car.

Mike stands there watching her drive off.

Across the street, a car, facing the restaurant parking
lot, sits in the shadows of a huge oak tree. From this
distance, it is impossible to identify the car or see
any details except the outline of a figure inside.

EXT. POLICE DEPARTMENT - MORNING

A police car pulls away from the station house. After
it disappears down the street, Kerry reveals herself
from behind a tree across the street. She glances at
her watch and looks up the street expectantly. All of a
sudden, she pulls back behind the tree.

A few moments later, Kerry peers around the tree and
listens carefully as Haskins drives by in his 4X4 and
parks in his assigned space. Not hearing any fan belt
squeal, she looks disappointed.

After Haskins goes inside, Kerry walks off.

EXT. ELM STREET - DAY

Kerry's car slowly cruises by Haskins' house.

INT. KERRY'S MOVING CAR - DAY

She glances at Haskins' house and sees the open front
door. She looks both anxious and a little unsure.

EXT. ELM STREET - DAY

Kerry's car resumes normal speed and turns the corner.

EXT. BURROWS' HOUSE - DAY

Tommy races to the screen door and smiles at Kerry.

> KERRY
> Hi, Tommy. Is your mom here?

> KATHY (O.S.)
> Come on in!

INT. BURROWS' HOUSE - KITCHEN - DAY

Kathy — looking sober and dressed to go out — is checking the cupboard and making a list while Kerry observes. The PHONE RINGS. Kathy grabs it.

> KATHY
> (into phone)
> Hello?.. Hi, Mary Ann, I'm ready whenever you are... When then?..

Understanding what's going on, Kerry waves to Kathy.

> KERRY
> I'll take you.

> KATHY
> Mary Ann, never mind. I've got someone who'll take me...

Kathy hangs up.

> KATHY (cont'd)
> You don't mind?

> KERRY
> Not at all.

> KATHY
> Jake! Tommy! Let's go.

INT. SUPERMARKET - DAY

Jake and Tommy are grabbing candy from the shelf and dropping it into the shopping cart.

> KATHY
> Put it back.

> JAKE
> But I want it!

                         KATHY
             I said — put it back, <u>now</u>.

Tommy can't reach inside the cart, so Kerry lifts him
up. He takes his out — but Jake stands defiant.

                         JAKE
             No!

                         KATHY
             I'm not telling you again.

                         JAKE
             I hate you!

With that, Jake runs down the aisle and disappears
around the corner.

                         KERRY
             I'll get him.

                         TOMMY
                    (timidly)
             Mommy. Can I have some candy?

Kathy smiles and nods "yes."

INT. SUPERMARKET - DIFFERENT AISLE - DAY

Kerry finds Jake sulking by a shelf.

                         KERRY
             What's the matter, Jake?

                         JAKE
             I hate her.

                         KERRY
             That's not a nice thing to say.

                         JAKE
             I don't care.

                         KERRY
             You should care. She's your
             mother and she loves you very
             much.

                         JAKE
             If she loved me, she'd buy me some
             candy.

                         KERRY
             It's really not good for you. If
             I were your mother, I probably
             wouldn't buy it for you either.

                              JAKE
                    Then I'd hate you, too.

Kerry can't help but smile. She offers him her hand.

                              KERRY
                    C'mon, tough guy.

Reluctantly, he takes it and they walk off together.

EXT. SUPERMARKET PARKING LOT - DAY

Kerry is holding Jake's and Tommy's hands while Kathy
pushes the grocery cart to Kerry's car.

As they load the groceries into the trunk, a car passes
behind them with a SQUEALING FAN BELT.

Kerry spins around and sees an older model station wagon
driven by Gail Haskins.

As the station wagon crosses the parking lot, Kerry
looks after it, transfixed. Kathy notices this.

                              KATHY
                    What's the problem?

Kerry snaps out of it and looks at Kathy.

                              KERRY
                    Nothing.

They finish loading the groceries into the trunk.

INT. BURROWS' HOUSE - KITCHEN - DAY

Kerry is helping Kathy put the groceries away.

                              KERRY
                         (holding two cans)
                    Where do these go?

                              KATHY
                         (gesturing at cupboard)
                    Over there. Second shelf.

Kerry puts the cans on the shelf, then tries to find a
home for a box of plastic garbage bags.

                              KATHY (cont'd)
                         (observing Kerry)
                    The cabinet below the sink, to the
                    right.

In putting the garbage bags away, Kerry sees a box of
Ziplock plastic bags. She picks the box up.

                    KERRY
          Mind if I take two of these?

                    KATHY
          Help yourself.

Kerry goes to her pocketbook on the counter and puts two
Ziplock bags inside. From the kitchen doorway, through
the living room window, she sees Mike stop out front.

                    KERRY
          Mike's home.

                    KATHY
                (reacts)
          Home?

                    KERRY
          I mean — he's here.

A few moments later, Mike enters. He smiles at Kerry
then addresses Kathy with genuine concern.

                    MIKE
                (to Kathy)
          How'd your day go?

                    KATHY
          Okay.

                    MIKE
          Where are the boys?

                    KATHY
          Upstairs.

                    MIKE
          They're awfully quiet. I'd better
          go check.

After Mike exits —

                    KATHY
          Will you stay for dinner?

                    KERRY
          How about me taking you out?

                    KATHY
          That'd be nice.

                    KERRY
          I'll come back around six.

Kathy nods. As Kerry walks out —

                    KATHY
          Thanks for helping me with the
          shopping.

Kerry smiles. Mike returns with Jake and Tommy.

                    JAKE
                 (to Kerry)
          Would you play with us?

                    KATHY
          She's leaving, Jake.

                    KERRY
          That's all right.
                 (to Jake)
          Sure.

Jake and Tommy lead Kerry outside. After they leave —

                    MIKE
          I don't have any work tomorrow, so
          why don't I take the boys for an
          overnight.

                    KATHY
          Fine. I can use a break. I'll
          pack up their stuff.

Kathy heads upstairs. Mike heads outside.

EXT. BURROWS' HOUSE - DAY

Mike comes outside. Kerry is lobbing a wiffle ball to
Tommy. He swings wildly at it and misses.

                    JAKE
          Dummy.

                    MIKE
                 (reproaching him)
          Jake!

Mike approaches Kerry.

                    MIKE (cont'd)
          Thanks for spending time with
          Kathy.

                    KERRY
          I enjoy her company.

Kerry remembers something — her focus quickly changes.

                    KERRY (cont'd)
          I've got something to tell you.

They're interrupted by Kathy. She comes outside with a
small shopping bag and hands it to Mike.

>   KATHY
>   There's a change of clothes in
>   there and unless you pick up
>   another toothbrush, they'll have
>   to share one.

Hearing that, Jake makes a face and says —

>   JAKE
>   I'm not sharing with cootie
>   breath!

Tommy looks like he might cry. Mike goes to him.

>   MIKE
>   Jake, enough now, hear me?

Jake freezes and doesn't say a word. Kathy kisses the
boys goodbye.

>   KATHY
>   (to Kerry)
>   I'll see you at six.

Kathy heads inside.

>   MIKE
>   C'mon, guys, let's go.

>   KERRY
>   I'll talk to you later.

Mike nods and helps his sons into his truck.

INT. TOOMEY'S - KERRY'S ROOM - NIGHT

Kerry is sitting on the bed holding the phone.

>   DAN (V.O.)
>   I just tallied the June figures
>   —we're up twenty-three percent
>   over last year — and July's
>   shaping up to be even bigger.

Her mind elsewhere, Kerry responds apathetically.

>   KERRY
>   That's good.

>   DAN (V.O.)
>   (jesting with her)
>   That's all you have to say?

                    KERRY
        Sorry, Dan. I'm just tired.

                    DAN (V.O.)
        You getting through this thing all
        right?

                    KERRY
        Yeah.

Seeing a note is slipped under her door —

                    KERRY (cont'd)
        I'd better let you go...

She listens to his response, then hangs up. Kerry picks
up the note and reads it.

CLOSE ON NOTE — it reads: "A Mr. Hibbs called and said
he would be in the area tomorrow and would like to meet
you for lunch. You can call his office in the morning
and work out the details. He said you have the number."

BACK TO SCENE as Kerry looks off contemplatively.

EXT. CAFE - EARLY MORNING

Kerry comes outside and glances at her watch.

EXT. POLICE DEPARTMENT - MORNING

Kerry's car drives by.

INT. KERRY'S MOVING CAR - MORNING

Kerry sees Haskins' 4X4 parked in its assigned space.

EXT. ELM STREET - MORNING

Kerry's car is parked way up the street. She gets out
wearing running gear — shorts, shirt and jogging shoes.

A man cutting his grass looks at her curiously. She
smiles at him then goes through the stretching ritual.

EXT. HASKINS' HOUSE - MORNING

Kerry jogs past Haskins' house and sees Gail standing in
the neighbor's driveway, behind the house, engrossed in
conversation with the woman next door.

Kerry stops on the other side of Haskins' house, out of
the women's view. She drops to one knee and reties a
shoe while scanning the street. Only two young boys can
be seen playing up the block.

She moves swiftly for Haskins' front porch. She glances around to make sure no one is watching her, then slips inside — quietly closing the screen door behind her.

INT. HASKINS' HOUSE - FOYER - MORNING

Kerry stands there — heart pounding — listening. She quickly shakes off her anxiety and races upstairs.

INT. BATHROOM - SECOND FLOOR - MORNING

Kerry steps into the bathroom. From her jogging shorts, she retrieves the Ziplock bags.

She picks up what is obviously a man's hair brush, pulls off a wad of matted hair and puts it into one Ziplock. She goes through the medicine cabinet, finds a man's razor and pops the blade into the other Ziplock bag.

INT. UPSTAIRS HALLWAY - MORNING

As she heads for the stairs, a SCREEN DOOR SNAPS SHUT.

> LT. HASKINS (O.S.)
> (loud & angry)
> Gail?!!

Next, the SOUND of HEAVY FOOTSTEPS COMING UPSTAIRS.

Kerry is in a state of panic. Two bedroom doors are closed, so she goes into the only one that is open.

INT. MASTER BEDROOM - MORNING

Kerry realizes where she is and mutters, "Oh, shit!"

INT. UPSTAIRS HALLWAY - MORNING

Haskins is unbuttoning his coffee-stained shirt.

INT. MASTER BEDROOM - MORNING

Haskins enters removing his badge from his shirt. He goes to his closet. Across the room, Kerry is crouched down and peering out at him nervously through the narrow open space in Gail's closet door.

She watches Haskins retrieve a shirt from his closet and put it on. Then, she sees the Ziplock bag with his hair sample lying on the floor, just under the near corner of the bed. Kerry — sweat trickling down her face — is wild-eyed with fear.

Haskins looks down at the floor at the far corner of the bed. His face makes an odd expression. As he is about to take a step towards the strange object —

                        GAIL (O.S.)
              Bill! Are you upstairs?

Distracted, he walks to the bedroom doorway.

                        LT. HASKINS
              Where the hell have you been?

Gail can be HEARD COMING UPSTAIRS QUICKLY.

He returns to his dresser and pins his badge to his
clean shirt. Gail sheepishly stands in the doorway.

                        GAIL
              I didn't hear you pull in. What
              happened?

                        LT. HASKINS
              I spilled coffee all over my damn
              shirt. Where were you?

                        GAIL
              Next door talking to Beverly.

                        LT. HASKINS
              You sure know how to pick losers.

                        GAIL
              How can you say that? They're
              very nice to us.

                        LT. HASKINS
              They're nice to us because I'm a
              cop and they might need a favor
              sometime. Think they'd give us
              the time of day if I wasn't?

                        GAIL
              Yes.

                        LT. HASKINS
              That's how much you know.

                        GAIL
              Should I have your lunch ready at
              twelve-thirty?

                        LT. HASKINS
              Have it ready — I may or may not
              be here.

Haskins exits the bedroom with Gail following him.

After a long beat, Kerry quietly slides the closet door
open and crawls out. Soaked with perspiration, she
grabs the Ziplock bag on the floor, then stands up.

EXT. HASKINS' HOUSE - MORNING

Gail stands on the front porch smiling at her husband as
he drives away in the police cruiser. Once he's out of
sight, her smile quickly vanishes and she heads inside.

INT. HASKINS' HOUSE - STAIRWAY - MORNING

Kerry nervously tiptoes downstairs.

INT. FIRST FLOOR - MORNING

Kerry peeks around the stairway into the kitchen where
she can see Gail preparing food.

Kerry looks at the screen door and realizes she'll never
get out of the house without making some noise.

As the tension builds, Gail turns the RADIO ON. With an
eye on Gail, Kerry quietly slips out the screen door.

EXT. ELM STREET - MORNING

Kerry jogs up the block looking highly relieved.

INT. TOOMEY'S - KERRY'S ROOM - DAY

In the b.g., the SOUND of a SHOWER TURNING OFF. Kerry
soon appears with a towel wrapped around her body.

EXT. BLACK KETTLE RESTAURANT - DAY

Kerry, holding a file folder, walks out with C.H. Hibbs.

                    HIBBS
          I hope that information helps you.

                    KERRY
          I think it will.
               (then)
          How long for the DNA test?

Hibbs retrieves the two Ziplock bags from his suit
jacket pocket and inspects them.

                    HIBBS
          I will drop it off at the lab on
          my way back and let you know.

                    KERRY
          If you can get them to rush it,
          I'll pay extra.

                    HIBBS
               (nods; then)
          Good day, Miss Parker.

EXT. GAS STATION - DAY

Kerry is pumping her own gas when Mike's pickup truck
pulls in loaded with lumber. He hops out.

                    MIKE
          I went by the Black Kettle around
          noontime and saw your car there.

                    KERRY
          I met with the investigator.

                    MIKE
     And?

                    KERRY
          Haskins left the New York City
          Police Department under very
          suspicious circumstances. He was
          accused of raping one woman and
          beating two others — but was never
          indicted.

                    MIKE
          How the hell did he ever get the
          job here?

                    KERRY
          With that background — good
          question.

                    MIKE
          Was there something you were gonna
          tell me from yesterday?

Kerry finishes pumping gas and hangs up the hose.

                    KERRY
          Oh. I spoke to Mrs. Pratt. She's
          the one who reported the gunshots
          the night Tom Daily was killed.

                    MIKE
          I know Esther.

                    KERRY
          She remembered one thing from that
          night she never told the police.
          The car that raced by her house
          after the shots had been fired had
          a fan belt that squealed.

                    MIKE
          That's not gonna get you much.

Kerry smiles with satisfaction.

                         KERRY
          Oh, it isn't? Yesterday, when I
          was helping Kathy shop, a car
          passed us in the parking lot with
          a fan belt that squealed. It was
          a station wagon driven by Haskins'
          wife. He could've been driving it
          that night. I'll bet Haskins
          flagged him down — and Daily —
          knowing who it was — didn't call
          in. Haskins conveniently made up
          that story about Daily stopping a
          car and not following procedure.

In disgust, Mike nods his agreement.

                         MIKE
          And he'll probably end up our next
          chief.

                         KERRY
                    (confidently)
          Not if I have anything to do with
          it.

Two cars pull in behind Kerry for gas.

                         MIKE
          See you for breakfast tomorrow?

Kerry nods, then goes to the gas station service window.

INT. HASKINS' HOUSE - KITCHEN - DAY

The PHONE is RINGING. Gail rushes in from outside.

                         GAIL
                    (into phone)
          Hello?

                         KERRY (V.O.)
          Mrs. Haskins?

                         GAIL
          Yes.

                         KERRY (V.O.)
          Was your husband using your car
          the night Tom Daily was killed?

                         GAIL
          Who is this?

                         KERRY (V.O.)
          You may be married to a murderer.

                          GAIL
              I don't think this is very funny.

CLICK — Kerry is gone. Gail hangs up looking upset.

INT. TOOMEY'S - KERRY'S ROOM - DAY

Kerry sits on the edge of the bed — expelling a breath.

EXT. MAIN STREET - NIGHT

Kerry's car cruises down Main Street.

EXT. FIRE DEPARTMENT - NIGHT

Ned Widgrin sits on a chair outside an open bay watching
traffic go by. He looks familiar because he was part of
the search party that looked for Elaine.

Kerry's car stops past the "No Parking" area out front.
She gets out and goes to Ned.

                          KERRY
              Remember me?

                          NED
              Sure. Sorry about your sister.

                          KERRY
                    (nods; then)
              I was told you live around the
              corner from Lt. Haskins.

                          NED
              Actually, I live directly behind
              him.

                          KERRY
              Do you know what kind of car his
              wife drives?

                          NED
              Yeah. A station wagon — one of
              those big ol' gas-guzzlin' bombs.

                          KERRY
              Have you ever seen him drive it?

                          NED
              He drives a four-by-four.

                          KERRY
              I know. But I could swear he
              waved to me the other day from a
              station wagon.

                         NED
          I've seen him drive her wagon.

Confirming this point — Kerry looks pleased.

                         KERRY
          Thanks.

As Kerry walks back to her car, a police car pulls in
and stops. Ned gets up from his chair and walks over.

INT. PARKED POLICE CAR - NIGHT

Behind the wheel, SGT. ED WALCOTT, 38. Ned leans inside
the open passenger window.

                    SGT. WALCOTT
          Hey, Ned.
                    (gesturing at Kerry
                    getting into her car)
          New girlfriend?

                         NED
          I wish. That's the Parker girl.
          The one whose sister was raped and
          murdered?

                    SGT. WALCOTT
          Oh, yeah.

EXT. MAIN STREET - NIGHT

Kerry's car follows Main Street out of town.

INT. HASKINS' HOUSE - KITCHEN - NIGHT

Gail — sitting at the table — trembles under the harsh
scrutiny of her husband standing over her.

                    LT. HASKINS
          What else did she say?

                         GAIL
          That's it.

                    LT. HASKINS
          And you're sure you didn't
          recognize her voice?

Gail nods nervously. The PHONE RINGS. Haskins lets it
ring for a while, then grabs it, to Gail's relief.

EXT. ORCHID HILL ROAD - NIGHT

Kerry's car stops next to a man walking his dog. The
man comes over to her. She asks a few questions. The
man shakes his head — she drives off.

EXT. ORCHID HILL ROAD - NIGHT

Kerry's car is traveling a section of the road flanked
by woods on the left and a marsh on the right.

INT. KERRY'S MOVING CAR - NIGHT

Coming her way is a TRUCK loaded with HAY — HIGH-BEAMS
ON. The truck swerves back and forth across the middle
of the road, then heads right for her.

Kerry leans on her HORN and says, "C'mon! C'mon!"

Looking left, she sees only trees — to the right, the
dense marsh.

EXT. ORCHID HILL ROAD - NIGHT

The hay truck is gaining speed as it approaches her car.

Just before a head-on collision, Kerry's car pulls hard
right and — barely missing a huge willow tree — RIPS
through the THICK MARSH and comes to an abrupt stop.

The hay truck keeps going down the road.

EXT. KERRY'S CRASHED CAR - NIGHT

Her car is partially submerged in the marsh. Small
streams of SMOKE drift upward from the HEADLIGHTS.

INT. KERRY'S CRASHED CAR - NIGHT

The windshield is shattered and Kerry is slumped over
the wheel, unconscious.

EXT. ORCHID HILL ROAD - NIGHT

Seeing Kerry's car in the marsh, a passing car stops.

EXT. HOSPITAL - NIGHT

Mike races inside the "Emergency Entrance."

INT. HOSPITAL - EMERGENCY ROOM - NIGHT

As Mike moves from partition to partition looking for
Kerry, a NURSE approaches him.

                    NURSE
        Sir. You can't come in here.

                    MIKE
        I'm looking for Kerry Parker.

He sees a POLICEMAN by a partition and rushes over.

Mike steps into the partition. Kerry is lying on her
back on a table, being treated by a DOCTOR.

                    MIKE
        How is she?

                    DOCTOR
        She has a concussion and a few
        lacerations.

Mike takes Kerry's hand. She looks at him, half-dazed.

INT. HOSPITAL - KERRY'S ROOM - LATER THAT NIGHT

Kerry is lying in bed, eyes shut, with Mike standing
over her. After a moment, she opens her eyes.

                    MIKE
        How do you feel?

                    KERRY
        Lousy.
            (beat)
        How'd you know I was here?

                    MIKE
        I stopped at a friend's house. He
        had a scanner on.

The Policeman enters with a pad and approaches Kerry.

                    POLICEMAN
        If you're up to it, miss, I'd like
        to take your statement now.

Kerry gives him a barely perceptible nod.

INT. HOSPITAL - CANTEEN ROOM - NIGHT

Mike sips the vending machine coffee and cringes.

INT. HOSPITAL - CORRIDOR - NIGHT

Mike and a NURSE are standing outside Kerry's room.

                    NURSE
        She's asleep now. It'd be best if
        you come back tomorrow.

Mike nods and walks off looking a bit exhausted.

EXT. CAFE - MAIN STREET - EARLY MORNING

As Mike heads for his truck, a car pulls in behind him.
Sgt. Jim Quill, in uniform, gets out.

                    SGT. QUILL
          Hi, Mike. I heard you're doing a
          job for Richard Haney.

                    MIKE
          Yeah. I'm rebuilding his deck.

                    SGT. QUILL
               (flashing big grin)
          Did you see his daughter?

                    MIKE
          Maggie?
               (on his nod)
          She's around.

                    SGT. QUILL
          Well?

                    MIKE
          Well what?

                    SGT. QUILL
          Is she running around naked?

                    MIKE
          Where'd you get that?

                    SGT. QUILL
          From Jim Sweeney.

                    MIKE
          Why don't you go over there and
          arrest her for indecent exposure.
          Then you could frisk her.

                    SGT. QUILL
          Don't think I wouldn't like to.
               (beat)
          Hear about the accident on Orchid
          Hill Road last night? That Parker
          girl ended up in the marsh.

                    MIKE
          What's the story on that?

INT. HOSPITAL - PATIENT ROOM - DAY

Kerry is sitting up in bed. Mike enters.

                    MIKE
          You look better.

                    KERRY
          Other than a little soreness, I
          feel better.

                    MIKE
          I ran into a sergeant I know. He
          said the truck that ran you off
          the road was probably stolen by
          kids out for a joy ride.

                    KERRY
                (sarcastically)
          Sure. All I want to know is —
          where was Haskins last night?

                    MIKE
          Kerry. It's time for you to go to
          the State Police.

                    KERRY
          After the DNA comes back on Elaine
          and Haskins.

                    MIKE
          You got a sample on him?
                (on her nod)
          How?

                    KERRY
                (evenly)
          I walked into his house and took
          some hair from his brush.

                    MIKE
                (incredulously)
          You just walked in?

                    KERRY
          The front door was open.

                    MIKE
          Where was he?

                    KERRY
          Working.

                    MIKE
          And his wife?

                    KERRY
          Outside talking to a neighbor.

Mike shakes his head in disbelief.

                    MIKE
          You know what would've happened if
          he caught you inside?

                    KERRY
          He almost did. He came home while
          I was there.

                    MIKE
                  (angrily)
          What the hell's wrong with you?
          If he murdered your sister and Tom
          Daily, he certainly wouldn't
          hesitate to kill you — especially
          if he caught you inside his home.

                    KERRY
          Well he didn't.

Mike is clearly annoyed at Kerry for being so reckless.
After a long silence —

                    KERRY (cont'd)
          The doctor said he'll probably
          release me late this afternoon.

                    MIKE
                  (abruptly)
          Still have my card?
                  (on her nod)
          When you're released, beep me with
          the hospital number and I'll pick
          you up.

Kerry nods. Mike exits — his anger still apparent.

EXT. HOSPITAL - EVENING

Mike assists Kerry into his truck parked out front.

Across the parking lot, a man observes them from a car.
But from this distance he is impossible to identify.

INT. MIKE'S MOVING PICKUP TRUCK - EVENING

                    KERRY
          I need to pick up another rental.

Mike — looking relaxed — glances over at her.

                    MIKE
          Want to do it now?

                    KERRY
          Sure.

INT. CAR RENTAL OFFICE - EVENING

Mike stands next to Kerry as the RENTAL AGENT puts the
keys to the rental car on the counter.

                    RENTAL AGENT
          The car's around back.

                    KERRY
          Thanks.

Kerry and Mike walk out. There is clearly a change in
how they look at each other.

EXT. CAR RENTAL PARKING LOT - EVENING

As Kerry unlocks her new rental car —

                    MIKE
          Are you hungry?

                    KERRY
          Starved.

Her response very suggestive — Mike smiles at her.

                    MIKE
          Wanna follow me?

                    KERRY
          Why don't we drop my car off at
          Toomey's first.

Mike nods — then goes to his pickup truck.

EXT. TOOMEY'S - EVENING

Mike's truck pulls in next to Kerry's rental. They get
out. Kerry looks at Mike.

                    KERRY
          Before we leave, I'd like to see
          if there are any messages.

Mike gestures for her to lead the way.

INT. TOOMEY'S - KERRY'S ROOM - EVENING

As they enter, Kerry looks on the floor inside the door.

                    KERRY
          No messages.

They look at each other for a moment and slowly step
into an embrace. They kiss — at first softly, then with
growing passion.

Suddenly, to Mike's surprise, Kerry gently pushes away from him.

> MIKE
> What?

> KERRY
> As much as I want to — this isn't right.

> MIKE
> What are you talking about?

> KERRY
> You still love your ex-wife and she was my sister's best friend.

Thinking beyond his desire to be with Kerry, Mike realizes she is right. He makes light of it.

> MIKE
> I need a stiff drink or a cold shower... or maybe both.

They both smile.

INT. RESTAURANT - NIGHT

Their platonic relationship back on track, Kerry and Mike are engaged in a philosophical conversation.

> MIKE
> I keep hoping she'll come around.

> KERRY
> Seeing you two together, I think there's a chance. It's a matter of being patient and not having unrealistic expectations.

> MIKE
> I'm hoping someday she'll invite me along for one of her counseling sessions. It would be a real turning point.

Kerry nods her understanding.

EXT. RESTAURANT - PARKING LOT - NIGHT

As Mike and Kerry head towards his truck, she glances over her shoulder, out to the road. A TRACTOR TRAILER TRUCK, approaching the restaurant, suddenly crosses over the dividing line, almost annihilating a car in the oncoming lane. Kerry realizes the huge truck is heading directly for them.

                              KERRY
              Look out!!!

The tractor trailer, aiming right for them, SMASHES into
one car, then another and another — to the horror of
patrons leaving the restaurant. Kerry and Mike barely
escape with their lives as the tractor trailer wipes out
six vehicles and turns back onto the highway.

The tractor trailer flips over on its side and SLIDES
across the pavement, FLASHING SPARKS. In a blinding
FLASH, it EXPLODES into a MASSIVE FIREBALL.

Mike and Kerry hold each other tightly as FLAMES from
the BURNING truck LIGHT up the night sky.

EXT. RESTAURANT - LATER THAT NIGHT

Mike and Kerry give their statement to LT. STEVE CONROY,
40, of the State Police. In the b.g., firemen are
inspecting the charred remains of the smoldering
wreckage while policemen interview other witnesses.

A Westbridge police car pulls in. Haskins gets out.

                         LT. CONROY
                    (seeing Haskins)
              Bill.

Haskins nods courteously, then addresses Conroy.

                         LT. HASKINS
              What've we got here?

Both Mike and Kerry look at Haskins coldly.

                         LT. CONROY
                    (gesturing at wreckage)
              These people claim that truck
              tried to hit them.

                         LT. HASKINS
              Any witnesses?

                         LT. CONROY
              Four — we're taking their
              statements now.

                         LT. HASKINS
              What about the driver?

                         LT. CONROY
              Burned beyond recognition.

                    LT. HASKINS
          Why would you think that truck was
          trying to hit you, Miss Parker?

                    LT. CONROY
          You know her?

                    LT. HASKINS
          Her sister was murdered here a
          week ago last Friday.

Kerry looks extremely exhausted and eager to leave.

                    KERRY
               (to Conroy)
          Can we go?

                    LT. CONROY
          I'm done.
               (looks to Haskins)
          Bill?

                    KERRY
          I'm too tired to answer any more
          questions.

                    LT. HASKINS
          Then tomorrow morning at the
          station. I'll need your statement
          too, Mike.

Kerry and Mike walk to his pickup with Haskins looking
after them, expressionless.

EXT. POLICE DEPARTMENT - MORNING

Kerry and Mike are heading inside together. Mike stops.

                    MIKE
          How are we gonna handle this?

                    KERRY
          We'll tell it exactly as it
          happened.

                    MIKE
          No. I mean with Haskins. He's
          got to know — from the way you
          look at him and act — you think
          he's involved with everything
          that's happened.

                    KERRY
          So? I want him to think that.

                    MIKE
Why?

                    KERRY
Maybe he'll do something reckless.

                    MIKE
               (pointedly)
Kerry. Twice he's probably tried
to kill you or have you killed —
both times trying to make it look
like an accident.

                    KERRY
I'm going to get the bastard.

                    MIKE
               (hard)
If he thinks he's cornered,
there's no telling what he might
do next.
               (on her silence)
Am I getting through to you?

                    KERRY
Let's go.

Kerry leads the way. Mike looks after her, frustrated.

INT. POLICE DEPARTMENT - HASKINS' OFFICE - MORNING

Kerry and Mike are seated across from Haskins. She is
aloof and cold in dealing with him.

                    LT. HASKINS
Before we get started, can I get
either one of you some coffee?

                    MIKE
None for me.

Kerry just shakes her head.

                    LT. HASKINS
Miss Parker. Why don't you tell
me what happened from the time you
arrived at the restaurant.

EXT. POLICE DEPARTMENT - FRONT DESK - MORNING

Russ Worth — the fellow who helped Kerry find Kathy — is
waiting for Sgt. Quill.

                    SGT. QUILL
              (into phone)
         That's not a police matter. You
         have to call the Department of
         Conservation... What?..
              (rolls his eyes)
         Ma'am, it's the Department of Con-
         ser-vation, not Con-ver-sation...

Sgt. Quill hangs up shaking his head.

                    SGT. QUILL (cont'd)
         What a dodo.

Russ smiles. The door to Haskins' office opens. Mike,
seeing Russ, comes right out and goes to him.

                    MIKE
         Hey, Russ. How you doin'?

                    RUSS
         Not good. Some shithead broke
         into my truck and stole my tools.

                    MIKE
         I've got some extra tools you can
         borrow.

                    RUSS
         That'd be great. I've got this
         job I have to finish by tomorrow.

INT. HASKINS' OFFICE - DAY

As Kerry goes to leave, Haskins blocks the doorway. He
is almost playful with her.

                    LT. HASKINS
         What's your problem, Miss Parker?

                    KERRY
              (meeting his gaze)
         I think you already know.

                    LT. HASKINS
         I'm not sure — so why don't you
         tell me.

                    KERRY
         I just want you to know — you're
         not going to get away with it.

                    LT. HASKINS
         With what?

                         KERRY
          What you did to my sister and Tom
          Daily.

While he tries to act unaffected, Haskins is a little
less sure of himself.

                      LT. HASKINS
          You certainly have a vivid
          imagination.

                         KERRY
          I wonder if you'll still be
          smiling after I nail your balls to
          the wall.

Her response wipes the smile from his face. Seething
with anger, he continues to block her retreat.

                      KERRY (cont'd)
                   (low but forceful)
          Get out of my way.

When it is obvious he won't budge, she raises her voice.

                      KERRY (cont'd)
          I said — get out of my way!

Realizing all eyes are upon them from the front desk
area, Haskins steps aside. After she walks out, he
closes the door without looking at anyone.

INT. POLICE DEPARTMENT - FRONT DESK - DAY

Surprised by Kerry's outburst, Sgt. Quill, Mike and Russ
stand mute. She addresses Mike abruptly.

                         KERRY
          Let's go.

                         MIKE
                   (to Russ)
          Stop by the house and take what
          you need. It's in the shed —
          Kathy'll give you the key.

                         RUSS
          Thanks, Mike.

After they exit, Sgt. Quill and Russ exchange a look.
Quill gestures at Haskins' office.

                      SGT. QUILL
          I wonder if he grabbed her ass?

Russ smiles.

EXT. POLICE DEPARTMENT - DAY

Kerry walks with deliberation to her car with Mike
chasing after her.

> MIKE
> Kerry!

She reaches her car and stops — shaking with anger.

> KERRY
> That smug bastard!

> MIKE
> What happened?

> KERRY
> I told him he wasn't getting away
> with what he did to Elaine and to
> Tom Daily.

> MIKE
> Great. Just great...

Kerry, highly agitated, gets into her car. Mike grabs
the door as she is about to shut it.

> MIKE (cont'd)
> Where the hell are you goin'?

> KERRY
> I've got things to do.

> MIKE
> If you won't go to the State
> Police, I will.

> KERRY
> Mike. Stay out of this. It has
> nothing to do with you.

She yanks the door shut, starts her car and drives off
with Mike looking after her in total frustration.

INT. TOOMEY'S - KERRY'S ROOM - DAY

> HIBBS (V.O.)
> The lab will be delivering the DNA
> results to me late this afternoon.

> KERRY
> (into phone)
> Thanks, Mr. Hibbs. I'll be over.

Kerry holds the receiver button down while she retrieves
a piece of paper from her pocketbook. She re-dials.

                        KERRY (cont'd)
                       (into phone)
                    Dr. Compton please.

EXT. MASSACHUSETTS TURNPIKE - DAY

Kerry's car is moving along with traffic, heading WEST.

INT. KERRY'S MOVING CAR - DAY

Kerry looks a bit impatient. She glances down next to
her, on the front seat, at an 8" X 10" manila envelope.
In bold letters it reads: SECOR LABORATORIES.

INT. DR. COMPTON'S OFFICE - DAY

Kerry sits across from an empty desk looking anxious.
Dr. Compton enters holding Kerry's manila envelope.

                        KERRY
          Well?

                        DR. COMPTON
          No match.

                        KERRY
                       (stunned)
          Are you sure?

Kerry looks defeated as Dr. Compton nods and hands back
her manila envelope. Slowly, Kerry rises to her feet.

                        DR. COMPTON
                       (curiously)
          Since I accommodated you, how
          about telling me whose DNA it was.

                        KERRY
          He'll probably be the next chief
          of police in Westbridge.
                       (then)
          Thanks for the help.

As Kerry slips out of the office, Dr. Compton — knowing
Kerry means Haskins — looks a bit surprised.

INT. DEPARTMENT STORE - MUSIC/STEREO SECTION - NIGHT

Kerry — holding a portable tape recorder and a package
of tapes — is on line behind teenagers buying CDs.

EXT. TOOMEY'S - NIGHT

Kerry's car pulls into a space. As she gets out with
her shopping bag, she sees Mike getting out of his
pickup truck. He approaches her cautiously.

                    MIKE
          Can we talk?

                    KERRY
          Did you contact the State Police?

                    MIKE
          No.

Kerry heads for the door leaving Mike standing there.

                    KERRY
               (stops; looks at him)
          You coming?

They go inside together.

INT. TOOMEY'S - KERRY'S ROOM - NIGHT

Mike watches Kerry unpack the recorder and break open
the package of tapes. There is tension between them.

                    MIKE
          I'm afraid to ask what that is
          for.

                    KERRY
          The DNAs didn't match.

                    MIKE
          Then Haskins is innocent.

                    KERRY
               (adamantly)
          Somehow, I _know_ he's involved.

                    MIKE
          Can't you admit you've made a
          mistake and leave it alone?

                    KERRY
          Weren't you the one who said he
          tried to kill me or have me
          killed?

                    MIKE
          Then I was wrong, too.

                    KERRY
          I don't think either one of us is
          wrong!

Tension mounting — they both retreat into silence.
Kerry glances at the tape recorder, then looks at Mike.

>   KERRY
>   I think I know a way to push him
>   over the edge. Will you help me?

In dealing with Kerry's stubbornness, Mike works hard to
suppress the anger and frustration he is feeling.

>   MIKE
>   Is there any way I can talk you
>   out of whatever you're planning?

>   KERRY
>   No.

After much agonizing, Mike reluctantly agrees.

>   MIKE
>   Whattaya want me to do?

INT. POLICE DEPARTMENT - FRONT DESK - MORNING

Sgt. Ed Walcott is on duty. Kerry approaches the front
desk carrying the shopping bag.

>   SGT. WALCOTT
>   Can I help you?

>   KERRY
>   I'd like to see Lt. Haskins.

>   SGT. WALCOTT
>   You'll have to wait. He's on the
>   phone.

Kerry nods then strolls over to the wall, to the side of
Haskins' office, where pictures of policemen receiving
accommodations are prominently displayed.

She looks a bit anxious — like she might even change her
mind. Suddenly, Haskins' door opens. He stands in the
doorway and addresses Sgt. Walcott.

>   LT. HASKINS
>   Did Russo see Mrs. Redfield yet?

>   SGT. WALCOTT
>   No, Lieutenant. He just called in
>   — he's on his way there. This
>   lady would like to see you.

At first, Haskins is taken aback seeing Kerry standing
there looking at him. He gestures at the doorway —

>   LT. HASKINS
>   Come in.

INT. HASKINS' OFFICE - MORNING

Haskins takes his seat and watches Kerry put the tape
recorder on the edge of his desk and plug it into the
wall outlet. She holds up a blank tape.

                    KERRY
          Do you know what this is?

                    LT. HASKINS
                  (impatiently)
          Of course.

Kerry loads the blank tape into the recorder.

                    KERRY
          It's for your confession.

He smiles in amusement. She hits the record buttons.

                    KERRY (cont'd)
          I'm ready anytime you are.

                    LT. HASKINS
                  (condescendingly)
          Miss Parker. Why don't you pack
          up your stuff and leave before you
          get into trouble.

                    KERRY
          Someone's holding a tape — just
          like the one in this recorder —
          with Sgt. Daily's statement on it.

Haskins shifts uneasily in his chair.

                    KERRY (cont'd)
          Think I'm bluffing?
                  (on his look)
          Let me tell you what's on the
          tape. Sgt. Daily said he
          recognized — from the autopsy
          photos — my sister Elaine, as the
          woman you were talking to the day
          she disappeared. In great detail,
          he pointed out how you denied it
          was her — and how you threatened
          him into silence.

Haskins is stunned. After a moment, he stands, turns
off the recorder, then rests his hand on his sidearm.

                    KERRY (cont'd)
          If anything happens to me, that
          tape will end up with the F.B.I.

There is no doubt in Kerry's mind that Haskins is contemplating some immediate action.

                    KERRY (cont'd)
          Better look out your window.

Haskins moves to his window. He sees Mike standing next to his pickup truck glancing at his watch anxiously.

                    KERRY (cont'd)
          He knows nothing about this — and
          he's not the one holding the tape.
          He's just my ride.

                    LT. HASKINS
                    (angrily)
          What the hell do you want from me?

                    KERRY
          I want to know what happened to my
          sister.
                    (re: tape recorder)
          I'll leave this. If I don't have
          your confession in twenty-four
          hours, I will personally deliver
          the tape to the F.B.I.

Kerry exits his office, closing the door behind her.

More than being worried, Haskins is consumed with anger.

INT. MIKE'S MOVING PICKUP TRUCK - MORNING

As they drive away, Mike turns to Kerry.

                    MIKE
          How'd it go?

                    KERRY
          I got to him.

Mike looks very worried.

                    MIKE
          Kerry. You've got to go to the
          State Police for protection — and
          tell them what's going on.

                    KERRY
          No. I think he's going to crack.

                    MIKE
                    (angrily)
          If he's guilty of murder and
          thinks you're holding evidence
                    (MORE)

                    MIKE (cont'd)
          that will convict him, he's got
          nothing to lose by killing you.
                    (on her silence)
          In my life, I have never met
          anyone as stubborn as you.

                    KERRY
          Mike, I'll be all right!

                    MIKE
                    (insistently)
          I've a got a job to do — so I want
          you to stay with Kathy until I
          finish. At least do that.

                    KERRY
                    (reluctantly)
          All right. But I'd like to get my
          car in case she wants to go out.

                    MIKE
          We'll get it and I'll follow you
          over.

EXT. BURROWS' HOUSE - DAY

Kerry's car pulls into the driveway with Mike's pickup
behind her. The front door is open. Kerry gets out and
goes to Mike in his truck.

                    KERRY
          What time will you be back?

                    MIKE
          Around five.

Kerry walks to the front door. Mike backs out of the
driveway and heads down the street.

EXT. BURROWS' HOUSE - DAY

Kerry goes to the screen door and calls inside.

                    KERRY
          Kathy?

No response. She RINGS the DOORBELL. Again, nothing.

                    NEIGHBOR (O.S.)
          She went out!

Kerry sees a NEIGHBOR, a woman, 40, looking her way.

EXT. NEIGHBOR'S HOUSE - DAY

Kerry walks over to the Neighbor watering flowers.

> KERRY
> Do you know where she went?

> NEIGHBOR
> No. Her friend Mary Ann picked
> her and her sons up an hour ago.

> KERRY
> She left the front door open?

> NEIGHBOR
> She is a bit of a scatterbrain.

Kerry nods then heads back to Kathy's house.

INT. BURROWS' HOUSE - LIVING ROOM - DAY

Kerry — looking bored and restless — is on the couch
paging absently through a women's magazine.

INT. KITCHEN - DAY

As Kerry checks out the fridge, the DOORBELL RINGS.

INT. FRONT DOOR - DAY

Kerry goes to the front door and finds a uniformed
policeman, OFFICER JOHN DANSK, 25, standing there.

> OFFICER DANSK
> Mrs. Burrows?

> KERRY
> No. She's out.

> OFFICER DANSK
> I need to find her. There's been
> an accident.

EXT. BURROWS' HOUSE - DAY

Kerry, very anxious, steps outside.

> KERRY
> An accident?

> OFFICER DANSK
> Her ex-husband has been hurt.

> KERRY
> How?

                    OFFICER DANSK
          I don't know. I was dispatched to
          take her to the hospital. I was
          told she doesn't drive.

                    KERRY
          I don't know where she is or when
          she's coming back. I'm a friend
          of the family. Can you take me?

                    OFFICER DANSK
                    (unsure)
          I guess so.

Kerry closes the front door behind her and hops into the
back seat of the police car.

EXT. MAIN ROAD - DAY

The police car crawls behind a long line of traffic.
Ahead of them is road construction. The police car
turns onto the next side street.

INT. MOVING POLICE CAR - DAY

Having been to the hospital, Kerry realizes they are
heading in the wrong direction.

                    KERRY
          Officer. This is not the way to
          the hospital.

                    OFFICER DANSK
          It's a shortcut to bypass the
          construction.

EXT. RURAL ROAD - DAY

The police car follows the rural road past open fields,
thick woods and an occasional house.

INT. MOVING POLICE CAR - DAY

                    KERRY
          It seems like we're going further
          away from the hospital.

                    OFFICER DANSK
          We'll be there shortly.

EXT. HOUSE - DAY

The police car pulls onto a dirt road leading to a house
six hundred yards from the road. The structure sits on
two open acres, on a slightly elevated ridge. It is
surrounded by a dense woods on three sides.

INT. MOVING POLICE CAR - DAY

Kerry is alarmed and grabs the door handle.

> OFFICER DANSK
> I wouldn't do that.

Two men step out of the house — SONNY LELLO and JIMMY WATTS. In their mid-30s, Sonny is physically fit and a meticulous dresser while Jimmy, on the other hand, is a pudgy slob with shirttails hanging outside his trousers. Sonny has the look of a contract killer.

EXT. HOUSE - DAY

The police car stops out front. Without a word, Kerry is dragged from the back seat by Sonny and Jimmy.

> KERRY
> Get your hands off me!

They drag her inside — the police car hurries off.

INT. HOUSE - BEDROOM - DAY

Kerry, mouth gagged, is tied to all four corners of the bed — in a very vulnerable position. As hard as she struggles, the ropes securing her are firmly tied. Outside the closed door, she HEARS the MUTED SOUNDS of the men TALKING and WALKING AROUND on hardwood FLOORS.

Sonny and Jimmy enter. Sonny sits on the middle of the bed, facing Kerry. He studies her body and smiles approvingly. He turns and looks at Jimmy.

> SONNY
> She's really nice. I might do
> this one for free.

Hearing "I might do this one for free" registers with Kerry. Her eyes go wide not from fear, but with anger.

> JIMMY
> How 'bout me this time?

> SONNY
> What would she want with someone
> like you?

> JIMMY
> I ain't a bad-looking guy.

> SONNY
> You need a new mirror, meatball.

Sonny unties Kerry's gag. She stares at him, hatefully.

                         KERRY
              You son of a bitch!

Sonny, highly amused, looks at Jimmy again.

                         SONNY
              Better with the gag on.

Kerry, fighting for her freedom, pulls hard on the ropes
securing her. Sonny is impressed by her spunk.

                         SONNY (cont'd)
              Tough one, huh?

                         KERRY
              Where's Lieutenant Haskins?

                         SONNY
              Where's the tape?

Kerry gives him a hateful look.

                         KERRY
              Drop dead!

Sonny's playful demeanor quickly vanishes.

                         SONNY
              I said — where's the tape?

On her silence, Sonny puts his hand on the inside of her
right thigh, above the knee. She flinches at his touch.

                         SONNY (cont'd)
              Touchy?

He runs his hand up the inside of her thigh. She closes
her eyes tightly. As he goes higher —

                         KERRY
              Stop!

Sonny stops, but leaves his hand where it is.

                         SONNY
              Well?

                         KERRY
              I hid it.

Pleased with himself, Sonny looks at Jimmy and smiles.

                         SONNY
              Where?

                    KERRY
In an air vent.

                    SONNY
                 (impatiently)
The rest of it.

                    KERRY
It's in the ladies room — at the
Black Kettle Restaurant.

                    SONNY
Jimmy. Go check it out. I'll
stay here with our lady friend.

                    JIMMY
Why me?

                    SONNY
'Cause I said so, meatball.

                    JIMMY
How the hell am I gonna get into
the ladies room?

                    SONNY
Put a dress on. Tell 'em you're
the building inspector. Figure
somethin' out, dummy.
                 (as Jimmy exits)
I'll call Nicky and have 'im meet
you there.

Once Jimmy's gone, Sonny returns his attention and his
hand to Kerry. He smiles at her suggestively.

                    SONNY (cont'd)
We've got some time to kill.

                    KERRY
If you don't want me to mess this
bed, you'd better let me use the
bathroom.

Her point made, Sonny slowly unties her.

EXT. BURROWS' HOUSE - DAY

Mike is talking to the Neighbor Kerry spoke to earlier.

                    MIKE
Did you see who was driving?

                    NEIGHBOR
Sorry, Mike. I don't know any of
the policemen.

INT. HOUSE - BATHROOM - DAY

Kerry examines the bathroom window. Too small for her
to pass through — she looks extremely anxious.

> SONNY (O.S.)
> How you doin' in there?

Over the following dialogue, she quietly pops open the
medicine cabinet and searches its contents.

> KERRY
> I'm having a tough time with you
> standing outside the door, talking
> to me every thirty seconds.

> SONNY (O.S.)
> If you're not out of there soon,
> I'm comin' in.

INT. BURROW'S HOUSE - KITCHEN - DAY

Mike is on the phone — he looks desperate.

> MIKE
> (into phone)
> She was taken away by a policeman.
> When I called the department, they
> knew nothing about it!

Mike sees Kathy walk into the living room carrying a
bunch of packages. Behind her, Jake and Tommy.

> MAN (V.O.)
> Mr. Burrows, our agents will be
> arriving at your home shortly.

Kathy enters as Mike slams the phone down, angrily.

> KATHY
> Mike, who were you talking to?

> MIKE
> The F.B.I.

Jake and Tommy race to their father screaming, "Daddy!"

INT. HOUSE - HALLWAY - DAY

Kerry steps into the hallway from the bathroom. Sonny
follows her back to the bedroom.

INT. BEDROOM - DAY

Sonny notices Kerry's clenched fist. He grabs her arm
and forces her hand open.

A double-edged razor blade drops to the floor. He gives
her the back of his hand across her face. She stares
back at him, defiantly.

EXT. BURROWS' HOUSE - EVENING

Mike stands next to an unmarked car with F.B.I. AGENTS
CABOT and KELLER, both in their late 30s.

                    CABOT
          She's at a house we have under
          surveillance. It's wired — we
          hear everything. We know she's
          all right. At a moment's notice,
          we can rescue her.

                    MIKE
               (angrily)
          Why don't you rescue her now —
          what the hell are you waiting for?

                    KELLER
          Mr. Burrows. An investigation has
          led us to a number of corrupt law
          enforcement people. We're waiting
          to see who else shows up there.

                    MIKE
          At the risk of her life?

                    CABOT
          They're after a tape she has, so
          they won't do anything to her
          until after they get it.

                    MIKE
          But there is no tape!

                    KELLER
          We know. Trying to buy time, she
          told them it was hidden at this
          restaurant. We've arrested the
          man who went there to pick it up.

                    CABOT
          The man watching her has no way of
          knowing what's happened, so we've
          gained some additional time.

                    MIKE
          This is bullshit! You're risking
          her life for an investigation. I
          wanna talk to whoever's in charge.

EXT. HOUSE - NIGHT

A few LIGHTS inside the house GLOW BRIGHTLY against the
pitch darkness outside.

EXT. WOODS - F.B.I. POSITION - NIGHT

A hundred yards away, F.B.I. AGENTS KIRBY and WYATT are
watching the house. Kirby uses an infra-red scope while
Wyatt communicates with a portable to other agents.

>   WYATT
>   (into portable)
>   We've got three vehicles arriving.

POV THROUGH INFRA-RED SCOPE of two sedans and one 4X4
stopping in front of the farm house. No outside lights
on, three men appear as dark figures as they get out of
their vehicles and go inside.

BACK TO SCENE on Wyatt.

>   WYATT (cont'd)
>   Can you ID them?

Kirby, still looking through scope, responds.

>   KIRBY
>   From this angle I can't even see
>   their plates, but I think one of
>   them is Haskins.

INT. MOVING F.B.I. CAR - NIGHT

Mike is riding in back of Agents Cabot and Keller's car.
Cabot drives — Keller handles the portable.

>   KELLER
>   (into portable)
>   Wyatt. What's the update?

>   WYATT (V.O.)
>   Counting Sonny Lello and Miss
>   Parker, we now have five inside.
>   Not confirmed, but we think one of
>   the new arrivals is Haskins — the
>   other two are unsubs.

>   MIKE
>   What are "unsubs"?

>   KELLER
>   Unknown subjects.

INT. FARM HOUSE - BEDROOM - NIGHT

Kerry is tied to the bed as before. Outside the room, the MUTED SOUND of INDISTINGUISHABLE VOICES.

INT. FARM HOUSE - LIVING ROOM - NIGHT

Sonny and Haskins are standing with Dennis Ludlow (the man Haskins visited earlier) and ROBERT PROVOS, 50.

> PROVOS
> Where's Jimmy?

> SONNY
> Don't know. He should've been
> back by now.

> LT. HASKINS
> How long ago did he leave?

At the SOUND of a CAR COMING —

> SONNY
> This should be him.

EXT. WOODS - F.B.I. POSITION - NIGHT

Kirby is tracking the approaching car with the scope.

> WYATT
> What've you got?

Over Kirby's dialogue, the action he describes is seen THROUGH the POV in the INFRA-RED SCOPE.

> KIRBY (V.O.)
> A dark-colored sedan — can't see
> the plate — has stopped out front.
> I make Lello and, confirm,
> Haskins, standing in the doorway.
> The man from the sedan — I think
> it's Nick Faranda — is gesturing
> them outside. They're stepping
> away from the house. Something's
> going on. They're looking around.
> Lello and Haskins went inside —
> Faranda is returning to his car...
> He's just sitting there.

INT. HOUSE - LIVING ROOM - NIGHT

Sonny, Haskins, Ludlow and Provos are standing very close together, looking nervous and talking softly.

                        HASKINS
        Nick said Jimmy was picked up
        outside the Black Kettle. He's
        guessing it was the F.B.I.

                        SONNY
                (glancing around room)
        There's only one way they could've
        known. This place is bugged.

                        HASKINS
                (to Sonny; angrily)
        We wouldn't be in this mess if you
        had properly disposed of that
        Parker girl's body.

Sonny glares back at him.

INT. F.B.I. SURVEILLANCE VAN - NIGHT

AGENT DORSEY, 30s, is sitting in a chair monitoring a
high-tech recording/surveillance system.

                        WYATT (V.O.)
        Dorsey. What are they saying?

                        DORSEY
                (into portable)
        All I'm getting is whispering —
        they might be on to us.

INT. HOUSE - LIVING ROOM - NIGHT

Sonny leads Kerry into the living room gagged,
blindfolded, with hands tied behind her back.

EXT. WOODS - F.B.I. POSITION - NIGHT

Kirby is looking through the infra-red scope.

                        KIRBY
        Shit!

                        WYATT
        What?

                        KIRBY
        They're all leaving at once.

                        WYATT
        What about the girl?

                        KIRBY
        I'm not sure. They're all close
        together.

EXT. HOUSE - NIGHT

Three cars and Haskins' 4X4 race down the driveway.

EXT. WOODS - F.B.I. POSITION - NIGHT

> KIRBY
> (looking through scope)
> They're making a run for it.

> WYATT
> (into portable)
> Attention all units! We've got
> four vehicles on the move. Close
> in, now!

From behind Kirby and Wyatt, an F.B.I. assault team —
armed with automatic weapons — races past them and heads
for the house.

EXT. RURAL ROAD - NIGHT

From the house, two cars turn right, a black sedan and
Haskins' 4X4 turn left — heading away from town.

EXT. RURAL ROAD - DIFFERENT LOCALE - NIGHT

An unmarked F.B.I. car pulls onto the rural road from a
hidden spot in the woods.

EXT. RURAL ROAD - ANOTHER LOCALE - NIGHT

Another unmarked F.B.I. car races down the rural road.

EXT. RURAL ROAD - NIGHT

One of the F.B.I. cars passes the black sedan and
Haskins' 4X4 heading in the direction they came from.

The F.B.I. car spins around and pursues.

INT. MOVING F.B.I. CAR - NIGHT

AGENT DANFORD, 33, drives — AGENT TULLY, 30, handles the
portable.

In front of them — the black sedan leading the 4X4. The
rural road intersects with another road forming a "T."
The black sedan turns left, the 4X4 turns right.

INT. INTERSECTION - NIGHT

The F.B.I. car turns right, following Haskins.

EXT. LAKE ROAD - NIGHT

As the F.B.I. car races after Haskins —

> TULLY (V.O.)
> This is Tully! We're pursuing
> Haskins eastbound on Lake Road.
> Black sedan is heading west.

INT. MOVING F.B.I. CAR - NIGHT

Mike is leaning over the back of the front seat.

> KELLER
> (into portable)
> This is Keller. We'll reach Lake
> Road in one minute.

INT. HOUSE - LIVING ROOM - NIGHT

The F.B.I. assault team stands at ease as AGENT WARGO,
35, reports in.

INT. MOVING F.B.I. CAR - NIGHT

Mike listens attentively.

> WARGO (V.O.)
> This is Wargo. The house is
> empty. I repeat — everyone has
> left!

> CABOT
> She has to be in one of four
> vehicles.

As they reach Lake Road, the black sedan goes WHIZZING
by at HIGH SPEED.

EXT. LAKE ROAD - NIGHT

The F.B.I. car turns onto the road and accelerates.

INT. MOVING F.B.I. CAR - NIGHT

In front of them, the DISTANT TAIL LIGHTS of the black
sedan.

> KELLER
> Close in — he's getting away!

Cabot nails the accelerator — the car leaps forward.

About two hundred yards ahead, the black sedan's TAIL
LIGHTS disappear around a sharp bend in the road.

EXT. LAKE ROAD - PAST SHARP BEND - NIGHT

When the F.B.I. car hits the straightaway past the sharp
bend, it slows down to a crawl.

INT. SLOW-MOVING F.B.I. CAR - NIGHT

There is a long stretch of road in front of them and no
TAIL LIGHTS in sight. On both sides of the road, there
are bungalows and driveways leading to other bungalows.

INT. STOPPED F.B.I. CAR - NIGHT

Cabot, Keller and Mike look around in frustration.

>   CABOT
>   He must've pulled into one of
>   these driveways.

>   MIKE
>   What if he turned off his lights
>   and kept going?

>   CABOT
>   He wasn't that far ahead of us.

>   KELLER
>   And it's too dark. He wouldn't be
>   able to see.

EXT. RURAL ROAD - NIGHT

The last vehicle to arrive at the house — driven by Nick
Faranda — is racing recklessly down the road with a
State Police and F.B.I. car in hot pursuit.

At a sharp bend in the road, the car brakes hard, skids
wildly, flips over three times and EXPLODES.

EXT. TWO-LANE ROAD - NIGHT

The fourth suspect vehicle — being pursued by a State
Police car — approaches a road block. It stops. As the
police approach with weapons drawn, Robert Provos and
Sonny Lello get out with their hands raised.

EXT. LAKE ROAD - NIGHT

The F.B.I. car pulls off the road and parks. Cabot and
Keller get out. So does Mike. Cabot addresses him.

>   CABOT
>   Stay here!

Cabot and Keller go off into different directions.

EXT. DRIVEWAY - NIGHT

Flanking both sides of the driveway are bungalows with
LIGHTS ON and the SOUNDS of TELEVISIONS and RADIOS.

A few OUTSIDE SPOTLIGHTS provide some light.

After two boys pass by, Dennis Ludlow steps out of the
shadows steering Kerry by her arm. She is still gagged,
blindfolded, with hands tied behind her back.

EXT. DARK BUNGALOW - NIGHT

Ludlow drags Kerry to the door. He cautiously looks
around. No one in sight, he breaks a window pane on the
door with his gun, reaches inside and unlocks it.

EXT. LAKE ROAD - NIGHT

Mike stands by the F.B.I. car looking extremely anxious.
Tired of waiting, he walks along the road glancing down
driveways flanked by rows of bungalows.

INT. BUNGALOW - LIVING ROOM - NIGHT

TOTAL DARKNESS. The SOUND of SHUFFLING FEET, then a
LIGHT goes on. Kerry is gasping for air as the gag not
only covers her mouth, but has shifted upwards partially
blocking her nostrils. Ludlow removes the gag. Kerry
finally has relief and draws in deep breaths.

                    LUDLOW
          Scream once and it goes back on.

Kerry is jolted by the SOUND of the MAN's voice.

                    KERRY
          I don't believe it.

                    LUDLOW
          You recognized my voice after all
          these years?

He is obviously not Dennis Ludlow, but KENNETH HOBART
—the man her father supposedly murdered.

                    KERRY
          Take off my blindfold, I want to
          see you.

                    HOBART
          We'll leave it on for now.

                    KERRY
          How can you be alive?

He wanders over to the window and looks outside.

                    HOBART
          Have you ever heard of the Witness
          Protection Program?

Kerry follows the sound of his voice.

                    KERRY
          What does that have to do with
          you?

                    HOBART
          The Mafia has their own version
          —and for a hefty price, a person's
          death and new identity can be
          arranged.

                    KERRY
          How did you get away with it?

He moves from the window and stands in front of her.

                    HOBART
          It's quite simple. When the
          police found the charred remains
          of a body at the company lodge, my
          dental charts provided a match.
          Of course, weeks before, my charts
          had been exchanged for those of
          the man who died in my place. I
          relocated here under a new
          identity and, I might add, have
          been living a very normal life —
          although somewhat less flamboyant.

                    KERRY
          Who died in your place?

                    HOBART
          I have no idea.

                    KERRY
               (angrily)
          You... you killed my father!

                    HOBART
          In a manner of speaking.

                    KERRY
          Why? Just tell me why you did it.

                    HOBART
          Things didn't have to turn out the
          way they did. Blame it on your
          father's unwavering ethics.

                    KERRY
          What are you talking about?

                    HOBART
          I had gotten myself into some
          financial problems — through bad
          investments — and had to borrow
          from our clients. When your
          father found out, I begged him to
          give me time to straighten things
          out, but he wouldn't listen.

                    KERRY
          So you framed him for embezzling
          and for your murder!

Thinking about it, Hobart smiles with satisfaction.

                    KERRY (cont'd)
          My sister told me she saw you here
          and I didn't believe her.

                    HOBART
          It was her bad luck all around —
          especially running into Haskins.
          He works for the Mafia, looking
          after the new identities living in
          this area.

EXT. RURAL ROAD - NIGHT

Agents Danford and Tully walk Haskins, in handcuffs, to
their car. His 4X4 is lying on its side in a ditch.

EXT. DRIVEWAY - NIGHT

At each bungalow, Mike checks the cars parked there.

Walking a little further, he squints into the darkness
at a car parked haphazardly near the back of a bungalow.
Getting closer, he sees that it is the black sedan. He
carefully approaches the dark bungalow. The door is
locked and he sees no signs of tampering.

Thinking the driver might be close by, he moves swiftly
but cautiously down the driveway.

INT. BUNGALOW - LIVING ROOM - NIGHT

Hobart stands by the window looking outside.

                    KERRY (O.S.)
          I need to use the bathroom.
               (on his silence;
                she pleads)
          Please, let me use the bathroom.

Hobart, seeing all is quiet outside, goes to Kerry.

> HOBART
> I'm going to untie your hands.
> Try <u>anything</u> and I will kill you
> here and now, understand?

> KERRY
> Please hurry!

Hobart unties her hands. Kerry slips off the blindfold.
After she makes brief eye contact with him —

> KERRY (cont'd)
> Where's the bathroom?

Hobart, gun in hand, gestures towards the hallway.

> HOBART
> It must be there.

She moves swiftly. He stands at the end of the hallway
and watches her go inside the bathroom.

EXT. BUNGALOW - NIGHT

In the soft glow of the spotlight across the way, Mike
notices the broken pane of glass on the bungalow door.
He approaches quietly and looks inside.

He sees Hobart standing in the living room, gun in hand,
looking down the hallway. Soon, Kerry appears. Hobart
starts to retie her hands behind her back.

Mike looks desperate — like he has to do something.

INT. BUNGALOW - LIVING ROOM - NIGHT

Hobart finds it awkward trying to tie Kerry's hands
while holding the gun at the same time. But as
aggravated as he is, he is not willing to put it down
for a moment. Kerry shifts on her feet.

> HOBART
> Hold still!

There is a LOUD THUD on the far side of the roof —
followed by the SOUND of SOMETHING ROLLING OFF the edge.

Hobart drops the ropes that are loosely wrapped around
Kerry's wrist and looks up at the ceiling.

Kerry looks over her shoulder at Hobart who is now very
nervous and ready to shoot.

EXT. BUNGALOW - NIGHT

Mike flings another BIG ROCK onto the roof.

INT. BUNGALOW - NIGHT

BANG! Another LOUD THUD on the far side of the roof
followed by the SOUND of SOMETHING ROLLING off the edge.

At the SOUND of the FRONT DOOR CREAKING OPEN, Hobart
swings around and aims the gun at Mike darting inside.

At the same time, Kerry pulls her hands apart from the
loosely wrapped ropes. With all her might, she shoves
Hobart — knocking him off balance.

The GUN FIRES. The bullet BREAKS a FRONT WINDOW PANE.

Mike leaps at Hobart — Hobart steps aside and catches
Mike on the side of the head with the butt of the gun.

Mike drops to the floor, dazed. As Hobart aims at Mike,
Kerry grabs Hobart's gun arm. They struggle.

Mike grabs Hobart by the ankles and topples him over.

The gun flies from Hobart's hand and slides across the
wood floor, disappearing into the corner somewhere. As
Kerry tries to find the gun—

Hobart, lying on his side, pulls free from Mike's grasp
around his legs and kicks him hard in the face.

Hobart gets to his feet. He sees that Mike is quickly
recovering. He glances at Kerry looking frantically for
the gun. Not wasting the opportunity, Hobart goes to
the fireplace and grabs a poker.

Kerry reaches under a chair in the corner and retrieves
the gun. Just as Hobart is about to smash Mike with the
poker, she FIRES the GUN at Hobart — FIVE TIMES.

Each shot catches him in the arm or shoulder, jerking
his body. The final shot hits dead center in his chest.

Hobart drops to the floor, dead. Kerry stands over his
body, trembling. Mike goes to her, takes the gun from
her and holds her tightly. A moment later, Cabot and
Keller race inside the bungalow, guns ready.

EXT. BURROWS' HOUSE - DAY

Jake and Tommy are running around the yard while Kathy,
with tears in her eyes, hugs Kerry goodbye.

Kerry gets into Mike's truck. They drive off.

EXT. BURROWS' HOUSE - DAY

Kathy picks up the newspaper and reads the front page.

CLOSE ON HEADLINE —

"F.B.I. BREAKS MAFIA CRIMINAL RELOCATION PROGRAM."

Then, CLOSE ON article text —

"Local law enforcement officers were arrested following an F.B.I. investigation into a Criminal Relocation Program run by the Mafia. Those arrested include: Lt. William F. Haskins, Sgt. Edward J. Walcott and Officer John Dansk, all members of the Westbridge Police Department. Additional charges have been filed against Haskins for the murder of Sergeant Thomas Daily — an eight-year veteran of the department. Mafia hit man Sonny Lello has been charged with the rape and murder of Elaine Parker..."

EXT. MASS TURNPIKE - DAY

Mike's pickup truck heads EAST, towards BOSTON.

INT. LOGAN AIRPORT - BOARDING AREA - DAY

Behind them, airplane passengers are boarding. The moment at hand, both Kerry and Mike are showing anxiety about saying goodbye. Mike looks at her with admiration.

> MIKE
> Kathy asked me to go to counseling with her. Said you convinced her.

Kerry shrugs it off —

> KERRY
> I caught her at the right moment.
> (beat)
> I told her I'd keep in touch, but probably wouldn't be as faithful as Elaine was.

> MIKE
> (confidently)
> We'll keep in touch.

Kerry and Mike embrace. After a moment, Kerry slowly pulls away from Mike and heads for the boarding gate. He looks after her, smiling.

<u>THE END</u>

BIOGRAPHY

Robert A. Berman was raised in Rye, New York. In his early twenties, he lived *on the beach* on St. John's, U.S. Virgin Islands, and then hitchhiked across the United States. He has traveled in Mexico, Hawaii, Switzerland, France, Germany, Italy and Portugal—having conducted wine tours in the latter four countries.

After a brief stint at college, he worked as a musician, songwriter, jingle writer, and has had articles published in national magazines on music, fishing, wine, business, and humor. Before pursuing screenwriting, he was a sales and marketing executive in the wine business.

Berman lives with his wife of twenty-eight years in New York's Westchester County where, five years ago, he started running weekly jazz sessions at his home attracting noted musicians.

If you would like to contact me regarding a *simple* question, you can write to me at:

> Robert A. Berman
> c/o Michael Wiese Productions
> 11288 Ventura Blvd., Suite 821
> Studio City, CA 91604

Please DO NOT send any screenplays because they will not be forwarded to me—and understand that my ability to reply will be based upon my work and travel schedule at the time. In addition to your address, you may provide me with a phone number to expedite a response. Indicate the best hours to reach you.

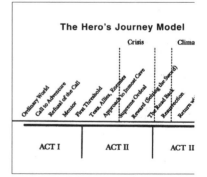